Deities, Dolls, and Devices

Neolithic Figurines from Franchthi Cave, Greece

Excavations at Franchthi Cave, Greece

T. W. Jacobsen, General Editor

Lisa S. Williams, Managing Editor

FASCICLE 9

Deities, Dolls, and Devices

Neolithic Figurines from Franchthi Cave, Greece

LAUREN E. TALALAY

INDIANA UNIVERSITY PRESS
Bloomington & Indianapolis

Library of Congress Cataloguing-in-Publication Data

Talalay, Lauren E. (Lauren Elizabeth), date.
Deities, dolls, and devices : Neolithic figurines from Franchthi Cave, Greece.
p. cm. — (Excavations at Franchthi Cave, Greece; fasc. 9)
Includes bibliographical references.
1. Franchthi Cave (Greece) 2. Neolithic period—Greece.
3. Pottery figures, Prehistoric—Greece. 4. Paralia Site (Greece)
I. Title. II. Series
GN816.F73T34 1993 730′.0938′8—dc20 92-43060
ISBN 0-253-31981-1 (pbk.)

1 2 3 4 5 97 96 95 94 93

TO MY MOTHER AND FATHER

CONTENTS

FIGURES

MAPS

TABLES

PLATES

(photographs and drawings)

FOREWORD

The study of gender and the role of women in prehistoric societies are issues that have lately come to be of increasing concern to archaeologists and feminist scholars. Under the circumstances, it is perhaps not surprising that the venerable concept of the Mother Goddess, dormant (if not dead) in the archaeological literature for decades, has reappeared and seems to be flourishing in some quarters once again. In the following pages, Lauren Talalay reevaluates the appropriateness of that concept in the interpretation of Neolithic anthropomorphic figurines and, at the same time, addresses other fundamental questions relevant to the study of prehistoric figurative art in the Aegean world.

The primary objective of this volume, the ninth in the series of final publications of the excavations at Franchthi Cave, is the detailed presentation and analysis of the Neolithic human and animal figurines from our site. That is accomplished in Chapters 1–5. In Chapter 6 the author offers a valuable review of the Franchthi sample in the context of comparable material from elsewhere in southern Greece and the Aegean islands and, in less detail, the more abundant remains from northern Greece and the Balkans. This volume cautiously explores new territory in an attempt to understand early Aegean figurative art, and in a concluding chapter (7) Dr. Talalay suggests additional paths for exploration in the future.

Major contributions of this study are discussions of the classification, dating, and production of the Franchthi and southern Greek figurines, essentially for the first time. (All dates are given in uncalibrated years b.c.) In addition, the author examines the use and meaning of those pieces and concludes, largely on the basis of ethnographic evidence, that they must be viewed as a *multi-functional* class of objects. Therefore, it seems that, at least in the case of the anthropomorphic examples, the Mother Goddess interpretation by itself is unsatisfactory.

The general editor wishes to take this opportunity to thank once again Lisa Williams for her invaluable help at all stages in the preparation of this volume for publication. I would also like to acknowledge the assistance of Stephen Krebs and Kimberly Elkins of the Program in Classical Archaeology at Indiana University. Costs for the preparation of camera-ready copy were borne by the E. A. Schrader Endowment and a grant from The Office of Research and the University Graduate School at Indiana University. I gratefully acknowledge the Office of the Vice President for Research at the University of Michigan for a grant awarded to the author to help defray the costs of printing.

T. W. JACOBSEN

PREFACE

David Clarke's now classic article "Archaeology: The Loss of Innocence" (1973) begins with a simple observation: "The loss of disciplinary innocence is the price of expanding consciousness; certainly the price is high, but the loss is irreversible and the prize substantial." Exploring the trajectory of disciplinary growth, Clarke argues that scholars move from discussions of the purely pragmatic to querulous debates about definition, classification, and methodology, and, finally, to a rethinking of the philosophical, metaphysical, and theoretical issues which guide their research. While not everyone would agree with the specifics of Clarke's paradigm, it is certainly true that significant advances in all disciplines result when long-standing and traditional forms of reasoning and interpretation are challenged. To that extent, the loss of disciplinary innocence is critical to every field of study.

One of the fundamental preoccupations of the "New Archaeology" of the '60s and '70s was precisely this self-conscious concern with underlying theories in the discipline. Several subfields within archaeology willingly, if not eagerly, sought ways to shed their innocence, and often vociferous debate resulted. Others were more reluctant to join in the fray. With a few notable exceptions (e.g., Ucko 1962, 1968), the small cadre of specialists who studied Stone Age figurines was slow to initiate meaningful dialogues on method and theory. Even today, two decades after Ucko's pioneering work was published, the boundaries of archaeological consciousness in figurine studies have not expanded to the point where new observations, methods, perspectives, and theories are vigorously discussed. Despite claims to the contrary, we are still a long way from explaining how figurines were used in prehistoric contexts or how they fit into the larger social or adaptive strategies of early, nonliterate societies.

This volume, a fascicle in the series on Franchthi Cave, attempts to address some of the theoretical and methodological issues confronting archaeologists who study prehistoric figurines. These larger concerns are not, however, the only or even the prime goal of this work. In fact, theoretical matters became an issue only after it became clear to me that a proper study of the figurines from Franchthi could not rely on guidelines available in the literature. They were too few and too poorly defined.

The primary intent of this work is to examine the Neolithic figurines from Franchthi. Three distinct but related objectives emerge in the following pages: first and foremost, to present the data on figurines from Franchthi Cave as completely as possible; second, to address specific intra- and intersite questions regarding the production, form, and function of these images; and third, to explore issues of a larger and more theoretical nature that are relevant both to the Franchthi collection and to the study of all prehistoric figurines.

In the process of preparing this volume, I encountered many areas of study which seemed ripe for research. As will become evident to the reader, I chose three areas in particular: the production, use, and meaning of these images. Each of these topics has received varying degrees of exploration in the literature, though none of the investigations have met with great success.

While the topic of use has been broached by a number of archaeologists (e.g., Meighan 1954; Broman 1958; Ucko 1962, 1968; Hourmouziadis 1973; Gimbutas 1974a; Bartel 1981; Peltenburg 1988, 1991; Morales 1990), discussion of the actual manufacture of these objects is rare. As with other artifacts, the creation of a figurine entails a number of choices, each of which is linked to the social and/or economic constraints of a society. Some of the decisions that individuals or groups must make in creating a figurine are: the type and acquisition of raw materials, the selection and manufacture of necessary tools, the designation of craftsmen or craftswomen, the scale and extent of labor investment, the allocation of time and place for production, and the kinds or styles of figurines to be designed, including whether figurines should be similar to or different from those produced in neighboring communities. There is a multiplicity of options along this chain of production (cf. Young and Bonnichsen 1983:1–20), and each has far-reaching implications.

The interpretation of a figure's function is equally complex and, in many ways, confronts the archaeologist with a more difficult task. Those of us who study prehistoric figurines have neither direct access to the behaviors which produced these images nor to the meanings which they held for the people who used them. No matter how optimistic we would like to be about the accessibility of human experience or cognitive particulars from prehistoric evidence (cf. Renfrew 1985:1), certain modes of behavior leave more indelible and direct marks than others on the archaeological record. For the most part, the behaviors associated with the use of prehistoric figurines leave frustratingly little evidence. The problem, however, is not that the data are unyielding, but that as prehistorians we have made little attempt to develop systematic ways of dealing with the available material. Some of these failings are reflected in the vocabulary we employ, which is far too coarse for fine-scale analysis. For example, archaeologically useful definitions explaining distinctions among "function," "use," and "meaning" have yet to be formulated.

Progress is also impeded by the seeming acceptance of dubious assumptions. More often than not, we tend to gloss over variability among figurines: images which span several millennia are treated synchronically, regardless of their stylistic or contextual differences. It is not uncommon to find that a Greek Neolithic figurine from 6000 b.c. (uncalibrated) is assumed, *a priori*, to have served the same function as an example three millennia later. To the contrary, one of the main tenets of this study is that Neolithic figurines are considered a multifunctional class of objects, their uses varying across space and time. Although it is not easy to disentangle the possible uses of these images, the guidelines offered in this volume will, I hope, encourage others to adopt more rigorous approaches to our data.

Perhaps the most difficult task confronting those who study prehistoric figurines is deciphering the symbolic dimension of those images, what Gimbutas calls their "shorthanded allusiveness" (1986:229). By definition, figurines are symbolic, embodying a complex blend of behaviors and cognitive concerns tied to the common encoding and decoding strategies of the groups producing them. Moreover, symbolic expression, be it verbal or nonverbal, encompasses an enormous range of capacities, which are described by the anthropologist Victor Turner as "*multivocal*, (literally 'many voiced'), 'speaking' in many ways at once; *multivalent*, having various meanings or values; and *polysemous*, having or being open to several or many meanings" (1982:16). Inferring human cognition and such a multiplicity of meanings from archaeological remains is, of course, no simple matter, and it is certainly possible that we may never fully understand the messages which prehistoric figurines were intended to broadcast. Nonetheless, either to ignore entirely the cognitive dimension of these images or to offer undisciplined speculation about their meaning seems unproductive. This study attempts to find a middle ground by suggesting several, hopefully reasonable, ideas about the symbolic intent of a few of the Franchthi figurines. These interpretations are not conclusive; they are presented only as possibilities.

In the process of analyzing the sample of figurines from Franchthi, I inevitably touch upon a number of theoretical and methodological topics which deserve more complete treatment. The intention of this book, however, is *not* to design a single, overarching framework for the study of Neolithic figurines. There are good reasons why such frameworks have not been developed by archaeologists working in either the Old or New Worlds. Since there are so many avenues which one can pursue in analyzing prehistoric figurines (e.g., stylistic, symbolic, iconographic, functional, and technological), the prospect of designing a comprehensive framework would be akin to a Herculean labor.

At this stage in our research it seems best to take small steps, not to run before we can walk (Renfrew 1985:11). If we are to begin making strides in the study of Neolithic figurines, new questions need to be raised, and answers, no matter how preliminary, need to be suggested. As others have argued, there are no *final* answers in archaeology, only responses that will stimulate others to think, render what is said inadequate, and so move on (Shanks and Tilley 1987:3). Therefore, while this volume is part of the series of final reports on Franchthi Cave, and therefore presents the data as fully as possible, it is also written with larger concerns in mind. Those matters are explored in the hope of losing a bit more of our archaeological innocence.

ACKNOWLEDGMENTS

To thank adequately the many people who offered advice and help on this study would fill a volume in itself. I am especially grateful to Thomas W. Jacobsen, who initially suggested the topic of Neolithic figurines at Franchthi Cave. Since my first years as a graduate student, Tom has provided invaluable assistance and guidance at all levels. The excavations at Franchthi Cave and the program at Indiana University, both directed by Tom, created an unusually stimulating environment for Neolithic studies in Greece. I am deeply indebted to all my colleagues and friends in both places.

I would like to single out four people in particular who consistently provided support, insightful advice, and incalculable hours of discussion: Tracey Cullen, Shelby Brown, K. D. Vitelli, and Michalis Fotiadis. Both Tracey and Shelby read earlier drafts, and their comments contributed substantially to the present manuscript.

On a more technical level, I owe a great debt to Peter Ward for his computer assistance on cluster analysis, Reg Heron for photographing the Franchthi collection, and Lisa Williams for her editorial expertise. I would also like to extend my gratitude to the American Council of Learned Societies for a postdoctoral fellowship, and to the late John L. Caskey and the late Dimitrios Theocharis, who allowed me to study unpublished material in Greece under their authority. It is with gratitude that I acknowledge the support of the Office of the Vice President for Research at the University of Michigan, which provided a grant towards the printing costs of this fascicle.

Finally, I would like to thank my extraordinary family: Kathy and Nina, who both deserve medals for patience and support, Frank, Eddie, Bobbi, Charles, Rho, Dick, Stacy, Eric, and Dennis.

In the case of my parents and my husband, words fail. To my mother and father I offer my deepest love and respect. To Steve, a Mickey Mantle baseball card.

INTRODUCTION

Excavations at Franchthi Cave, in the southern Argolid, began in the summer of 1967 and continued for seven additional seasons. These campaigns exposed two areas of human activity: the cave itself and a section along the modern shoreline, referred to as Paralia. Investigations in the forepart of the cave[1] revealed a succession of stratified deposits from what are called in traditional terms the Upper Palaeolithic, Mesolithic, and Neolithic periods. Paralia, which lies within 100 m of the cave's mouth, seems to have been occupied only in the Neolithic, however. Evidence for earlier activity on this part of the site is lacking (Jacobsen and Farrand 1987).

These two areas produced a small corpus of anthropomorphic and zoomorphic images dating exclusively to the Neolithic. Of the 45 pieces recovered, only 24 qualify unequivocally as figurines. The remaining 21 are classified in this volume as possible figurine fragments, since their status as figurines or parts of figurines is uncertain.

While the size of the Franchthi sample is modest, the collection is important for several reasons. First, figurine collections of more than a few examples from a single site are extremely rare in southern Greece.[2] Franchthi is only one of two sites in that region to yield a sample greater than 20. Second, since almost all of the Franchthi figures[3] can be reliably dated on stylistic or stratigraphic grounds, the sample proved critical for devising the first chronological and typological sequence of Neolithic figurines in southern Greece. It is only with such temporal frameworks that we can begin to answer questions about the evolution and variability of these images and their significance to early Greek societies. Finally, the evidence from this important site helped shape new ideas about the possible uses of such artifacts in nonliterate societies like that at Franchthi.

This study contains seven chapters, the first three of which are devoted to the evidence from Franchthi. Chapter 1 provides an overview of the sample and includes general discussions of chronology, raw material, subject matter, and design. Chapter 2 offers a detailed description of each figurine. Chapter 3, which examines the production of the figurines, considers how they were made, how much time was invested in their production, and who within the village may have been responsible for manufacturing these images. Chapter 4 proposes guidelines for deciphering use and meaning among prehistoric figurines in general, while Chapter 5 applies those guidelines to the Franchthi corpus in particular.

The penultimate chapter, Chapter 6, leaves the confines of Franchthi society to gain a more regional perspective on figurines of the Greek Neolithic, especially those from southern Greece. Aided by computerized cluster analysis, detailed comparisons with other southern Greek groups are offered in terms of style, archaeological context, and function. General comparisons are made with figurines from northern Greece, particularly Thessaly.[4] The chapter explores where, when, and ultimately why neighboring and distant villages produced similar or different figurines, whether settlements manipulated their figurines in comparable social contexts, and if, indeed, these eminently portable objects were ever traded or exchanged among settlements. While it would have been worthwhile to include Balkan and Anatolian figurines in the comparative survey, such an ambitious undertaking was well beyond the scope of this volume. On the other hand, the extraordinarily rich corpus of Balkan figurines stands in marked contrast to the southern Greek collection and raises questions about the varying functions of figurines in the two regions. Therefore, Chapter 6 examines, in a cursory fashion, select evidence from southeastern Europe and suggests that anthropomorphic and zoomorphic images played very different roles in Balkan, as opposed to southern Greek, society.

Finally, the concluding chapter stands as a Janus-faced portal, offering both a recapitulation of the previous pages and a view toward future avenues of inquiry.

Deities, Dolls, and Devices

Neolithic Figurines from Franchthi Cave, Greece

CHAPTER ONE

An Overview of the Franchthi Figurines

Franchthi Cave, one of 21 sites in southern Greece to yield Neolithic figurines (Maps 1 and 2), has produced the second largest collection of anthropomorphic and zoomorphic images in the Peloponnese (Tables 1 and 2). Twenty-four, mostly fragmentary, examples came to light from areas within the cave, as well as from trenches opened along the modern shoreline (Paralia).[5]

As an introduction to these 24 examples, this chapter provides an overview of the figures' chronological distribution, archaeological contexts, raw materials, subject matter, and designs.

The relevant evidence from Franchthi is presented briefly in each section, and, where possible, general comparisons with other collections in southern Greece are drawn.

CHRONOLOGICAL DISTRIBUTION (Figure 1)

The chronological sequence employed here is site-specific and generally coincides with both the absolute and relative dating reported in preliminary publications on Franchthi Cave (e.g., Jacobsen 1969, 1973a-b, 1976). Following Jacobsen (1976), this study adopts a quadripartite schema for the Neolithic: Early, Middle, Late, and Final (EN, MN, LN, and FN). This relative sequence is derived principally from ceramic evidence at the site, with each phase defined by a limited range of wares. EN is characterized by burnished monochrome and red-patterned wares, MN by monochrome and patterned Urfirnis, LN by several varieties of matte-painted ware and black burnished pottery, and FN by coarse, largely undecorated examples, crusted, and pattern-burnished wares (see Jacobsen 1969, 1973a-b for a full description). With the exception of one biscuit, No Lime/Sandy, defined by Vitelli, the ceramic terminology used in this study is that employed by Jacobsen in his preliminary reports.[6]

The absolute chronology used in this study is that of Jacobsen (1976), namely: EN: 6000–5000; MN: 5000–4500; LN: 4500–4000; and FN: 4000–3000 b.c. (all uncalibrated dates). To a large extent, these general dates are supported by the extensive series of radiometric age determinations derived from the excavations (Jacobsen and Farrand 1987:Plate 71).

Since many of the deposits at Franchthi that produced figurines are disturbed (Appendix A), only a few examples can be securely dated on the basis of stratigraphy. Only one figurine, FC 101, came from an excavation unit[7] which produced a radiocarbon date. Most of the pieces in the collection are dated by comparing their fabric, design, and style with previously established norms recognized among the ceramic wares at the site. Since each ware is usually associated with a specific phase within the Neolithic, each figurine can be assigned to one of the major phases, provided that the example closely resembles the ceramic styles (Table 2). Occasionally, greater

KEY TO MAPS 1 AND 2

1. Halai
2. Elateia
3. Ayia Marina
4. Chaeronea
5. Orchomenos
6. Poliyira
7. Pyrgos Magoula
8. Thespiae
9. Eutresis
10. Thebes
11. Marathon (Cave of Pan)
12. Nea Makri
13. Poussi Kaloyeri
14. Glyphada
15. Athens (Agora, Acropolis, Patissia)
16. Kaza Panakton (Eleutherai)
17. Perachora
18. Gonia
19. Corinth
20. Ayios Yerasimos
21. Phlius
22. Nemea
23. Klenies
24. Mycenae
25. Prosymna
26. Tiryns
27. Lerna
28. Franchthi Cave
29. Levidion
30. Loukas
31. Ayioryitika
32. Asea
33. Koufovouno
34. Asteria
35. Apidia
36. Ayios Strategos
37. Goulas (Plitra)
38. Epidaurus Limera?
39. Alepotrypa
40. Malthi
41. Arnokatarako
42. Pheia (Ayios Andreas)
43. Akratas
44. Aegina
45. Kephala
46. Saliagos
47. Paros
48. Naxos
49. Amorgos
50. Eleusis
51. Kitsos Cave

Map 1. Southern Greece and the Cyclades: Neolithic sites. o = excavated sites; x = surface finds.

Map 2. Southern Greece and the Cyclades: Neolithic sites with figurines. o = excavated sites; x = surface finds.

TABLE 1

FRANCHTHI FIGURINES LISTED BY CATALOGUE NUMBER

Catalogue Number	*Plate Number*	*Date*	*Trench*
FC 4	4, 5	FN	F:4
FC 11	16, 17	EN/MN trans.	A:31
FC 12	4, 5	MN	A:53
FC 28	6, 7	LN	FF1:5
FC 30	16, 17	MN	G1:3
FC 31	16, 17	MN	G1:5
FC 41	18, 19	FN	H:21
FC 42	2, 3	MN	H:21
FC 57	10, 11	LN	H1:18
FC 60	14, 15	LN	H1:27
FC 68	10, 11	MN	H1:51
FC 88	18, 19	FN	FAN:59
FC 101	12, 13	LN	FAN:114
FC 112	4, 5	FN	FAS:68
FC 117	12, 13	MN	Q6NE section
FC 118	1	LN	FAS:103
FC 122	6, 7	EN	H2B:59
FC 124	8, 9	MN	FAS:123
FC 167	2, 3	MN	O5NE:27
FC 177	18, 19	MN	P5:31
FC 190	6, 7	EN	Q5S:186
FC 208	8, 9	MN	L5:69
FP 173	8, 9	MN	H1A:78
FS 101	14, 15	LN	G1:19

TABLE 2

SOUTHERN GREEK SITES WITH NEOLITHIC FIGURINES

Site	*Total Number Reported*	*Number by Chronological Phase*
Corinth	37	10 MN; 17 LN; 3 FN; 1 MN or LN; 3 LN or FN; 3 LN, FN, or EH
Franchthi	24	2 EN; 1 EN/MN; 11 MN; 6 LN; 4 FN
Kephala	8	8 FN
Saliagos	8	8 LN
Asea	7	4 MN; 1 FN; 2 MN, LN, FN, or EH
Lerna	7	6 MN; 1 MN or LN
Koufovouno	5	5 MN or LN
Agora (Athens)	4	2 MN or LN; 2 FN
Akratas	4	2 MN; 2 MN or LN
Alepotrypa	3	2 LN; 1 LN or FN
Aegina	2	2 MN or LN
Nemea	1	1 MN
Kitsos	1	1 FN
Nea Makri	1	1 EN or LN
Amorgos	1	1 LN
Naxos	1	1 LN
Eleusis	1	1 LN
Patissia(Athens)	1	1 LN
Tiryns	1	1 MN or LN
Mycenae	1	1 MN or LN
Malthi	1	1 MN or LN
TOTAL	119	2 EN; 1 EN/MN; 34 MN; 37 LN; 19 FN; 1 EN or LN; 16 MN or LN; 2 MN, LN, FN, or EH; 3 LN, FN, or EH; 4 LN or FN

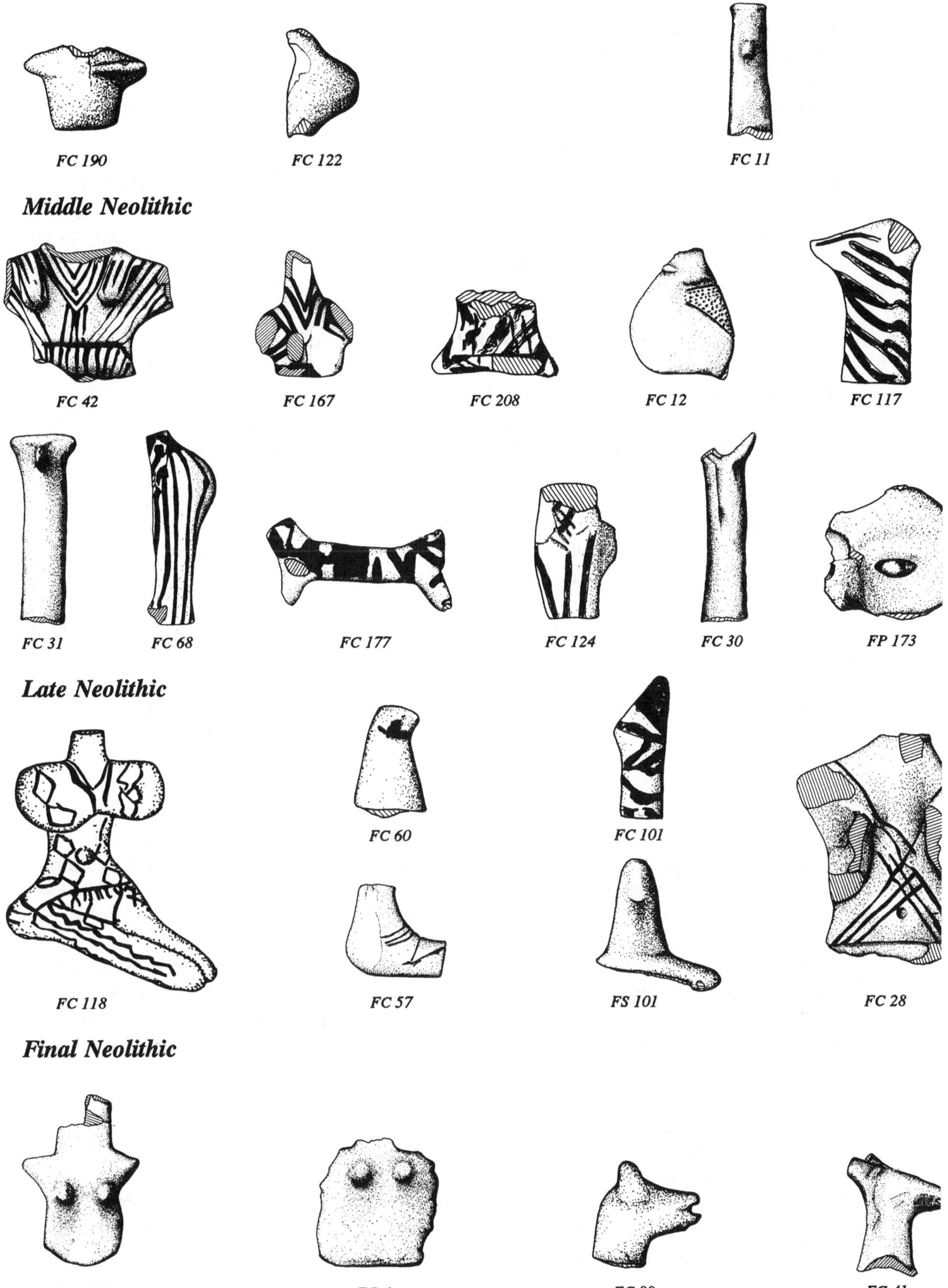

Figure 1. Drawings of Franchthi figurines, showing chronological distribution.

refinement is possible, and a figure can be dated to the earlier or later part of a major phase.[8]

Of the 24 figurines in this study, one is probably EN, one Early/Middle transitional (EN/MN), eleven MN, six LN, and four FN. Only one example (FC 122) defies definite chronological classification, although it is assigned provisionally to the Early Neolithic on the basis of northern Greek comparanda.

Both the size of the sample and its chronological distribution accord well with what is known from the rest of southern Greece. Most Neolithic collections in the Peloponnese, Attica, and the Cyclades are small and lack EN figurines (Tables 2 and 3). This pattern stands in marked contrast, however, to the evidence of northern Greece, particularly Thessaly, where both large samples and a fairly extensive collection of EN figurines are reported (see Chapter 6).[9]

ARCHAEOLOGICAL CONTEXT

Three examples from Franchthi (FC 124, FC 190, FC 101) come from possibly undisturbed units. The remaining pieces are associated with redeposited or secondary fill, postdepositional disturbances (e.g., erosion, pit-digging, building), or modern (i.e., twentieth-century) remains (Appendix A).

The few images deriving from undisturbed contexts are found with features such as hearths and ashy deposits and with artifacts traditionally linked with domestic activities. For the most part, contextual evidence from the rest of southern Greece is also limited. Only Saliagos and Kephala, both single-phase sites from the later part of the Neolithic, provide data which may have functional significance (see Chapter 6).

The figurines at Franchthi have been recovered from both the cave and Paralia. Five examples were recovered along the modern shoreline; the remaining nineteen were found inside the cave (Figure 2; Table 4). If this distribution is meaningful, it signals that, for much of the Neolithic, activities associated with figurines tended to be enacted inside, rather than outside, the confines of the cave.

RAW MATERIAL

The majority of figurines recovered from Franchthi are made of clay: 22 of the 24 examples are ceramic. Of the two remaining pieces, one (FS 101) is carved from white marble/alabaster, while the other (FC 122) defies classification. It is made from either an atypical, high-fired clay or an unidentified, dark gray stone.[10]

The Franchthiotes may have manufactured or employed anthropomorphic and zoomorphic images from less durable materials, such as wood, textiles, or fibers, but that evidence has long since vanished.[11] The general pattern exhibited at Franchthi echoes that from the rest of Neolithic Greece: clay was clearly the material of preference, while ventures into the production of stone figurines were rare.[12]

No archaeometric tests were conducted on the Franchthi figurines to determine the possible provenience of raw materials. Given, however, that the figures' fabrics, surface treatments, and range of colors so closely resemble those of the pottery found at the site, conclusions drawn from analyses on sherd samples may be cautiously applied to the figurines.

A small sample of patterned Urfirnis sherds from five sites in the northeastern Peloponnese, including Franchthi Cave, was subjected to a series of trace-element analyses (e.g., optical emission spectroscopy, neutron activation) as well as to petrographic studies (Cullen 1985a-b). The results

TABLE 3

CHRONOLOGICAL DISTRIBUTION OF NEOLITHIC FIGURINES FROM SOUTHERN GREECE

***EN* (n=2?)**

Franchthi	2 (?)

***EN/MN* (n=1)**

Franchthi	1

***EN or LN* (n=1)**

Nea Makri	1

***MN* (n=34)**

Franchthi	11
Corinth	10
Lerna	6
Asea	4
Akratas	2
Nemea	1

***MN or LN* (n=16)**

Koufovouno	5
Agora	2
Akratas	2
Aegina	2
Lerna	1
Corinth	1
Mycenae	1
Malthi	1
Tiryns	1

***LN* (n=37)**

Corinth	17
Franchthi	6
Saliagos	8
Alepotrypa	2
Naxos	1
Patissia	1
Eleusis	1
Amorgos	1

***LN or FN* (n=4)**

Alepotrypa	1
Corinth	3

***FN* (n=19)**

Kephala	8
Franchthi	4
Corinth	3
Asea	1
Kitsos	1
Agora	2

***LN, FN, or EH* (n=3)**

Corinth	3

***MN, LN, FN, or EH* (n=2)**

Asea	2

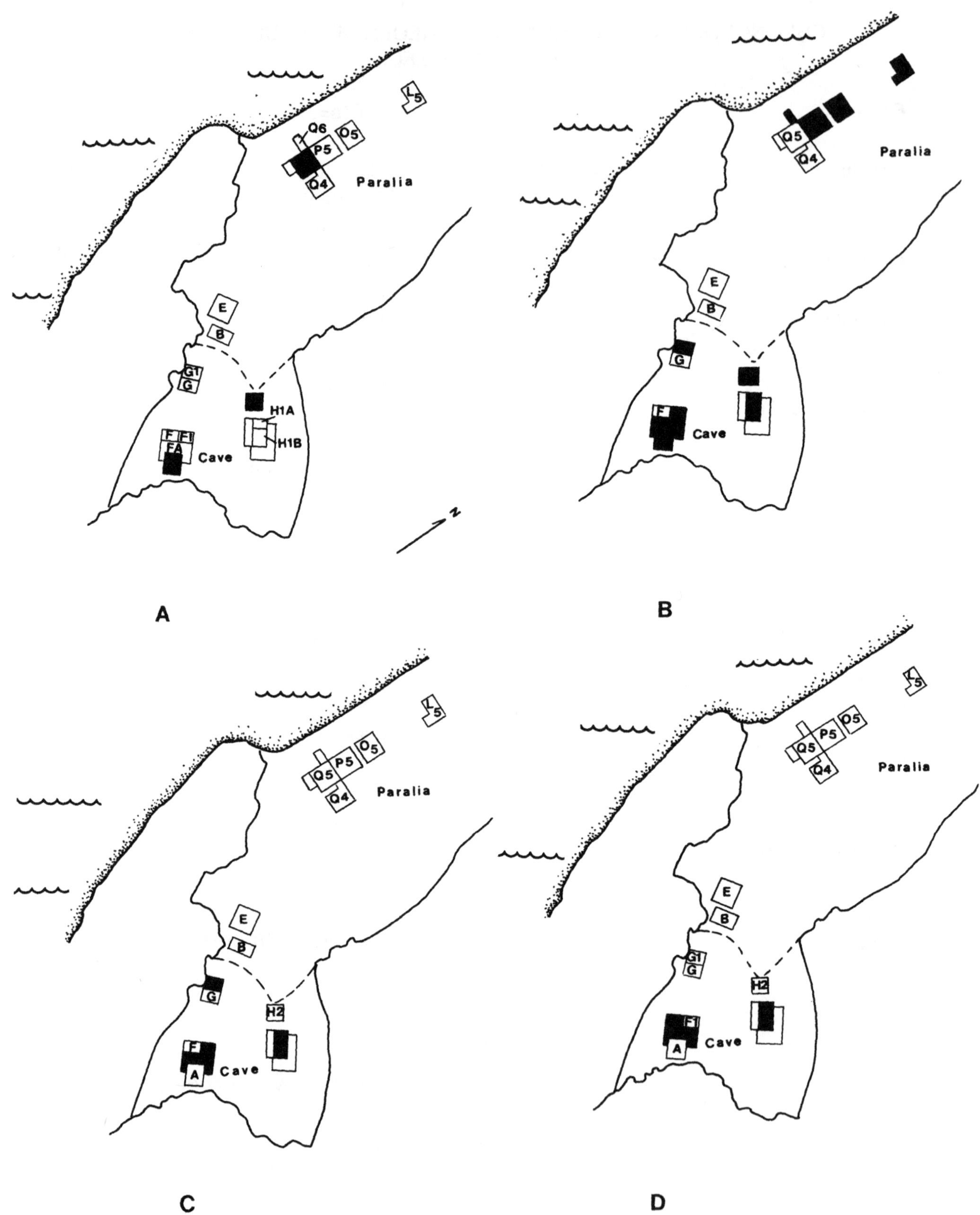

Figure 2. Chronological distribution of Franchthi figurines by trench. Dark areas indicate presence of figurines. A = Early Neolithic; B = Middle Neolithic; C = Late Neolithic; D = Final Neolithic.

TABLE 4

CHRONOLOGICAL DISTRIBUTION OF FRANCHTHI FIGURINES BY TRENCH

EN

FC 190	Q5S:186
FC 122	H2B:59

EN/MN

FC 11	A:31

MN

FC 12	A:53
FC 30	G1:3
FC 31	G1:5
FC 42	H:21
FC 68	H1:51
FC 117	Q6NE section
FC 124	FAS:123
FC 167	O5NE:27
FC 177	P5:31
FC 208	L5:69
FP 173	H1A:78

LN

FC 28	FF1:5
FC 57	H1:18
FC 60	H1:27
FC 101	FAN:114
FC 118	FAS:103
FS 101	G1:19

FN

FC 4	F:4
FC 41	H:21
FC 88	FAN:59
FC 112	FAS:68

suggest that MN patterned Urfirnis was a local undertaking, though potters "probably called upon discrete and disparate [clay] sources from a broader catchment area than the immediate vicinity of the site" (Jones in Cullen 1985a:235). The tests revealed no convincing evidence that this patterned fine ware was produced at a single site and subsequently exchanged or distributed among settlements (Cullen et al. 1984; Cullen 1985a: 224–261). As discussed below, the evidence of the southern Greek figurines supports a comparable claim: for the most part, clay figurines were designed for internal use at each site, not for local exchange. Only occasionally does an odd clay example suggest some kind of exchange or transport of these small, easily portable images.

Unlike clay, which was locally and immediately available to the inhabitants of Franchthi, marble was probably more difficult to obtain. Outcrops of marble are not documented in the vicinity of the cave (van Andel and Vitaliano 1987:20), and only a few sources are known from southern Greece: one at Doliana in the Peloponnese, three in Attica (Mt. Pendeli, Mt. Hymettos, and Sounion), and sources in the Mani Peloponnese (Herz and Wenner 1978; Herz, pers. comm. to Jacobsen, 1991). Varying grades, including very high quality marble, are also available in the Cyclades. Whether FS 101 or, indeed, any of the other marble figurines from southern Greek sites (e.g., Corinth, Koufovouno) were crafted from stones originally extracted from one of these sources is not known. Isotopic analysis conducted on five marble vessel fragments (FS 30, 49, 140, 262, and 263) from mixed, EN/MN, and MN contexts at Franchthi yielded provisional results. The five samples appear to have come from several different sources. FS 263 falls into the field of either the Mani or Doliana marbles. FS 30 and 140 are likely from the same source, which includes three possibilities: Sounion, Paros (Ayios Minas), or the southeastern coast of Naxos. FS 49 and FS 262 are more problematic. If they are marble, they do not match any of the sources in the current data base (Herz, pers. comm. to Jacobsen, 1991). Given the growing body of data indicating long-range transport of goods and raw materials in Neolithic Greece (Renfrew 1973; Runnels 1983, 1985; Torrence 1986), it would not be surprising to find that either the unworked marble or the finished product, whether figurine or vessel, was imported from some distance from the settlement at Franchthi.

SUBJECT MATTER

The Franchthi corpus is composed chiefly of fragments; complete examples are virtually absent, although three anthropomorphic pieces are nearly complete (FC 112, FC 118, FC 122). The rest of the sample consists of eight human heads, four human torsos, six human lower bodies, and three fragments of animals. Despite the nature of the collection, clear patterns are identifiable in the choice of subject matter, stance, sex, and degree of sculptural complexity.

Throughout the Neolithic, the preference at Franchthi was for small, simple, anthropomorphic images. Sex, where determinable, is most often female (n=12) and never clearly male. Some of the ostensibly "sexless" examples (e.g., FC 190) may have been deliberately designed as "genderless."[13]

Facial features are fairly perfunctory: mouths and ears are never indicated on anthropomorphic images, though they are detailed on zoomorphic examples. Eyes are infrequently marked and small, and modeled noses appear commonly. Postures are limited to standing, sitting with legs extended, and possibly crouching. Arms appear as short stumps or are curled to the figure's breasts.

These characteristics of gesture, posture, sex, and subject recur at most other Neolithic sites in southern Greece and, to a lesser extent, in the north. Franchthi does, however, possess one peculiar category of figurine: the disembodied body part. The corpus contains a left buttock (FC 122, nearly complete) and an upper torso finished at the waist (FC 190, minus the head), as well as several "half-body" pendants.[14] While we are a long way from understanding the meanings behind this unusual class of objects, its existence at Franchthi raises a number of intriguing questions (see Chapter 5).

DESIGN

Twelve pieces from Franchthi have painted, incised, or plastic designs which are not manifestly representative of anatomical features. Combining this sample with all other decorated examples from southern Greece, the total number is less than forty.

A comparative study of design elements on all decorated figures suggests that, at least during the Middle and Late Neolithic, Franchthi seems to have maintained close bonds with at least one neighboring settlement (see Chapter 6). Although the size of the sample cautions us to view the conclusions as provisional, comparable results were obtained by a more sophisticated design analysis conducted on MN Urfirnis ware (Cullen 1985a-b).

CHAPTER TWO
Catalogue

DESCRIPTIVE CATEGORIES

This chapter offers detailed and standardized information on each piece. For each figurine the following information is provided:

A. brief description
B. present condition
C. maximum height
D. maximum width
E. maximum thickness
F. ceramic description
G. design
H. color
I. hardness
J. miscellaneous features
K. sex
L. wear
M. plate number(s)

Although these categories are, by and large, self-explanatory, each warrants a short discussion of its potential utility to the study of prehistoric figurines and of the particular problems with the collection under study.

Brief Description (A)

The descriptions offered here, which are constrained by ethnocentric notions of art and observation, isolate two categories for each figurine: (1) the part(s) of the body depicted (e.g., human head with incised eyes and modeled nose; left buttock of seated figure, with painted pubic triangle); and (2) the figure's general shape (e.g., cylindrically-shaped [head]; rectangular, plank-like [torso]).

Present Condition (B)

This category identifies all breaks and describes the present surface condition of the piece (e.g., surface eroded, paint flaking, chipped across buttock).

Both stone and clay figures tend to fracture at their narrowest or weakest points, such as the narrow juncture of the neck or waist, places where hidden flaws exist, or (in the case of clay) locations where air has become trapped in pockets during manufacture. Most collections of prehistoric figurines contain a high percentage of images broken at the neck or waist.

Archaeologists commonly assume that once a figure broke it was no longer considered useful and was consigned to the rubbish pile (Ucko 1968:435). In fact, ethnographic studies do not support this notion; some cultures use broken figurines and consider the spontaneous fracturing of objects a positive omen (Massé 1954:274). As argued below (and elsewhere [Talalay 1982, 1983a, 1987]), at least one type of figurine known both from Franchthi and other sites in the northeastern Peloponnese appears to have been intentionally broken or split.[15]

Measurements (C-E)

Current research on prehistoric figurines suggests that accurate and detailed measurements of various heights and widths and their respective ratios can be instructive (Ucko 1968:174; Getz-Preziosi 1972, 1977, 1987).[16] These determinations, however, are useful only when complete figurines are available for study. Since the Franchthi collection is composed primarily of fragments, only the maximum height, width, and thickness (in meters) are recorded.[17]

Ceramic Description (F)

The ceramic vocabulary selected for the attribute lists is based on observations first formulated more than 40 years ago and since amplified and refined by several archaeologists (Weinberg 1947, 1970; Jacobsen 1969, 1973a-b, 1976, 1979, 1984a; Vitelli 1974, forthcoming). For the most part[18], Jacobsen's terminology and descriptions are adopted throughout this work.

Design (G)

The designs listed here refer only to painted, incised, or applied elements which are not readily recognizable as anatomical features (e.g., incised lines on cheeks, painted dots on legs). Occasionally, some of the marks on the figurines are ambiguous and, therefore, overlap with category A (brief descriptions which include anatomical parts). Because the photographs and drawings in this work provide a more vivid and accurate record than verbal descriptions, designs are described only summarily in the attribute list.

Design analysis has proven to be an extremely valuable tool for measuring regional interaction (Hardin 1977; Plog 1980; Hantman and Plog 1982; Cullen 1985a-b), despite theoretical and methodological problems associated with studies on style. In an attempt to identify possible intersite communication, this work compares the design elements on the Franchthi figures with those selected at other sites. Only four other settlements in southern Greece have produced decorated figurines: Asea, Corinth, Akratas, and Lerna.

Attributing specific meanings to design or decoration on human or zoomorphic figures is a risky undertaking. Decoration can be interpreted on several levels: aesthetic, symbolic, and/or representational (e.g., depicting clothing, tattooing, or jewelry). Demonstrating the intent of the maker is often impossible. Reasoned speculation can, however, provide provocative insights and help us better understand how symbolic meanings can mediate between design structure and social functions.

Color (H)

Without some objective scale, it is difficult to provide uniform and universally understandable color descriptions. Although not a totally satisfactory solution to the problem (because of human subjectivity and variations in lighting), the Munsell Soil Color Charts offer the best standard available. They are used in this study to provide some objective measures for a color's value, hue, and chroma.

Since the color of fired clays depends on many variables—including differences within and between clay beds, varying choices of tempering, and divergence in firing atmosphere— variations in color are to be expected both within and among sites. On the other hand, conformities in color suggest, among other things, intentional control and duplication of manufacturing processes and/or firing techniques, and, perhaps, a very limited selection of clay sources or beds.

Hardness (I)

The temperature and atmosphere of firing directly affect a clay's hardness or resistance to abrasion (Vitelli 1974:30). Since the temperature of most prehistoric firings tended to be low, the range in hardness is usually restricted, though some variability can be expected. The index used in this work is the Moh's Hardness Scale[19], in which 1 is the softest (talc) and 10 is the hardest (diamond).

Relatively low readings (2.0, 2.5) suggest that, among other possibilities: the producer and/or user of the figurine were not concerned with the object's durability; that the act of making the figure was more important than manipulating the artifact; or that the figure was rarely touched or moved, so that its resistance to abrasion and handling was inconsequential. On the other hand, high Mohs (4.0–6.0) might indicate that the figure was intended to have an "active" life and, consequently, that the maker intentionally exposed the piece to a thorough firing in order to ensure its permanence.

Miscellaneous Features (J)

This category is somewhat heterogeneous and subsumes those characteristics which cannot be logically included under the other headings. Most frequently noted are tool marks, fingerprints, and odd impressions still visible on the clay, but not observable in the photographs or included in the drawings. Also noted are suggestions regarding the original shape or form of the intact figurine.

Sex (K)

Determining sex in prehistoric figurines is not always a simple matter (Ucko 1968:173). The ethnographic record reveals that male figures can have both male genitalia and small breasts or nipples; the unwary archaeologist contemplating only the torso of such a figure might easily label it, erroneously, female. Because of such ambiguities (Macintosh 1977:194), I selected several criteria in determining the intended sex of a figure. The presence of male genitalia was used to signal the male sex, and the portrayal of pubic triangles to signal the female sex. Sex was also affixed as female when both the lower and upper parts of the body survived and had no male genitalia, but did show breasts, or, alternatively, when only the upper portion of the figure survived and showed what appear to be breasts, rather than small male-like nipples. It should be kept in mind that the makers and users of these figures may have viewed some examples as sexless. Long-since vanished accoutrements, such as clothing, may also have originally indicated gender as well as the sex of a figure.[20]

Wear (L)

The significance of wear patterns is not always apparent, given the difficulties of establishing which marks are associated with the active life of a figure and which are attributable to wear that occurred after a piece was discarded. Moreover, the absence of wear on a piece can be deceiving. While abraded or worn surfaces may indicate frequent contact with another, harder surface, the absence of wear may indicate that the figure, although mobile, came into regular contact with a softer surface, such as a pouch or human touch. The entries in the catalogue indicate the location of the wear, not the degree or kind of abrasion.

CATALOGUE

Nearly Complete Anthropomorphic Figurines

(excluding complete, dismembered body-parts)

<u>FC 118</u>

A. seated figure with arms curled to breasts, legs together, extending outward; flat, plank-like torso, pellet for navel; splayed buttocks; unarticulated hands and feet
B. broken at neck; surface in good condition, paint crackling where applied thickly
C. 0.095 (neck to buttocks)
D. 0.070 (across shoulders)
0.065 (across buttocks)
E. 0.018 (from back to middle of chest where hands lie)
F. [LN] matte paint
G. entire figure covered with complex painted design: vest-like attire of linked diamonds covers front and back of torso; short, two-strand "necklace" hangs in front and back; low-slung "belt" encircles hips, from which hang short, vertical lines; set of wavy lines runs across right buttock down side and front of right leg; left leg undecorated; pubic triangle outlined in black paint
H. surface: 7.5YR 6/4 light brown; paint: 7.5YR 3/0 very dark gray
I. 6.0
J. —
K. F
L. none observed
M. Plate 1

Anthropomorphic Heads

<u>FC 11</u>

A. slightly tapering cylindrical head/neck, with flat top and square protrusion for nose
B. broken at base of neck, original surface intact
C. 0.060
D. 0.021
E. 0.017 (across nose)
F. [EN/MN] No Lime/Sandy (Vitelli, pers. comm. 1990),[6] surface smoothed, not burnished
G. none visible

H. variable: 5YR 5/4 reddish brown; 5YR 3/1 very dark gray
I. 4.0
J. vertical tool marks visible—reedy quality to marks; tiny circular impression near break at back, made by seed, pebble, or some kind of attachment
K. not determinable
L. none observed
M. Plates 16, 17

FC 30

A. long, cylindrical head/neck, terminating in two horn-like projections
B. broken at base of neck and at point of one "horn"; original surface worn in places
C. 0.081
D. 0.021
E. 0.015
F. [MN] monochrome Urfirnis, slightly lustrous; covered with streaky wash; uneven, irregular surface
G. none visible
H. 2.5YR 3/0 very dark gray
I. 5.0
J. fingerprints visible
K. not determinable
L. none observed
M. Plates 16, 17

FC 31

A. long cylindrical head/neck, terminating in two triangular ears; pinched-out nose
B. broken at base of neck; well-smoothed surface, worn in places
C. 0.076
D. 0.027 (across ears)
E. 0.018 (across nose)
F. [MN] monochrome Urfirnis, slightly lustrous
G. none visible
H. 2.5YR 6/6 light red and 2.5YR 5/6 red
I. 4.0
J. —
K. not determinable
L. slightly worn across back of left ear
M. Plates 16, 17

FC 60

A. conical head with beak-like projection for nose
B. broken at neck; most of original surface worn, remains of paint and burnishing visible
C. 0.029
D. 0.018
E. 0.015 (across beak-like nose)

F. [LN] matte paint
G. red paint visible in patches, too worn to reconstruct original design
H. surface: 7.5YR 6/4 light brown; paint: 2.5YR 4/8 red
I. 3.0
J. —
K. not determinable
L. none observed
M. Plates 14, 15

FC 101

A. conical head with rounded crown, flattened back of head, and small pinched-out nose; diagonal incisions on either side of nose, probably indicating eyes (see G below for other incisions)
B. broken at neck; surface worn in places, paint crackling
C. 0.037
D. 0.015
E. 0.012 (across nose)
F. [LN] matte paint (black on gray)
G. front and back not treated as discrete decorative spaces, all lines connect: solid painted "cap" over crown, swirling diagonals encircle face and neck in sloppy barber-pole effect; in addition to eye incisions, incised diagonal line on either cheek (like modern tribal scars)
H. surface: 5YR 4/1 dark gray; paint: 5YR 2.5/1 black
I. 5.0
J. —
K. not determinable
L. none observed
M. Plates 12, 13

FC 117

A. cylindrical head with pinched-out nose, two small punctures for nostrils, two sets of diagonal lines on either side of nose
B. broken at neck, along top and back of head, and tip of nose; surface slightly worn all over
C. 0.045
D. 0.026
E. 0.028 (across nose)
F. [MN] patterned Urfirnis (possible early variety: Vitelli, pers. comm. 1990)
G. linear design encircles entire piece; like FC 101, slightly disorderly barber-pole configuration
H. surface: 7.5YR 6/4 light brown; paint: (back) 2.5YR 5/6 red, (front) 2.5YR 3/0 very dark gray
I. 3.0
J. —
K. not determinable
L. none observable
M. Plates 12, 13

FS 101

A. head, neck, and left arm of stone figurine; conical head slightly flattened at crown, beak-like nose; short, rounded, and unarticulated arms

B. broken along right shoulder and across top of chest
C. 0.032
D. 0.034
E. 0.015
F. marble/alabaster (identification made by C. J. Vitaliano)
G. none visible
H. —
I. —
J. —
K. not determinable
L. none observed
M. Plates 14, 15

FP 173

A. fragment of face-pot, includes entire right eye, lightly modeled left brow, part of right eye, nose, and left ear or lock of hair; interior surface unmodeled; gradual thinning toward top, suggesting piece is near rim of vessel
B. broken along all outer edges; surface slightly worn
C. 0.036
D. 0.036
E. 0.014 (across nose); 0.004 (minimum thickness at top)
F. [MN] coarse Urfirnis
G. thin horizontal band painted near top on interior; traces of red paint on exterior
H. exterior surface: 5YR 6/3 light reddish brown; paint: 10R 4/6 red; interior surface: 5YR 5/1 gray; stripe: 5YR 5/2 reddish gray and 5YR 5/3 reddish brown
I. interior: 4.0; exterior: 3.0
J. —
K. not determinable
L. none observed
M. Plates 8, 9

Anthropomorphic Torsos

FC 4

A. square, plank-like torso with small, pellet breasts
B. broken at neck, chipped along left side and part of both shoulders; most of surface worn
C. 0.054
D. 0.043
E. 0.016
F. [FN] coarse red ware (not characteristic of early FN wares at Franchthi: Vitelli, pers. comm. 1990); unusual fabric, flakes of vermilion paint on surface; slip and possible burnish visible in places
G. none visible
H. 10YR 2.5/2 very dark brown
I. 4.0

J. finished lower edge; flattened base allows figure to stand free; may have had arm extensions, as in FC 112, or squared-off shoulders
K. F
L. none observed
M. Plates 4, 5

FC 28

A. torso with arms curled to breasts (unarticulated hands merge with breasts); flat back; slight swell at belly; navel indicated by small hole; incised horizontal line beneath belly may mark top of pubic triangle
B. broken at neck, both shoulders and below waist; chipped along both sides; surface worn, especially on back
C. 0.079
D. 0.064 (across shoulders)
E. 0.024 (across left breast)
F. [LN] matte paint
G. three sets of parallel lines form large X across back, lines continue over shoulder; similar X-pattern on front; snakey lines along left arm; thin horizontal band encircles part of neck
H. surface: 7.5YR 8/2 pinkish white; paint: 7.5YR 3/0 very dark gray
I. 4.0
J. possibly seated
K. F
L. none observed
M. Plates 6, 7

FC 42

A. torso with pendant breasts attached to shoulders; flat back with slight concavity at small of back; flat chest front with slightly swollen belly; leg sockets visible on underside of piece, below waist
B. broken at neck, top of both arms and beneath belly; paint crackling in places
C. 0.059
D. 0.072 (across shoulders)
E. 0.029 (across belly)
F. [MN] patterned Urfirnis (early variety: Vitelli, pers. comm. 1990)
G. complex painted linear decoration covers figure in coherent, well-planned pattern; basic design: back—concentric V's start at neck and terminate at waist, forming cape-like covering; front—concentric V's hang down from neck between breasts, horizontal belt-like stripe painted across top of belly, set of parallel lines starts at each shoulder, runs diagonally along front of torso, under belt, and vertically over belly.
H. surface: 5YR 7/4 pink; paint: 10R 4/6 red
I. 4.5
J. position of arms uncertain, did not curl to breasts; possibly both arms unarticulated stumps extending out from body, or right arm raised, since right shoulder higher than left
K. F
L. worn across breasts
M. Plates 2, 3

FC 112

A. schematized, fiddle-shaped body with stumpy arms; small pellet breasts affixed below arms; cylindrical neck
B. broken at neck; rough surface; if originally slipped or burnished, all traces have disappeared
C. 0.073
D. 0.048
E. 0.020
F. [FN] coarse red ware (not characteristic of early wares at Franchthi: Vitelli, pers. comm. 1990); possible traces of vermilion on surface (similar to FC 4)
G. none visible
H. 7.5YR 3/0 very dark gray and 7.5YR 5/4 brown
I. 3.0
J. complete except for head
K. F
L. none observed
M. Plates 4, 5

FC 167

A. torso, shoulders, and neck/head of flattish figure; pellet breasts
B. broken at tip of head, both shoulders, along left side, and waist; chipped at right breast and sheared along left breast, surface worn, paint crackling
C. 0.052
D. 0.040
E. 0.019 (across left breast)
F. [MN] patterned Urfirnis (early variety)
G. painted linear design covers entire figure; basic design: stacked V's starting at neck and terminating at waist (back and front); diagonal lines over shoulders; suggestion of horizontal stripe at waist
H. surface: 7.5YR 6/4 light brown; paint: 10R 5/8 red
I. 4.0
J. only "tip" of head missing; head probably terminated in slightly rounded crown; no facial features (?); scars and breaks suggest arms curled up to or over breasts
K. F
L. worn on back right
M. Plates 2, 3

FC 190

A. small rectangular torso, finished at waist; right arm extends straight out from body; left arm bent at elbow with forearm placed horizontally across chest; both arms unarticulated; spiral impression between shoulders possibly once held head
B. complete except for head; several cracks emanating from head socket; rough, uneven surface; original surface (?)
C. 0.024
D. 0.033
E. 0.014

F. [EN] Low/No Lime Sandy[6] (not identical to any EN fabric from site [Vitelli, pers. comm. 1990])
G. none visible
H. 7.5YR 4/0 dark gray
I. 2.0
J. replication experiments suggest head made of shell, sp. *Conus mediterraneus*
K. not determinable
L. none observed
M. Plates 6, 7

Anthropomorphic Lower Bodies

FC 12

A. right half of buttocks from waist to top of leg; incised and punctated pubic triangle; small clay pellet applied to lower back
B. broken at waist, broken or split along medial edge, and chipped along front; surface worn, especially around pubic region
C. 0.058
D. 0.021
E. 0.046
F. [MN] monochrome Urfirnis (washy paint, mostly worn off)
G. pubic region rendered with incision marking outer edge of triangle and filled with punctures arranged in roughly horizontal rows (pubic hair, cicatrices?)
H. washy surface: 5YR 3/1 very dark gray; abraded surface: 5YR 6/4 light reddish brown
I. 4.0
J. construction of piece revealed at medial break: inner core of clay formed first, coil of clay added to exterior for final shaping; piece originally in two halves (?) made to coalesce; stance uncertain, either crouching (cf. Diamant 1974b:Figure 1; Valmin 1938:Plate xxv:46) or legless (cf. FC 122)
K. F
L. worn around pubic region
M. Plates 4, 5

FC 57

A. right half of seated figure from waist to upper thigh; right half of incised pubic triangle and lines across stomach
B. broken along medial edge, waist, and top of thigh; rough, pitted surface (original?); two-tone coloring (see H, below)
C. 0.038
D. 0.028
E. 0.016
F. [LN?] coarse ware
G. slightly irregular diagonal lines incised from mid-stomach to outer hip (flesh rolls, cicatrices?)
H. buttock and back: 2.5YR 4/0 dark gray; rest of figure: 5YR 6/6 reddish yellow
I. 4.0

J. underside of legs flattened to allow figure to sit unsupported; incisions on stomach and pubis made by two different tools; right edge of pubic triangle marked by set of parallel lines
K. F
L. worn over buttock area
M. Plates 10, 11

<u>FC 68</u>

A. left leg and buttock of standing figure, with half of pubic triangle indicated by paint and incision; four diagonal incisions and small scar on upper thigh mark fingers and hand
B. broken at waist, chipped along toes, and split along medial edge; medial surface flattened and well-smoothed; original surface and paint intact
C. 0.088
D. 0.022
E. 0.030
F. [MN] patterned Urfirnis
G. entire leg covered with painted linear design: vertical lines from waist to feet; horizontal line encircles back of waist; pubic area painted solid
H. surface: 5YR 6/6 reddish yellow; paint: 2.5YR 4/8 red and 2.5YR 3/2 dusky red; medial surface: 2.5YR 6/6 light red
I. outer surface: 5.0; medial surface: 3.5
J. pubic triangle added as separate slab
K. F
L. none observed
M. Plates 10, 11

<u>FC 122</u>

A. left buttock
B. broken at waist and top of thigh; large flake removed from pubic region; surface slightly worn; has soapy feel
C. 0.029
D. 0.011
E. 0.020
F. not determinable: clay or stone (?)
G. none visible
H. mostly 7.5YR 3/0 very dark gray; some 7.5YR 5/2 brown
I. 4.0
J. fragment may be nearly complete, remains of waist and thigh too thin to support much additional material
K. F (?)
L. none observed
M. Plates 6, 7

<u>FC 124</u>

A. hip, buttock, and top of right leg; four diagonal incisions and scar mark fingers and hand; tiny fifth incision in pubic region; small tab on medial side suggests left leg once attached

B. broken at waist, top of thigh; split along medial edge, surface worn, paint washy
C. 0.037
D. 0.023 (including tab)
E. 0.024
F. [MN] patterned Urfirnis
G. entire piece covered with painted linear design, consisting primarily of vertical lines
H. surface: 2.5YR 5/8 red; paint: 2.5YR 3/4 dark reddish brown
I. 5.0
J. flattened and smoothed medial surface as in FC 68; break at waist shows small finished (?) area on back edge where paint and burnish remain
K. F
L. abraded across buttock
M. Plates 8, 9

FC 208

A. bell-shaped piece, representing waist, stomach, and upper pubic region; small puncture marking navel; incisions indicating pubic triangle
B. broken above waist; chipped around pubic region; smoothed along bottom (not necessarily broken)
C. 0.023
D. 0.035
E. 0.033
F. [MN] patterned Urfirnis
G. either side of navel: two sets of short parallel lines, one atop the other; painted design of roughly diagonal lines encircles figure
H. surface: 7.5YR 6/4 light brown; paint: 2.5YR 5/6 red
I. 3.0
J. right edge of pubic triangle marked by a set of parallel lines identical to configuration in FC 57
K. F
L. none observed
M. Plates 8, 9

Zoomorphic Images

FC 41

A. head and neck of deer or goat-like animal; rounded snout with mouth slightly open; set of ears or horns
B. broken at neck and at both ears/horns; surface worn
C. 0.050
D. 0.023 (ear to ear)
E. 0.044 (ear to snout)
F. [FN] coarse red ware/crusted ware; remains of of pink smearing (?) and white crusting
G. not determinable
H. surface: 2.5YR 6/6 light red and 2.5YR 5/6 red

I. 3.0
J. thumb-size depression on underside of break (at neck)
K. not determinable
L. none observed
M. Plates 18, 19

FC 88

A. head of animal; two small, upright, rounded ears; rounded snout with slightly open mouth
B. broken at neck; surface worn
C. 0.027
D. 0.017
E. 0.026 (snout to back of neck)
F. [FN] coarse red ware; traces of white crusting or paint
G. none visible
H. surface: 5YR 5/3 reddish brown (also, patches of black from reduced firing atmosphere or post-firing burning)
I. 3.0
J. —
K. not determinable
L. none visible
M. Plates 18, 19

FC 177

A. body of quadruped with part of all four legs, head, and tail remaining; hole at one end, probably meant to mark anus
B. broken at neck, tail, and all four legs; surface very worn and friable
C. 0.031 (height from neck to leg)
D. 0.060 (length from head to tail)
E. 0.012 (thickness at center of body)
F. [MN] patterned Urfirnis
G. difficult to determine original painted design; some areas possibly solid, other parts of body encircled with thick lines of paint
H. surface: 5YR 6/4 light reddish brown; paint: 5YR 3/1 very dark gray
I. 2.0
J. —
K. not determinable
L. none observed
M. Plates 18, 19

CHAPTER THREE

The Production of the Franchthi Figurines

Figurines, like many other material products, cannot be fully understood apart from the processes involved in their creation (Young and Bonnichsen 1983:5). For the most part, however, archaeologists have failed to ask questions about the actual production of these images. This chapter, divided into three sections, examines the manufacture of the Franchthi figurines in an attempt to gain new insights about the makers, their preferences and techniques.

The first section reconstructs the possible steps and procedures used by the figurine-makers at Franchthi. Questions considered include: How were the figurines formed? How much time was needed? What tools were used? How much expertise was required? Many of these questions can be approached experimentally by assuming the role of the producer and attempting to replicate the ancient procedures and products.[21]

The two remaining sections are, in part, by-products of this experimental approach. Focusing on more aesthetic or social aspects of ancient production, these sections probe more elusive matters. For example, if anyone could make a Neolithic figurine, what would prevent everyone in the community from producing his or her own set of figurines? Were only certain people within the Franchthi social unit permitted to be figurine-makers? If so, how were they selected? Alternately, did random individuals in a family or group unit simply opt to undertake the work of creating figurines when the need arose? Who "owned" the figurines? Were they displayed in public or private spheres? And why did figurine-makers prefer to work in clay, adhering so closely to the styles of local pottery?

Since the manufacture of clay figurines entails different procedures and tools than that of stone figures, as well as different concerns on the part of the maker, the two media are considered separately. This distinction is not meant to imply that figurine-makers worked in only one of two media. For analytical purposes, however, it is easier to separate the two classes of material.

CONSTRUCTION TECHNIQUES

Clay

In all likelihood, makers of clay figurines at Franchthi used several simple techniques and needed very few tools, which could be easily fashioned from a range of readily available raw materials (e.g., clay, wood, or stone). Neither the techniques nor the tools seem to have changed radically throughout the Neolithic.

While most shaping was probably accomplished with the fingers, a small piece of wood, bone, or shell may have been used to facilitate modeling. Burnishing tools of some sort were also employed; burnishing marks are visible on a number of figures. Like the potter, the figurine-maker at Franchthi probably polished his or her work with a well-smoothed pebble, a snail shell, a piece of wood, a wild fruit seed, a baked clay tool, or his or her thumbnail (cf. Saraswati and Behura 1966 on Indian pottery techniques).

Additional tools were needed for incising and painting the figure. Since most incisions on the Franchthi examples are thin and linear, the makers apparently employed implements such as bone needles, flint points, or well-sharpened sticks of wood. Brushes for painting may have been designed from animal hair, vegetal fibers, chewed or shredded bamboo, or pieces of cloth rolled into thin stick-shapes, none of which would have required much time to make (cf. Saraswati and Behura 1966).

A figurine was roughly shaped using one of two techniques: pinching, rolling, patting, or pulling a *single* lump of (prepared) clay, or manipulating several separately worked pieces of clay into a final image. FC 112 and FC 4, FN examples created by the first technique, were formed from a single ball of clay that was first flattened between the palms, between one palm and a thigh, or between one palm and a slab of wood, stone, or other appropriate material. By pinching and/or pulling the flattened piece of clay, the maker created the arm stumps and the head. Only the small pellet breasts were applied separately. Since surface finishing on these pieces consisted of, at the most, slipping and occasional burnishing, little additional time was required once the maker had given the figure its final shape.

This approach has several advantages. A piece can be made quickly, tools are unnecessary or minimal, and the resulting image is usually sturdy and highly portable since appendages are short and stumpy.

It would appear, however, that most of the figurines from Franchthi were not constructed in this fashion. Rather, they were modeled from separate components that were worked together for the final image.[22] Replication experiments carried out by the author suggest that the maker first formed several separate clay chunks of appropriate sizes into the major anatomical parts of the body: a trunk, two separate legs, and possibly a head. Once these components were roughly shaped into the desired form, the maker would press them together and then modify them to produce the final image (see Plate 4c, where the roughly shaped inner core of a buttock is visible at the break). Features such as breasts, arms, and pubis could then be attached as pellets, coils, or triangular slabs. This additive technique is evident in several examples. Both FC 68 and FC 124 represent individual legs, each of which was once attached to a separately made but matching half. FC 12, which forms the right buttock of a crouching (?) female, was also made in at least two lateral parts; FC 57, another right buttock and upper leg, was likewise made in parts or sections.

Also instructive are the leg sockets visible at the break on FC 42 just below the waist. As the drawing in Plate 3a indicates, a small ridge or hump runs down the center of the break, with slight D-shaped depressions on either side of this ridge. This distinctive topography can be duplicated by first adding a strip of clay where the ridge now appears, then creating two slight depressions with one's thumb on either side of the clay strip, and finally, inserting separately formed legs into the prepared sockets.[23]

Two examples, FC 190 and FC 208, suggest that not only were figurines modeled in sections but that, occasionally, parts of figures may have been made from materials other than clay. The distinctive spiral-shaped socket between the shoulders of FC 190 probably once held a head. Replication experiments demonstrate that this peculiar impression is best duplicated by gently sticking a shell, specifically the species *Conus mediterraneus*, into clay that is still moist and pliable.[24] An inedible marine gastropod, *Conus* may have been fairly common in the vicinity of the cave.[25]

The other piece (FC 208), a curious bell-shaped example, represents the lower torso and upper pubic region of a female. Close inspection of the underside, just beneath the pubic area, reveals a slightly concave, seemingly finished surface.[26] If this surface is, indeed, finished and represents the bottom edge of the piece, then the artist must have intended to portray only *part* of the pubic region. This is not impossible, especially given the occurrence of half-body pendants and figurines at Franchthi, but a rival proposal is also possible. The piece may once have been part of a larger image, the section which now remains having been formerly attached to a lower half made out of some material which left a smooth and slightly concave impression at the point of attachment (e.g., a gourd-like container). While clay *could* have left this kind of impression, other materials should not be ruled out.

Arms and breasts, as with legs, were often formed independently and then applied to the torso. The arms on FC 28 and FC 118 are simple coils that were worked into the shoulders and upper chest of the figure, and the breasts on FC 4, FC 42, FC 112, and probably FC 167 were applied as separate pellets. Some, though not all, of the heads were also modeled separately and then attached to the torso. Three examples (FC 11, FC 30, FC 31) are notable for their length, averaging 0.072 m.

In summary, the construction of clay figurines at Franchthi was often an additive process: separate components were pressed together and shaped to create the desired image. This technique has disadvantages as well as advantages, compared with the "single lump" approach discussed above.

Figurines made from separate pieces are more susceptible to breakage (during firing or use) since parts formed separately (perhaps at different times) may be imperfectly joined. On the other hand, building a figurine in parts allows the maker to experiment with posture and shape. Seated or slightly irregular postures can be modeled more easily from multiple pieces of clay than from a single lump.

On a more speculative level, the additive process may reflect a fairly sophisticated level of cognitive abstraction, the process whereby sensory information is condensed into codes. These codes form the basis of all symbolic communication. Behavioral scientists believe that one of the highest levels of abstraction is achieved when an individual is able to divide a perceived object into attributes and mentally store those attributes in categories. This ability allows the person not only to compare entities that are different, but also to recognize and construct new patterns (Posner 1973; Young and Bonnichsen 1983:10–11). For example, rather than recognize the human form simply as a complete, intact image (as a child might), a higher level of abstractive ability allows one to divide the body into any number of distinct dimensions (e.g., a head, legs, hands, and feet) and to associate those attributes with other things or ideas. By linking various attributes within a category, one can devise a whole range of symbolic expressions.

Linguistically, for example, this ability to relate seemingly different attributes allows one to refer to the "brow" of a cave or the "lip" of a cup. Visually, one can link the image of a disembodied hand with a command to stop (as in American culture), or with the concept of an "evil eye" (as in modern Greek society). Although the symbolic intent of an object is usually culturally determined, the process by which such symbolic expressions emerge is inextricably linked to this capacity for abstraction. The technique at Franchthi for constructing figurines from parts, as well as the existence of half-body pendants and possible half-body figurines, suggests that such an ability, or at least the ability to conceptualize and then intentionally depict a perceived object in parts, was well developed.

Unfortunately, we probably will never know whether the figurine-makers believed that making a figurine in parts was an important step in production.[27] If, however, the piecing together of a figurine from its component and related parts was viewed by the maker as an essential aspect of manufacture (e.g., imparted life or power to the image), then the craftsmen and craftswomen may well have preferred a multi-stage building process to working from a single lump of clay.

The process of making a figurine out of component parts is easily accomplished with clay. Moreover, clay may have held an additional symbolic attraction for figurine-makers at Franchthi. This easily accessible material has unusual transformative properties. Unlike many other raw materials, it can be altered from one state to another, changing from a wet, muddy substance to a hard, durable form. The figurine-makers at Franchthi may have been aware of and intrigued by this unique aspect of clay and may have believed that clay was an ideal substance for creating a miniature world of human forms.[28] Just as the figurine-maker changed disparate and dismembered parts of the body into a complete human image, the clay itself changed from a soft, malleable, and ephemeral material to a hard, unyielding, and durable form.

Stone

Techniques for extracting, forming, and finishing stone share little with those required for obtaining and working clay. The Neolithic stoneworker who wanted to create a figurine needed to plan well in advance. His/her first step was to acquire a suitable block of raw material, the size of which would vary in accordance with the planned size of the figurine. Having selected a suitable stone, the craftsperson began the process of forming a figurine. The following steps have been suggested for Early Cycladic carvers by both Pat Getz-Preziosi (1972, 1977, 1987) and Elizabeth Oustinoff (1984) on the basis of replication experiments. These procedures may have held true for the Stone Age carver as well.

First, the artist trims the stone to the approximate length, width, and depth of the final product. Second, he/she lays the outlines of the basic design of the figure by drawing or incising the main details on the flat surface (Oustinoff found that obsidian flakes were very useful for this step). Some kind of measuring device, perhaps a string tied in knots or an angular ruler, might have been used to aid in the layout of more complex designs.[29] Third, using a cutting tool, the artist sinks the design into the slab. Light blows give the figure its general form, while the finer work is accomplished with an obsidian tool (which can literally shave soft marbles[30]) or abrasives. Finally, the figure is polished with materials such as sand, water (LeBar 1963:32; Buck 1930), or emery[31], or by repeated handling and rubbing (Oustinoff 1984:42). Although there is as yet no convincing evidence from Greece, it is possible that the Neolithic stone figurine-maker worked from a clay model. Using a prototype would have helped eliminate costly mistakes.

Experiments suggest that Early Cycladic figurines could take from five to sixty hours to produce, depending on the experience of the carver and on the elegance and detail of the piece (Oustinoff 1984). While the stone figurines from Neolithic Greece lack the complexity of many EC II examples, these earlier versions must have demanded several hours of work as well. In contrast, my attempts to duplicate many of the Franchthi *clay* examples took anywhere from ten minutes to somewhat less than an hour, not including preparing the clay, drying, and firing, all of which require considerable time. The overall work entailed in producing both stone and clay figurines is, therefore, labor-intensive. It would appear, however, that the allotment of time focuses on different types of activities, depending on which medium is selected. Much of the time and energy needed to create clay figurines like those at Franchthi would not be devoted to the actual modeling of the image, but rather to the pre-production of the raw materials and to the final stages that ensured the durability of the piece. On the other hand, the greatest amount of time for manufacturing stone images was probably given over to the actual carving and polishing of the image.

Although nearly 1000 stone pendants, beads, ornaments, and groundstone tools have been catalogued from Franchthi, only one definite stone figurine (FS 101) has yet come to light. The ornaments, beads, and pendants which span the entire Neolithic were most often manufactured from soft materials such as talc, serpentine, soapstone, steatite, and anhydrite. Some of these materials were available locally, while others were probably brought in as stream cobbles (van Andel and Vitaliano 1987:20). Coarser materials, such as andesite, which was imported from Aegina and elsewhere, and calcareous sandstone were reserved for millstones (Runnels 1981, 1985; van Andel and Vitaliano 1987:20). The archaeological evidence at Franchthi reveals, therefore, an ongoing tradition of carving and grinding a variety of stones into both ornamental and utilitarian items. The figurine-makers at Franchthi, however, seem to have participated rarely in this tradition. A comparable situation exists at neighboring sites such as Corinth and Lerna, where excavations unearthed a range of stone artifacts, thus indicating a stoneworking tradition, but very few stone figurines. On the other hand, the sample of anthropomorphic images from sites such as Koufovouno (n=5) and Saliagos (n=8) consists almost exclusively of marble and/or alabaster figurines. The reasons for such variability among sites are not known and will remain unclear until we have a better understanding of the purposes of stone figurines, the social and economic differences among settlements, and the local availability of marble and alabaster.

FIGURINE-MAKERS AND OWNERSHIP

Having explored some technical aspects of figurine production at Franchthi, we can consider the questions of who within the settlement may have actually made these images and whether these images were possibly "owned" by individuals or groups. Neither question can be answered adequately, but both have heuristic value.

Pre- or nonstratified societies (such as the one which may have characterized Neolithic Franchthi) usually do not support full- or even part-time craft specialists.[32] Given the size of the figurine sample and the seeming ease with which most of the clay figurines were made, it is arguable that almost anyone within the community could have modeled one. On the other hand, it seems unlikely that just anybody within the settlement designed figurines, at least not in the Middle or Late Neolithic. The similarity of the MN and LN figurines to contemporary ceramic wares in terms of clay fabric, surface treatment, and painted design suggests a degree of organization and control over raw materials, firing processes, and the general style of these images.[33] Conceivably, potter and figurine-maker were one and the same.[34] Comparable relationships are known from the ethnographic record: the Yami potters of Formosa, for example, model clay figurines for their own amusement during their pottery-making season and give them to children as dolls or toys (Kano 1956:411, 425).

It is equally possible, however, that a figurine-maker who worked closely with the local potter, shared the potter's clays, tools, and paints, and eventually fired[35] the finished pieces along with the potter's vessels, might also have produced figures in keeping with the local pottery tradition. Although the evidence is slim, it suggests that, at least during the Middle and Late Neolithic, whenever the need arose at Franchthi for a figurine, either the local potter or someone working under his/her supervision was called upon.[36]

We do not know if these images, once completed, became the property of the makers or users or whether they were owned by individuals, families, or corporate groups. Archaeologists still have a poor understanding of the archaeological correlates of ownership and only vague ideas about when the concept of exclusive rights or possession of objects, resources, or territory may have emerged in Greece. Current evidence suggests that corporate groups may have been staking claims to resources or land via the use of formal cemeteries by the Final Neolithic (see Chapter 6; Talalay 1986, 1991). It would be surprising, however, if proprietorship, particularly of resources and food, was not a matter of concern earlier in the Neolithic, even in a society considered egalitarian.

The motivations to possess or control such resources as arable land, water sources, or raw materials are not necessarily the same as those which compel people to "own" individual artifacts, such as figurines. The display or ownership of small artifacts like figurines may have been perceived as emblematic of one's personal or group identity, while the possession or control of resources is more likely to have been linked to the exercise of power. What little can be gleaned from ethnographic reports on the ownership of figurines among modern nonindustrialized groups reveals a broad range of behaviors. Certain images are owned by lineages and are inherited from one generation to the next. Other images are the exclusive property of one individual and do not automatically or necessarily become the property of one's offspring or kin (Greub 1988). No universal principles seem to dictate whether ownership is based on individual or corporate identities. It would be surprising, however, if competition for control or ownership of resources and food had not been a matter of concern among individuals or groups, at least during times of crisis.

The few figurines at Franchthi that possibly derive from undisturbed contexts are found near small hearths and scattered tools usually associated with activities such as spinning and grinding (see Chapter 5). It may be the case, therefore, that some of the Franchthi figurines were used in small gatherings and were, perhaps, the property of individual families or household units.

Even if the figurines were owned by individual households, we cannot determine if, or how often, other members of the community may have seen or used these images, or whether the Franchthi figurines were regularly placed in public or private areas. ("Public" describes areas accessible to and frequented by all members of a settlement; "private," those with restricted access, open only to a specific, small segment of the population.) Limited evidence from other Neolithic sites in Greece and the Balkans, however, may be cautiously applied to Franchthi. Other than so-called rubbish deposits from which many of the figurines derive, the most commonly reported contexts are in unspecified positions on house floors, in communal areas such as courtyards, and by hearths or ovens.

Figurines appear, therefore, to function in public and domestic spheres. Even when these images are interpreted as "ritual" paraphernalia, the common locus is not an unusual or distinctive building, but an "ordinary" house or dwelling (see Whittle 1985:150–156 for a general discussion of figurine contexts in Greece and the Balkans). Archaeological data from the Balkans indicate that, at least for many of the Vinča and later Karanovo sites, figurines are found in houses (or possible cult areas), where they were placed on benches or "altars" near ovens (Gimbutas 1986:226; J. Chapman 1981:72–77). Only occasionally are figurines recovered from burials. Such practices would have effectively removed these images from public view.

If the Franchthi figurines were, in fact, highly visible objects, they were probably seen by a cross section of individuals within the settlement (e.g., children, adults, males, and females). Whether a dominant "reading" (understood by all members of Franchthi society) existed for each figurine, or different segments of the population had contrasting perceptions and understandings of each image or class of figurines, is not known. Certainly, recent discussions by anthropologists strongly underscore the belief that the polysemic and multivalent nature of symbols leads to varying readings of a given symbol by different groups within a given society. Subordinate and dominant individuals, as well as males and females, will often experience accepted ideologies in different ways (Bynum et al. 1986:5).

The issue of figurine ownership is, of course, tied to the matter of figurine function. Figurines used as dolls likely were linked to very different systems of ownership than those functioning as ritual paraphernalia. Indeed, figurines associated with ritual activity inevitably raise questions about the controlling forces behind the ritual itself, the social role of cult in Neolithic society, and who might have had possession of the cult equipment. If sites like Vinča, which produced over 2000 figurines, were indeed ritual centers, an encompassing system must have been in place for organizing individual or group control of cult equipment. Unfortunately, until we have a more fine-grained understanding of the functions of Neolithic figurines, the issue of their ownership will remain obscure.

FIGURINES AND POTTERY

Figurines at Franchthi often share attributes with local MN, LN, and FN pottery, including clay fabric, surface treatment, and general color. Moreover, the decoration selected for both classes of objects is markedly similar: nearly every painted decoration or design element found on a figurine is found on sherds or vessels. While an overarching decorative tradition may have governed painting on clay of any form, be it figurine or vessel, I suggest that the makers of those two ceramic forms wanted to create an explicit symbolic link between them.

Ethnographic studies have shown that, at least among modern nonindustrialized groups, decorative elements on pots, baskets, and the like often have specific meanings and are carefully selected for placement on certain kinds of artifacts (Hodder 1982). While we may never know which of the design elements on the Franchthi pots or figurines were intended as symbolic or what they may have meant, we should grant to the Franchthi potters and figurine-makers a concern for symbolic notation. If at least some of the notation on these artifacts was part of a common visual vocabulary understood by the makers and users of pottery and figurines, I suggest that consciously placing the same designs on both types of artifacts was motivated by the belief that pots and figurines were linked by a common symbol: the human form.

The notion that pots in some sense represent people, or that vessels can be structurally equated with the human form, has been documented ethnographically by a number of researchers (e.g., Welbourn 1984; David et al. 1988). In addition, prehistoric pots with modeled breasts, feet, and arms occur in Greece and southeastern Europe (Hodder 1988:382), rendering obvious links among ceramic vessels, anthropomorphic figurines, and the human form. Among more recent societies, these connections have been explicitly reinforced by language. Human attributes are used in many languages to describe parts of a vessel (e.g., the lip, belly, neck, and arms of a pot [Joyce 1988:383]).

The possibility that pots, figurines, and the human form were conceptually linked in the minds of the potters and figurine-makers at Franchthi may help us better understand why design elements on pottery and figurines at Franchthi are so similar. We should not dismiss these similarities as simply part of an established tradition in painting clay objects of any form. Nor should we reduce the practices of figurine-makers to rote behavior, assuming that they mindlessly imitated designs preferred by the potters. The similarities were probably intentional and may have been motivated, at least partially, by a desire to render explicit, for whatever reasons, symbolic connections among the human body, pottery, and figurines.

CHAPTER FOUR

Deciphering the Use and Meaning of Prehistoric Figurines

INTRODUCTION

During the last century, an array of interpretations has been advanced to explain the function of Stone Age figurines in the Mediterranean (Bent 1884; James 1957, 1959, 1960; Broman 1958; Ucko 1962, 1968; Mellaart 1970; Hourmouziadis 1973; Gimbutas 1974a, 1982; Peltenburg 1988, 1991; Morales 1990). While most of the explanations are provocative, many are simplistic, ignoring the profound social and, perhaps, political complexities that likely motivated the manufacture of figurines in early, nonliterate societies. More importantly, since few of the explanations are supported by a well-defined body of theory, they often do not relate in a coherent or systematic fashion to the available data.

Not surprisingly, figurine specialists fail to agree unanimously about matters methodological or theoretical. As Renfrew has observed (1985:3), the investigation of prehistoric materials that may reflect religion, cult, and ritual is prone to two extremes: an inflexible skepticism about ever gaining valid insights into long-vanished belief systems, or a naive, uncritical optimism about recovering the cognitive particulars underlying those ancient behaviors. It is difficult to steer a path between this Scylla and Charybdis.

By and large, archaeologists who study Stone Age figurines and subscribe to the notion that ancient behavioral practices are indeed accessible, fall into two schools of thought. One group (e.g., Gimbutas, James, Mellaart) views figurines as ultimately religious or cultic, reflecting an underlying worship of one or several deities associated with various life-giving and regenerative forces. Though these kinds of explanations have amplified and modified earlier beliefs in a Great Goddess, they are unquestionably part of the long "Mother Goddess" tradition first embraced by archaeologists and anthropologists in the mid-nineteenth century. And while ample evidence can be summoned for a historically attested Mother Goddess in the Mediterranean (especially in Mesopotamia, Anatolia, and Egypt), demonstrating the existence of such a goddess in early Greek societies remains problematical (see Ucko 1968:413).

Other archaeologists, including the author, adopt a broader perspective. Without categorically denying that these small, portable images may have served religious or cultic purposes, these writers (e.g., Ucko, Hourmouziadis, Broman) suggest, either implicitly or explicitly, that figurines were ultimately associated with the adaptive strategies of a given community and that their functions varied. Stone Age figurines from several parts of the Mediterranean have been interpreted as tangible expressions of personal desires (Broman 1958), as rudimentary forms of writing (Hourmouziadis 1973), as objects of sympathetic magic (Talalay 1989), as dolls and toys (Meighan

1954), and as items in initiation rites (Ucko 1962, 1968; Talalay 1983c). It has even been suggested that certain examples had economic importance (Talalay 1987).

Additional suggestions will, no doubt, continue to appear in the literature. Although the development of diverse interpretations is to be encouraged, I believe that the field of figurine studies can be served better by building a body of method and theory aimed at recovering the possible functions of these images, and by precisely defining a basic, working vocabulary. To those ends, some of the terms and assumptions employed in this volume are briefly discussed below.

The following discussion requires clarification of three terms: *use, meaning,* and *function. Use* and *function* are used interchangeably in this study to refer to the basic or general purpose for which an object was designed or employed. For example, the basic or general use (or function) of a small, clay anthropomorphic image may have been as a doll, a votary, a gaming piece, or a charm.[37]

These terms are distinct from an object's *meaning*. Meaning refers to what is intended or signified or understood to be expressed by an object[38], and is not only more complex than use, but often less accessible to archaeologists. For example, a figurine may be *used* as a votive offering, but the *meaning* embodied by the object may refer to the cosmological or mythological concerns of a given group, the way in which the group perceives the human body, and/or social attitudes toward gender.

As a rule, meanings are both arbitrary and culturally defined. They are arbitrary in that they mean whatever people have agreed that they will mean; they are culturally specific in that it is difficult to understand the symbolic intent of an object *in vacuo*, since meanings usually evolve in the context of beliefs and opinions shared by a social group. The ideology embodied in a figurine (or, indeed, in any symbolic object) is subject to manipulation, and in complex societies the manipulation of such symbols can become an important source of social control (particularly among the elite). Presumably, as long as a symbol remains effective, it will continue to be used in a given social context.

Archaeologists have yet to devise an overarching term which encompasses the concepts of both use and meaning. Although a distinction between the two is analytically important, such a division was probably not made by the people who produced and used these images. Use and meaning were likely connected in the minds of the users; a term which reflects that linkage would be helpful.

Many archaeologists have failed to recognize the complexities of use and meaning and have assumed *a priori* that a collection of figurines from a single site (or region) served a single function or held only one meaning. Contrary to that notion, I believe that some images from a given site and time period may have had one purpose, while other contemporary pieces may have been designed for quite different uses. Figurines may even have moved from one category to another in a very short time. Ethnographic reports note this phenomenon. For example, Béart writes of seeing a West African child playing with a specific doll which, a month later, acquired supernatural qualities and was found, covered with blood, on a village altar (1955:34; see also Greub 1988:72 for the differences between sanctified "nkisi" and unsanctified "teki" figures among the Bemba). Assuming, therefore, that Neolithic figurines are not a unifunctional class of objects and that a distinction should be made between use and meaning, how can archaeologists disentangle these threads?

While no final answers or solutions are provided here, it is suggested that studies of use and meaning should explore at least four kinds of evidence: (1) the figures themselves; (2) their archaeological contexts; (3) the particular socioeconomic matrix in which the figurines functioned (i.e., the systemic context); and (4) ethnographic analogues.[39] A short discussion of the first three categories is presented below. A lengthier consideration of ethnographic analogues follows.

FIGURINES AND THEIR CONTEXTS

Many observable characteristics, such as indications of sex, depictions of obvious deformities, or representations of exaggerated or incomplete body parts, reflect conscious choices on the part of the figurine-makers. While it is often difficult to interpret these features in a rigorous fashion, they can provide clues to the use or meaning of an image. A good example of a study that builds an argument based solely on such observable attributes is that of Broman (1958). In brief, she notes that most of the clay images from Neolithic levels at Jarmo are only lightly fired or sun-baked and are often so crude or squashed as to defy classification. From that evidence she reasons that the importance of figurines in this early Near Eastern village lay not in the finished product, but in the actual modeling of the image. In addition, she observes that the wide technical and stylistic variety among figurines suggests that many different hands may have fashioned the pieces. From the features of the figures themselves, Broman concludes that each figurine represented an individual, personal wish, expressed in the making of the form. An ingenious suggestion, it fails to be totally convincing because Broman does not attempt to correlate her proposal with data from other categories of evidence (e.g., do the numbers of figurines increase or decrease during any subphases of the period, and are these patterns associated with other changes in the socioeconomic sphere?).

Renfrew, in his discussion of Bronze Age religion, has also stressed the importance of inspecting the images themselves for clues to possible function (Renfrew 1985). Attempting to design an operational framework for the archaeology of cult practice, Renfrew identifies 18 potential material correlates of religious ritual. At least two of those correlates are associated with the iconography of the images and the repeated use of certain gestures and symbols on the figures (Renfrew 1985:19–20).

Consideration of the figurines should proceed in concert with analysis of the figures' contexts. Although the matter of context is raised in many discussions of function, archaeologists usually equate context with the findspot of an image. The literature on Stone Age figurines does not make an important distinction between two very different kinds of contextual evidence: the archaeological and the systemic (Schiffer 1976:27–28). The former refers to the position of an object in the immediate context of a site; the latter, to the cultural and environmental systems of a society. Objects—whether figurines, tools, or pots—are part of ongoing behavioral systems, and the use and meaning of any object must make sense within the framework of such systems.

Unfortunately, in citing archaeological contexts either to support or to propose the functional or symbolic intents for figurines, archaeologists often construct circular arguments. A typical example of such circular thinking comes from the reports on the EN site of Nea Nikomedeia in Macedonia (Rodden 1962, 1964). The figurines recovered in the alleged shrine at that site are called deities because they were found in a putative religious structure; however, *one* of the reasons the building was labeled a shrine is because the figurines were assumed, *a priori*, to be sacred objects!

References to systemic contexts occur far less frequently in the literature on Stone Age figurines. Neglecting such information, archaeologists often propose untenable suggestions. The literature on Upper Palaeolithic figurines from Western Europe provides a good example of such pitfalls. For nearly a century, writers have claimed that Palaeolithic figurines were used to promote human fertility (Ucko 1968:409–411). Modern ethnographic studies show, however, that the mobility and life-styles of hunter-gatherers preclude welcoming many offspring (Ucko 1968:412; Lee and DeVore 1968). If this were true for Upper Palaeolithic hunter-gatherers (as is likely), the assumption that figurines were used to promote human fertility becomes less convincing. When viewed within a systemic context, the equation of figurines with human fertility is doubtful, at least for the Upper Palaeolithic.

ETHNOGRAPHIC ANALOGUES

Ucko, in his pioneering work on Neolithic figurines (1962, 1968), was the first to discuss extensively the value of ethnographic analogues to the study of prehistoric figurines. By so doing, he opened the eyes of many researchers to the varied practices that might be associated with anthropomorphic images in early, nonliterate societies. The use of ethnographic analogues in prehistoric research is, however, a source of heated debate (Ascher 1961; Binford 1972; Gould 1978; Gould and Watson 1982; Shaw and Ashley 1983; Wylie 1982, 1985). Since a lengthy discussion of the subject is beyond the scope of this study, suffice it to say that the bias of this study is clearly in favor of admitting ethnographic analogies into the ranks of prehistoric research. Despite legitimate problems with finding the best "fit" and with establishing reliable procedures for testing, analogies: (1) provide models that are relatively free of ethnocentric bias (Stanislawski 1974:19); (2) make archaeologists aware of various modes of behavior that would be difficult to deduce by logic alone (Gould 1978:254); and (3) present the possibility of varied and heterogeneous reasons or causes for a practice (Ucko 1969:263).

The examples presented below, which describe various functions of figurines among ethnographic societies, are culled from a wide range of sources. Far from exhaustive, they offer food for thought and underscore the suggestion initially raised by Ucko (1962, 1968) that archaeologists need to broaden their thinking about the use and meaning of these images.

Most of the nineteenth- and twentieth-century ethnographies I consulted did not cite the use of small figurines. Whether reporting ethnographers failed to note the use of figurines, or these societies did not include figurines in their cultural repertoire, is difficult to assess. I suspect, however, that small figurines were once used more widely than they are now and that intrusions of Western cultures into remote areas of the world have altered the practices among such groups. Many of the lengthy ceremonies that appear to have accompanied the use of these images in the earlier part of this century are dying out as primitive cultures become acculturated to modern practices and ideas (Cory 1956; Parrinder 1967; Greub 1988:34).

Although ethnographers do not always include information that is serviceable to archaeological research, a number of intriguing uses of figurines are cited in the literature. Most of the descriptions, however, are sketchy; consequently, some of the examples below may seem frustratingly incomplete. Whenever possible, I have tried to include details on the following categories: (1) general production; (2) time of usage and production (daily, seasonal); (3) distribution (exchange, ownership); (4) function; (5) storage; (6) reuse and recycling; (7) disposal (discard, breakage); and (8) processes of change (Stanislawski 1974:23).

Ideally, each one of the examples discussed here should be reformulated into a hypothesis to be tested against the archaeological data. Some attempt was made to frame such hypotheses in an earlier work (Talalay 1983a), but the outcome was not totally satisfactory: both the ethnographic record and the archaeological evidence were too incomplete. Eventually, as more archaeological data are uncovered and, perhaps, as more detailed ethnographic discussions on figurines are rediscovered in journals and books, such tests may be possible. In the interim, the examples detailed below highlight the variety of uses, as well as the social importance, of these images among modern, nonindustrialized societies.[40]

Initiation Ceremonies

Function. Various groups in Africa and the Americas regularly use figures as teaching devices during initiation rites. The practice is documented among the Valenge (Earthy 1933), the Wazaramo

(Harding 1961), the Mandibirca (Ploss et al. 1927), the Yao (Stannus 1922), the Pangwe (Tessmann 1913), the Bena (Culwick 1935), the Lega (Biebuyck 1973), the Nyaturu, the Zaramo, the Manyema, the Makua, the Nyamanga, and the Tendauri (Cory 1956:172), and among several groups in the Sierra Leone, Zaire, and Angola (Greub 1988:24, 66). In most cases, figurines are associated primarily with the teaching of sexual matters, marriage, and the value systems of the culture. Some of the most detailed information derives from a report on the Bantu (Cory 1956), and a number of examples are worth brief mention.

One of the main focuses of Bantu initiation ceremonies is the instruction of novices about the values of their society. Figurines are often used to illustrate narratives or proverbs extolling the virtues of hard work, courage, generosity, honesty, and the importance of the family unit. Didactic songs or poems frequently accompany the use of the figurines as an additional expedient for teaching young initiates.

In one instance young novices pass around a figure of a small quadruped biting a nondescript lump. As the figure changes hands, the participants recite a poem: "A cat will even steal to provide for her kittens," i.e., it is your duty to take good care of your children, play with them, and always bring them plenty of food (Cory 1956:44–45). Still other figures are used to demonstrate proper sexual behavior (Cory 1956:38–39, 45, 57) and human physical development (Cory 1956:85). Finally, images of pregnant females are used on several occasions. At a puberty rite for young women, an older tribe member shows a figure of a swollen-bellied female, accompanying it with a song advising pregnant women not to dawdle on the way to the market because of their susceptibility to witchcraft (Cory 1956:62). Similar figures are also used to warn young women about the shame of becoming pregnant before they are are properly initiated (Cory 1956:147–149).

Figurines are also an important part of initiation ceremonies among the Bemba of northeastern Rhodesia. Part of the puberty ritual for the female (which deals with the moral, legal, and economic aspects of marriage, procreative functions, etc.) entails the use of small, primarily anthropomorphic images. As in the Bantu tradition, songs which accompany the figures advise young women about proper behavior and conduct (Richards 1956).

Production. Cory's research on the Bantu suggests that figures are usually prepared by both male and female adults (some being the parents of the initiates), who are appointed as overseers for the novices (1956:32). No specific ceremonies mark the making of the figurines; the gatherings tend to be gay and casual. Certain figures are traditional to specific families, and members make identical replicas each time they attend one of these sessions. Other figures are designed on the spot, without any apparent precedent. No recognizable pattern governs the relationship between a figure and its associated lesson (Cory 1956:34). That is, some craftsmen/craftswomen select a single word from a lesson (song) and model a figure to accompany it; others choose not to explain the song, but rather to create an object that is visually impressive. As one would expect, there is considerable variation in the skill of the figurine-makers and, consequently, in the products of the different sculptors. Cory reports (1956:33) that, although participants never criticize each other, members of a tribe appreciate the skilled artist, who is often invited to remote areas for other initiations.

Among the Bemba, the initiation images are modeled by the mistress of ceremonies (usually a midwife with status in the community) and her helpers (Richards 1956:57). Once the figures are modeled they are placed in a slow fire and allowed to smolder all night. The next morning, the midwife and the helpers apply a white wash and black and red decorations (Richards and Schofield 1945:444). In general, types of images are selected from a large lexicon of traditional objects and designs. Consequently, some types are confined to small geographic regions, while others are distributed throughout northeastern Rhodesia (Richards 1956:60).

Both the Bantu and the Bemba model their figurines from easily workable and readily available materials. Clay is usually preferred to more "costly" raw materials.

Manipulation, Storage, and Disposal. Cory (1956) reports that the Bantu figures are usually stored in a corner of the initiation hut during the lengthy ceremonies and are covered with a cloth when not in use. Only occasionally are they brought out, when pupils are allowed to examine them. During the last days of the rites, each figure is destroyed by being tossed into the nearest pool of water; more rarely the figures are hidden in a cave until the next initiation rites are performed.

The Bemba differ in their storage and disposal of figurines. On the completion of the rite, a few images may be thrown into a river, or eventually one may be buried with the afterbirth of an initiate's first child. Otherwise, all figures remain the exclusive property of the mistress of ceremonies (and are presumably kept in her house) and are reused in subsequent rites. Since the figures are used repeatedly they tend to break, and new images need to be made often (Richards and Schofield 1945:444).

Curing Rites

Function. Although only scanty reports on the use of figurines in curing rites appear in the ethnographic literature, the practice is documented among numerous groups, including the Choco of Columbia, the Cuna Indians of South America (Reichel-Dolmatoff 1964), the Mende of Sierra Leone (Fagg 1977:#14), the Ibo of eastern Nigeria (Fagg 1977:#23), the Besongye of Zaire (Fagg 1977:#45), the Melanu and Kanyah of Malaysia (Fagg 1977:#51, #53), the Bandundu of Zaire (Greub 1988:76), the Batak of Sumatra (Greub 1988:196, 198), and the Lega (Biebuyck 1973:174). This usage has also been reported in a number of groups in western equatorial Africa (Greub 1988:38, 40, 44, 48) and on the island of Nias, east of Sumatra (Loeb 1935).

Some of the best documentation concerns the Navaho Indians of the American Southwest. Navahos believe that one may become ill by inadvertently disobeying supernatural sanctions. Such human mistakes must be ceremonially corrected (Kelly et al. 1972:24) before the sick person can be cured. Nearly all the ceremonies involve the use of anthropomorphic and zoomorphic figurines. The rites tend to be frequent and brief, and are attended only by the patient, the patient's family, and the requisite "singer," who is knowledgeable in the ritual.

Production. Most of the figurines are made of wood. They are fashioned either by the singer hired to perform the ritual or by a member of the sick person's family, who carves while the singer directs (Kelly et al. 1972:62). As a rule, a figure (as well as other necessary paraphernalia) is prepared in a few hours (Haile 1947:vi).

Manipulation. In some ceremonies, the figure is animated through song and prayer, as well as by the introduction of stones, shell fragments, beads, and feathers. Thus given "motion," the image is capable of carrying away the infecting element once it has been exorcized from the patient (Kelly et al. 1972:59). An identical concept exists among the Wambunga of Africa, who use a wooden idol in a ceremony to drive the sickness out of the patient and into an image (Culwick 1934:136). A slightly different and more passive use of curing images exists among the Cochiti. According to Father Dumarest, at the close of a long ceremony the healer leaves someone behind to guard the patient's door. The guardian is entrusted with six (stone) figurines, each representing a different animal. The Cochiti believe these figures possess strong intervening powers against evil spirits that might approach the door (Dumarest 1919:161, 211).

Storage and Disposal. It would appear from reports in the literature that when the Navaho curing rite is over, the figurines are taken to a site thought to be easily accessible to supernatural powers, often a ruin (Kelly et al. 1972:40). The storage or discard of figurines used by other cultures in curing ceremonies is not often documented.

Witchcraft

Akin to the idea of curing people with the aid of images is the notion of "witching" others with magical figures. Navaho sorcerers, for example, make images of the intended victim from clay or wood and "kill" or "torture" the figurines with a sharp pointed object or projectile (Kluckhohn 1944:18). Pueblos use comparable images that are stuck with thorns or are otherwise manipulated (Hawley 1950:146), as do the Cochiti, who make their "witching images" out of earth and urine and then torture the figures with cactus needles stuck in the stomach and ears (Dumarest 1919:165).

The use of figures or dolls in Haitian, Cuban, and Brazilian voodoo rites is fairly common. Contrary to popular belief, the dolls are not usually pricked with needles or pins. Rather, they are simply part of rituals involving possession, dancing, and prayer (Acquaviva 1977; Cabrera 1971; Valente 1955).

Fertility Rites

Figurines often serve as vehicles for human fertility. Morss (1954) discusses in detail the phenomenon among the American Indians, and Ucko (1968) lists at least four other tribes from Africa and Asia where idols or small figures are used to promote human fertility: the Habbe (Kjersmeier 1934); the Ashanti (Elisofon 1958); the Senufo (Lem 1948); and the Batak of Sumatra (Frazer 1922). E. Shaw (1948) also discusses the phenomenon among southern African tribes, including the Fingo, Zulu, Swazi, Matabele, Basuto, Tsawna, Valenge, and Ovambo.

In almost all cases where figurines are used to ensure female fertility, the figures represent infants, not pregnant women. Usually the figures are crude, and frequently no distinction is made between male and female babies. When sex is differentiated, it is as often on the basis of decoration or attributes (e.g., hairstyle, earrings) as anatomical features. The hopeful couple who become the owners of an infant effigy treat the figure as a real baby: they feed it, talk to it, keep it in a cradle, and take it to bed with them. In at least one tribe (the Senufo: Lem 1948), fertility figurines are given to female children at puberty and kept safely with them all their lives. The figures are ultimately buried with the owners at their deaths.

Increase ceremonies for the herd are less frequently noted in the literature. E. Parsons cites one example. She reports that in the early twentieth century the Zuñi enacted a series of complex rituals that included the use of zoomorphic images. Ceremonies took place during four days of the winter solstice. During that time, figures were placed on altars or in shrine-holes under floors. At the close of the winter ceremonies, the Zuñi either "planted" the figures like seeds or threw them out with the sweepings, thus consigning them to the rubbish heaps (Parsons 1919:285; Morss 1954:53).

Dolls and Games

Examples of clay figurines modeled and used by children for recreation are cited often in the literature. Dolls are reported among the Bembala of Sudan (Lem 1948); the Pomo (Loeb 1926); the Navaho (Fewkes 1923); the Talensi (Fortes 1938); the Aswan (C. Firth 1927); the Ashanti (Himmelheber 1960); the Baule (Elisofon 1958); the Yoruba (Elisofon 1958); the Nuer (Evans-Pritchard 1937); the Nyamwesi (Decle 1898); the Valenge (Earthy 1933); the Ibo (Thomas 1913); and the Koranga (Ehrenreich 1891).

Loeb discusses a typical interaction between Pomo girls and their dolls: during play, the girls make the dolls talk with one another, take them into the dancing hut, and make them dance

(1926:222). Morphologically, these dolls are identical to Pomo figures used for magical purposes. The sacred dolls, however, are blessed by the head priest and thus acquire supernatural qualities (Loeb 1926:246). As noted earlier, Béart observes the same phenomenon in West Africa. He writes of seeing the chief's child play with a specific doll. A month later, the same doll, covered with blood, was found on a village altar (1955:34).

According to Fortes, modeling clay figurines is a favorite diversion of young Talensi boys. Both girls and boys play with these dolls, although girls tend to use anthropomorphic images during their "housekeeping" play, while boys entertain themselves with zoomorphic images during their "cattle" play (1938:57). Cory records the same preoccupation among other African tribes where children make clay animals and pretend they are owners of large herds (1956:36).

Finally, ethnographers report the use of clay dolls among the Yami (Formosa). As noted in Chapter 3, Yami potters model clay images (for their own amusement) during the pottery-making season and then pass the figures on to children for recreation (Kano 1956:411, 425).

Miscellaneous

The functions discussed above far from exhaust the practices found among ethnographic societies. A host of additional uses can be cited, though many reports only mention these in passing.

For example, the Tiv employ small figurines as body charms which protect against evil forces and enhance one's ability to fight, make love, or gain material possessions (Bergsma 1973:175). Larger images are found among the Yoruba, who employ crude clay figures to combat nightmares (Morton-Williams 1960:Plate 2). Additional functions are mentioned by Ucko (1962, 1968), Fagg (1977), and Greub (1988), including the use of figurines or statuettes as: (1) ancestor images; (2) surrogate figures for chiefs who are sick or away; (3) protective spirits to whom petitions must be made; (4) images which either represent or house various spirits or deities; (5) agricultural charms used in gardens; (6) representations of killed transgressors; (7) hexes; (8) mourners; (9) fetishes; (10) vehicles for social ridicule; (11) illustrations to enliven narratives or story-telling; (12) divination images; and (13) twin images used if one twin dies at an early age (see also Verger 1954:191). Ucko also cites a number of cases in which figures are placed in tombs. In these contexts, the figurines, which rarely appear to be deities, are buried for specific and often practical purposes (Ucko 1962:781). Finally, in both Nashville, Indiana, and in Ann Arbor, Michigan, I have encountered a contemporary practice which may have a long ancestry: modern potters sometimes form crude, anthropomorphic images that they place on or near their kilns. These "kiln-gods" are meant to ensure a successful firing.

SUMMARY

Deciphering the uses and meanings of prehistoric figurines in the Mediterranean poses complex problems. Scanty and ambiguous archaeological data notwithstanding, the critical issue facing figurine specialists is the lack of a well-defined methodology and theory. It is crucial for archaeologists to develop a set of mutually agreed-upon research guidelines and definitions that will clarify analytic approaches to the functions and symbolic intents of these early images.

This chapter suggests that interpretations should include convergent data from four categories: (1) the figurines; (2) the archaeological context; (3) the systemic context; and (4) ethnographic analogues. Although the last class of evidence is not an essential component in the construction of a convincing argument, ethnographic analogies provide an array of potential models and offer researchers perspectives that are relatively free of ethnocentric bias.

CHAPTER FIVE

The Use and Meaning of the Franchthi Figurines

While the functions of most Franchthi figurines remain elusive, three uses are proposed below. These conclusions were arrived at by considering, whenever possible, the figures themselves, their archaeological and systemic contexts, and information gleaned from ethnographic reports. I suggest the following possibilities: (1) the MN split-leg figurines (FC 68, FC 124) served as economic contracts or identifying tokens; (2) the FN zoomorphic pieces (FC 41, FC 88) functioned as items of sympathetic magic associated with shifts in regional herding practices; and (3) a heterogeneous group of EN–LN images served as dolls or toys. There may, of course, be other possibilities, but the current data do not support them. For example, no convincing evidence (in the form of contextual data or attributes of the figures themselves) exists to suggest that Franchthi figurines served as deities or "sacred images of divine entities," as Gimbutas suggests for the Sitagroi examples (Gimbutas 1986:226). Neither do current data support the idea that these images were associated with death or beliefs in an afterlife, since none of the figures were recovered from burials at the site. Unlike comparable examples found farther north, Franchthi figurines do not occur: (1) as foundation offerings (cf. Plateia Zarkou: Gallis 1985); (2) with other figurines (cf. Achilleion: Gimbutas 1974b; Gimbutas et al. 1989; Balkan sites: Whittle 1985:150–156); (3) on what appear to be benches or "altars" (cf. Karanovo sites: Gimbutas 1986:226); or (4) in separate buildings set apart from the habitation areas or dwellings of a settlement (cf. Nea Nikomedeia: Rodden 1962, 1964). In fact, there is little about the contexts of the Franchthi examples that leads to simple inferences of possible function.

Since I have developed the idea of contracts and tokens more fully elsewhere (Talalay 1987), the following comments on that topic are summary. The other suggestions are discussed at greater length.

USE

Contracts and Tokens

FC 124 and FC 68 both represent split-leg figurines, a curious type of fragment recovered from six MN sites. Franchthi, Nemea, Corinth, Lerna, Akratas, and Asea yielded approximately 20 such images. These villages are all accessible to one another, lying within one-half to several days' journey by boat and/or foot.

Most of these legs were, I suspect, originally attached to complementary and matching halves (see Talalay 1987). They were, however, deliberately designed so that the two attached halves could be easily separated and realigned. Ethnographic and historical analogues reveal that objects designed for intentional splitting frequently serve either as contractual devices or as identifying tokens between individuals or groups. In all the cases I encountered, the objects symbolized an agreement, obligation, friendship, or common bond.

If the Peloponnesian examples served comparable ends, short of framing a testable hypothesis (which is not possible given the data; see Talalay 1987), the archaeological evidence should suggest, at the very least, that these six communities were bound into a large, interactive, and superlocal unit. The circulation and use of such devices would only make sense in a sphere of regional integration where literacy was not yet available to render explicit a range of obligations or ties among separate but interdependent settlements.

Recent discussions of intersettlement contact in the Peloponnese (Cullen 1985a-b; van Andel and Runnels 1987; Talalay 1987; Vitelli, forthcoming) suggest that, indeed, various types of bonds among communities would be adaptively beneficial during the Neolithic. For example, exogamous marriage practices might help ensure the biological viability of these settlements, since village populations were probably low. In addition, periodic food failures, which were inevitable in such climates, could have been alleviated by either the transport of goods between settlements or, perhaps, the partial movement of populations from one village to another. Given the benefits which would accrue from ongoing intersettlement contact, contractual devices or identifying tokens could have been used in a variety of contexts. They may have been employed by individual trading partners in a "down-the-line" mode of exchange; as tokens to identify messengers between villages (particularly in times of crisis); as symbols of future obligations among groups or individuals; as emblems of membership in sodalities; as signs of nonresidential family ties; or as markers of intervillage marital connections.

Items of Sympathetic Magic

Three zoomorphic figurines were found at Franchthi (FC 41, FC 88, FC 177; FC 194, which is classified here as a possible figurine fragment [Appendix D], may represent an owl). Elsewhere in southern Greece, 11 animal images were recovered from Corinth (n=7), Asea (n=3), and Nea Makri (n=1). Although there is debate about the date of these pieces (Phelps 1987), most can be assigned to either the Late or Final Neolithic. Many of the animals may represent ruminants or cervids, but identification is difficult.

While the sample is small enough to be misleading, the evidence suggests that zoomorphic images appear suddenly in southern Greece toward the end of the Neolithic. If this occurrence is "real," then an explanation can be proposed which, like the contractual hypothesis given above, is inspired by ethnographic parallels.

Parsons' report on the Zuñi festival (see Chapter 4) cites the use of small, zoomorphic figures in increase rites for the herd. Like other fertility rites found throughout the world, the Zuñi ceremony is rooted in a belief in sympathetic magic.

Although the Zuñi ritual is a yearly (i.e., cyclical) event, ceremonies which invoke sympathetic, contagious, or imitative magic can also be performed as needs arise (e.g., in times of crisis or change). The rites need not be enacted on an annual basis. If we postulate that the zoomorphic figurines in southern Greece served as items of sympathetic magic, designed to cope with some major change or crisis, then their seemingly sudden appearance in the archaeological record should correlate, broadly speaking, with alterations in the local environment. Animals, particularly sheep and goat, were important throughout the Neolithic as sources of food and possibly milk, wool, transport, and status. The seemingly sudden appearance of animal images during the Late Neolithic hints at a shift in attitudes, behaviors, or practices on the part of the local inhabitants.

Several archaeologists, including Jacobsen (1969), Theocharis (1973), Diamant (1974a), and Wickens (1986), have remarked on the possible increase in cave use during the Late and Final Neolithic in Attica and parts of the Peloponnese. Wickens suggests that the Attic caves were base camps inhabited by small groups of herder–hunter–gatherers. Moreover, he notes that most of these sites are no longer located "in coastal or lowland, well-watered or riverine locations, the preferred situation of the EN and MN villages" (1986:130). Rather, the majority of the Attic caves are situated in inland and upland areas, including lands that are marginal in agricultural terms, but provide good pasturage. On the basis of this (and other) evidence, Wickens proposes that there was an increase in herding and/or a change to a more mobile pastoral system during the Late and Final Neolithic (see also Halstead 1981, 1987a-b; Cherry 1988). The shift involved more extensive and widespread use of marginal lands by herders, and once it was recognized that these uplands provided suitable pasturage (and that grazing was an effective use of the land), the impetus for larger and more mobile herds became self-perpetuating (Wickens 1986:135). Whether these cave occupants were herders engaged in some pattern of transhumance, or possibly dairy pastoralists who perennially occupied upland areas, is a matter of debate, but it is arguable that milking and cheese-making may also have become more important components of the economy at this time (Halstead 1981:326–327; Wickens 1986:135). In sum, the Attic evidence seems to indicate a marked change in animal management, probably in the form of increased reliance on a more mobile pastoral system and, perhaps, larger herds.

Whether the same conclusions are relevant to areas farther south is difficult to determine from the available data. There is certainly evidence for a rise in cave use throughout the Peloponnese during this time, as well as a general increase in mobility, including new settlements on the Cycladic islands (Cherry 1981, 1988) and the Argolid (van Andel and Runnels 1988). At Franchthi, the Late Neolithic evidence shows an increased dependence on sheep and goat, as compared to the Middle Neolithic (Payne 1975, 1982). Concomitantly, Paralia appears to have been abandoned, though occupation continued inside the cave (Jacobsen 1973a, 1979; Vitelli, forthcoming). The increase of sheep and goat may indicate a greater reliance on herding, while the abandonment of Paralia is more enigmatic. The limited signs of occupation outside the cave, however, need not indicate a reduction in population, but rather an increased mobility and dispersal of those populations which had once concentrated in larger village sites (see Wickens 1986:131 for alternate suggestions). Visits to Franchthi by these mobile units may have become less frequent and more sporadic during the Late Neolithic.

Preliminary reports from Franchthi also indicate an increase in the frequency of spindle whorls during the Late Neolithic (Carrington Smith 1972). Since whorls are traditionally associated with spinning, the evidence would suggest greater reliance on wool and wool-bearing animals such as sheep and goat.

During Franchthi's FN phase the faunal evidence is somewhat different: preliminary analysis suggests a slight drop in sheep and goat and a rise in pig, deer, and bovines (Payne 1975). These data may reflect a more wooded environment around the cave than in the previous phase, concomitant changes in local herding practices, and/or an increased reliance on hunting animals ill-suited to domestication, such as deer.

While far from conclusive, current evidence supports the conjecture that the Late and/or Final Neolithic in Attica and the Argolid witnessed shifts in herding practices. The Late Neolithic may have seen an increased reliance on a more mobile pastoral system involving sheep and goat, larger herds, and, perhaps, greater exploitation of milk and milk-related products. If the preliminary evidence from Franchthi is correct, the Final Neolithic at the cave was characterized by another shift, which included a decreased reliance on sheep and goat and an increased dependence on deer, pig, and bovines. It would therefore not be surprising to find that certain animals began to acquire new social importance among the families, households, or other groups affected by these changes.

Since change, whether positive or negative, can provoke anxiety, it is possible that those affected took measures, magical or otherwise, to reduce their fears. The LN images may have been designed, at least initially, in response to those economic changes. It is difficult to know, however, at which point the shifts in animal management ceased to be a source of potential stress, although herders in southern Greece may have felt the precariousness of their situation even after several successful generations of herding. Consequently, figurines may have continued to be produced during the Final Neolithic in order to help ensure the ongoing health and well-being of local herds.

There is no evidence suggesting that the zoomorphic figurines from southern Greece were used, like the Zuñi examples, in actual rituals or ceremonies. The power of sympathetic magic, however, did not necessarily depend on elaborate rites. The manufacture and subsequent retention of an image may have been sufficient.

Dolls and Toys

Only three Franchthi examples derive from contexts which are possibly undisturbed: (1) FC 190, recovered from Unit Q5S:186, on Paralia; (2) FC 124, from Unit FAS:123, within the cave; and (3) FC 101, from Unit FAN:114, also within the cave. The figures are dated EN, MN, and LN, respectively. Their contexts may point to their use as dolls or toys.

The following information on context was gathered primarily from the unpublished excavation notebooks and the published stratigraphic profiles (see Jacobsen and Farrand 1987). FC 124 was found near a hearth and two quern fragments, while the units stratigraphically associated with it (Appendix A) contained the bottom half of the hearth, the end of a chisel made of honey flint, another quern fragment, a stone bead, the phalanx of a neonate, and the lower molar of a 25–30-year-old adult (Cullen, pers. comm. 1991). A similar constellation of features and artifacts was found associated with FC 101 (Appendix A), namely: a possible hearth, an awl of honey flint, stone or shell beads, a worked bone fragment, and scattered human skeletal remains (Cullen, pers. comm. 1991). Finally, FC 190, which was not associated with a hearth (though such ashy deposits do not preserve well on Paralia), was recovered near a bead, the basal phalanx of an adult left toe (Cullen, pers. comm. 1991), several stone drills, and a pierced clay disc that may have functioned as a whorl.

Since the sample is so small, the repetition of features and artifacts may be purely accidental. If it is not, however, it suggests that, on given occasions throughout the Neolithic, figurines were associated with domestic work areas, particularly those where some kind of grinding activities were conducted. Moreover, the appearance of an awl, drills, and beads might also suggest the production of ornaments, though it is equally possible that the tools were used for other activities or that the beads actually once adorned the figurines. In any case, we appear to have evidence, albeit slim, for similar types of activity areas in which three very different kinds of anthropomorphic images appear (one being a split-leg type).

One explanation for this diversity of types in seemingly similar contexts might be that the figures served as dolls or toys. They may have been given to children for their amusement while older members of the group carried out tasks such as grinding, spinning, or bead production. Moreover, the evidence suggests that these work areas may have been devoted to activities conducted by females.

The division of labor in modern primitive societies is often based on gender. Although any skill can be mastered by persons of either sex, the ethnographic literature indicates that some tasks devolved more often on women and others more often on men. Women's tools frequently included grinding stones for preparing food and pigments, whorls for spinning, and needles for sewing, while the male kit comprised implements for hunting and butchering, tools for making other tools, and celts for clearing land (see Flannery and Winter 1976). The constellation of tools and artifacts in the three Franchthi contexts discussed above seems more in keeping with female tool kits. It may well be that women were working in these areas of the site while attending to their offspring.[41]

Even if this conclusion is accepted, the human skeletal remains found in the three contexts is peculiar. Anthropomorphic figurines are not associated with burials at Franchthi, and it is difficult to determine whether these bone scatterings percolated into the units over time (suggesting greater disturbance than I have assumed) or were deliberately placed near the figurines.

MEANING

While the possible *uses* of the Franchthi images have been considered, the more elusive matter of *meaning*—the symbolic intent of these figures—remains to be considered.[42] The idea of objects as nonverbal communicators or meaning-bearing symbols, particularly among nonliterate cultures, is not new; Durkheim touched upon the subject as early as 1915. Visual images can be as informative as verbal language in proclaiming an idea, thought, sentiment, or belief. In fact, language is a comparatively late development in human cultural history. The earliest transmission of information was likely effected through various nonverbal gestures and visual images. Like other nonverbal images to which meanings adhere, figurines can be held, contemplated, discussed, ignored, and misunderstood by those who use them. Unraveling the possible meanings of such symbols is an enormously difficult task which entails, among other things, deciphering the range of encoding and decoding strategies of a given social group. Research is hampered by the fact that, in general, archaeologists have a poor understanding of the nature, organization, and operational behaviors of sign systems other than verbal language (Preziosi 1979:1).[43]

At this stage of our research we can only guess at why the range of postures and gestures on Franchthi figurines was so limited[44], why facial features were so unimportant, or what meanings were broadcast by some of the decorative elements on these images. There is, however, one unusual symbol for which there are provocative analogies in the anthropological literature.

Nearly a dozen Franchthi pendants and figurines, all of which are dated EN or MN, probably depicted, when complete, only half or part of the human form. FC 190 portrays the torso of a human body, and FC 122 depicts a left buttock. One pendant, FS 41 (see Schaeffer 1977:Figure 5) clearly represents a human body from the waist down, while seven other examples, FS 42, 161, 238, 499, 622, 721, and FV 216 (see Schaeffer 1977:Figure 5) may depict schematized versions of the lower body. These so-called half-body pendants are apparently unique to Franchthi. With the exception of a broken pendant from Mycenae (Diamant 1974b), whose status both as Neolithic and as a half-body is debatable, no comparable examples exist elsewhere in southern Greece.[45]

Interestingly, this concern with bodily divisions is echoed by other, more subtle aspects of figurine production at the site. As discussed in Chapter 3, many of the clay figurines are constructed in parts: the final image is a composite of several segments made to coalesce. Therefore, while the makers may have intended to create a gestalt of the human body, the process by which they made a figure entailed differentiating the image into halves or a number of distinct segments. In addition, the decoration on FC 118 shows a grass-like skirt running down *only one side* of the image. The Franchthi examples seem to suggest that the makers and users of these figures recognized two major bodily divisions: the upper and lower parts of the body, separated at the waist (e.g., FC 190 and the half-body pendants) and the left–right division (e.g., the split-leg examples; the skirt on FC 118).[46] It is anyone's guess what these divisions may have symbolized to members of Franchthi society. If, however, we accept that the explicit choice of body parts as symbols represents a kind of artifactual language likely understood throughout the group, then we may gain some insights by examining similar kinds of symbols among other cultures, particularly ones where the meanings of those symbols are documented. This is not meant to imply that precise equivalencies in meaning exist among those groups who employ body parts in this way. Indeed, no symbol can be adequately understood outside its cultural context. What one finds, however, is that the body and its component parts are often seen as a template by which to order, structure, and understand one's world.

Numerous societies throughout the world, both past and present, have used the human image to explain the origin and organization of diverse phenomena. Political systems, genealogies, cosmologies, kinship, social relations, inanimate objects, and even the physical layout of a village are often compared to the physical body, which serves as a metaphor to structure, classify, or explain the phenomenon (Griaule 1965; Perey 1975; Blacking 1977; Talalay 1984a-b). In my search for cultures which use the interrelationship of body parts to understand their world, I encountered an unusual case study that may have some relevance to the half-body pendants and figurines at Franchthi.

The Rom, a group of North American Gypsies, view the body as a powerful social symbol. These Gypsies conceptualize purity and pollution in a vivid fashion: the two opposing forces are symbolized by a separation of the body at the waist into two halves. Purity, an ideal of Gypsy society, is attained by avoiding polluting substances and areas, that is, the lower half of the body. Pollution is the failure to keep separate the upper and lower halves, even to the extent that clothing like shirts and trousers must be washed separately. This notion of pollution is related to other concepts of social importance, such as the crucial inside/outside boundary between Rom and non-Gypsy, internal political divisions, and age statuses (Sutherland 1977).

It would be absurd to argue that the upper-body/lower-body symbolism apparent at Franchthi had the same social implications; there are no supporting data, and any statements to that end are purely speculative. What is evident, however, is that the Franchthiotes purposely selected this unusual body image and continued to employ it for nearly two millennia. As such, this symbol likely embodied certain concepts or understandings shared (consciously or unconsciously) by the Neolithic inhabitants of the site. We cannot, at this stage of our research, know the referents implied by these symbols. Nor can we determine how these symbols were manipulated in a particular social context or setting. However, the notion that Franchthi ideology included the concept of the body as some kind of organizing metaphor remains a distinct possibility.

SUMMARY

The suggestions in this chapter account for only a handful of examples from Franchthi, leaving the majority of the figurines' functions, let alone their meanings, unexplained. As ethnographic analogies suggest, the possibilities are legion: charms, hexes, fetishes, ancestor images, deities, or paraphernalia in curing ceremonies, to name but a few. Tenuous evidence from sites farther north and east suggests that comparable figurines may have been part of social rituals, broadly defined as religious or cultic. Ucko has proposed (1962:438) that LN figurines from Hacilar were used in initiation rites (see also Talalay 1983c); Peltenburg believes that recent discoveries at Kissonerga, Cyprus, support the use of figurines in possible birthing rituals (Peltenburg 1988, 1991); and the general consensus among Balkan archaeologists is that the large number of figurines from later Neolithic levels at sites like Vinča, Karanovo, Tirpeşţi, and Sabatinovka II represent deities associated with the growing role of ritual activity and control in the area (Whittle 1985:150–156). At Nea Nikomedeia, five figurines found within a large tripartite structure were also interpreted as deities.[47] Whether the Franchthi figurines ever functioned in capacities comparable to those suggested at these other Neolithic sites is unknown.

Clearly, many intellectual hurdles still block our path to understanding the precise use and meaning of prehistoric figurines. As I have tried to demonstrate, however, progress is not possible until we establish categories of evidence which, when marshalled together, provide reasonable arguments. While I have tried to use several categories of evidence, all of the possibilities offered in this chapter are based on correlational rather than causal data. Consequently, they are weaker than one would like. On the other hand, they avoid unfounded speculation and are directed by a set of specific guidelines which incorporate evidence from the figurines themselves and their archaeological contexts, as well as the larger sociocultural matrix of the society which produced these images. It is precisely this kind of systematic approach to the data which helps us derive plausible functional explanations and lends a greater degree of rigor to the field.

CHAPTER SIX
Franchthi Figurines: A Regional Perspective

INTRODUCTION

The previous pages have examined the figurines from Franchthi in some detail, exploring aspects of manufacture, use, and meaning. Yet to be addressed in depth, however, is the sample in a regional perspective. This broader view allows us to consider the relationship of Franchthi to other sites and collections, to identify stylistic, functional, and technical variability among figurine samples, and to speculate on the range of social and economic behaviors which might account for intersite similarities.

Such a survey demands, at the very least, coherent groupings of sites and images, well-defined geographical parameters, and a clear sense of what is being compared.[48] To attempt, however, an exhaustive comparison of all Eastern Mediterranean figurines and relevant contexts would require a volume in itself. Therefore, what is offered here is arbitrarily confined to a detailed examination of figurines and contexts from sites within a few days' journey of the cave (i.e., sites in the Peloponnese, Attica, and the Cyclades) and a rather cursory look at select comparative material from northern Greece (i.e., Thessaly and Macedonia). Data from elsewhere in southeastern Europe are also considered, though only superficially and from a functional, not a stylistic, perspective. Unlike southern Greece, the Balkans have yielded an extremely rich collection of anthropomorphic and zoomorphic images, as well as evidence suggesting links between figurines and religious ritual. While there is no compelling reason to insist, as some authors do (e.g., Gimbutas), that Balkan and Greek figurines were functionally comparable, the evidence for ritual or cultic usages of figurines at certain Balkan sites affects our thinking about the Greek Neolithic, and the matter warrants at least brief consideration in this volume.

For the sake of clarity, the chapter is divided into two main sections: style and use/meaning. Such a division is not meant to imply that the form and decoration of figurines are distinct from their function and symbolic importance. Indeed, they are intimately intertwined. Rather, the division provides a manageable analytical and descriptive framework.

The stylistic section, which focuses exclusively on Greek figurines, includes all known examples from southern Greece. Each of those images was studied personally, and an extensive and identical range of attributes was recorded for each figurine. In contrast, I was not permitted to examine examples from northern Greece and had to rely on published photographs and descriptions, which are both limited and far from standardized. Consequently, stylistic comparisons between the Franchthi pieces and their Thessalian and Macedonian counterparts consider only a limited number of attributes and inevitably partake of biases in published reports. The attributes consist of an image's overall shape and decorative elements.

The section on use and meaning is site-specific, concentrating first on sites in southern Greece, then on northern Greek and Balkan evidence. Conclusions are drawn from a range of data, including an image's shape, decoration, and technical details, the archaeological and systemic contexts of the figurines, and possible functions suggested by the ethnographic record. It is not assumed, *a priori*, that "similar-looking" figurines from different settlements had identical functions, or that "different-looking" examples from separate sites had dissimilar uses or meanings. Indeed, stylistically distinct examples from separate communities may reflect similar usages.

Correlating the chronological sequences from Franchthi with those reported from other sites in Greece and the Balkans posed a particularly knotty problem. Unfortunately, there are no standardized chronologies. Terminologies vary among regions, and the number of radiocarbon dates, though impressive at some sites, is not sufficient for constructing a reliable pan-Greek/Balkan framework. I have deferred primarily to the comparative sequences published in Whittle (1985:Figures 3.2, 5.2), which are highly simplified.

The time intervals chosen for this chapter are those published by Jacobsen (1976) and used throughout the volume: Early Neolithic (ca. 6000–5000 b.c.), Middle Neolithic (ca. 5000–4500 b.c.), Late Neolithic (ca. 4500–4000 b.c.), and Final Neolithic (ca. 4000–3000 b.c.). Although far from an exact fit, the Early Neolithic at Franchthi encompasses the Preceramic, Proto-Sesklo, Pre-Sesklo, Early Pottery, and Early Neolithic in northern Greece, and overlaps partially with Karanovo I-II and Kremikovci sites in Bulgaria and the early Starčevo culture in eastern Yugoslavia. Franchthi's Middle Neolithic is roughly coincident with the Middle Neolithic throughout the rest of southern Greece, classical Sesklo in northern Greece, and the Veselinovo culture in Bulgaria. Although a distinction is made in this work between the Late and Final Neolithic, comparable divisions are not easily recognized farther north. The Late Neolithic in southern Greece is roughly contemporary with the Larissa/Tsangli and Arapi phases in northern Greece (Gallis 1987), Karanovo III-IV in Bulgaria, and early Vinča (Vinča-Turdaş) sites in Yugoslavia. Franchthi's FN aligns with the Dimini and Rachmani phases in northern Greece, Karanovo V-VI and Gumelniţa sites in Bulgaria, and the later Vinča (Vinča-Pločnik) sites and Bubanj culture in Yugoslavia.

Before issues of intersite diversity can be addressed, however, the main collections in question (i.e., all of the known figurines from southern Greece) must be sorted into useful taxa. The method employed in this study is briefly described below.

The 119 Neolithic figurines from southern Greece are ordered into classes by using attribute analysis to describe the images and cluster analysis to arrange the figures into stylistic groups.[49] The resulting dendrograms, which are based on approximately 30 coded dimensions (Appendix E), are reported elsewhere (Talalay 1983a). All dimensions refer to stylistic features, each of which is given equal weight in the analysis. A "type" is defined as complete or nearly complete figurines which share at least 80% of their attributes and "look alike." "Group" refers to two different classifications: (1) *fragments* which share between 60% and 100% of their attributes and also "look alike," or (2) *complete* figurines sharing more than 60% but less than 80% of their attributes and which also "look alike." (For a more complete discussion see Talalay 1983a:5–8, Ch. 3–5).

A summary of the computer analysis is included in the following discussions. Since the final taxa are difficult to envision without illustrations, they have been simplified and graphically depicted in Figure 3. Figure 3 should be used in conjunction with Table 5, which provides a brief description of taxa and a list of figurines assigned to each taxon. To simplify matters further, drawings of all published figurines from southern Greece are provided in Appendix F.

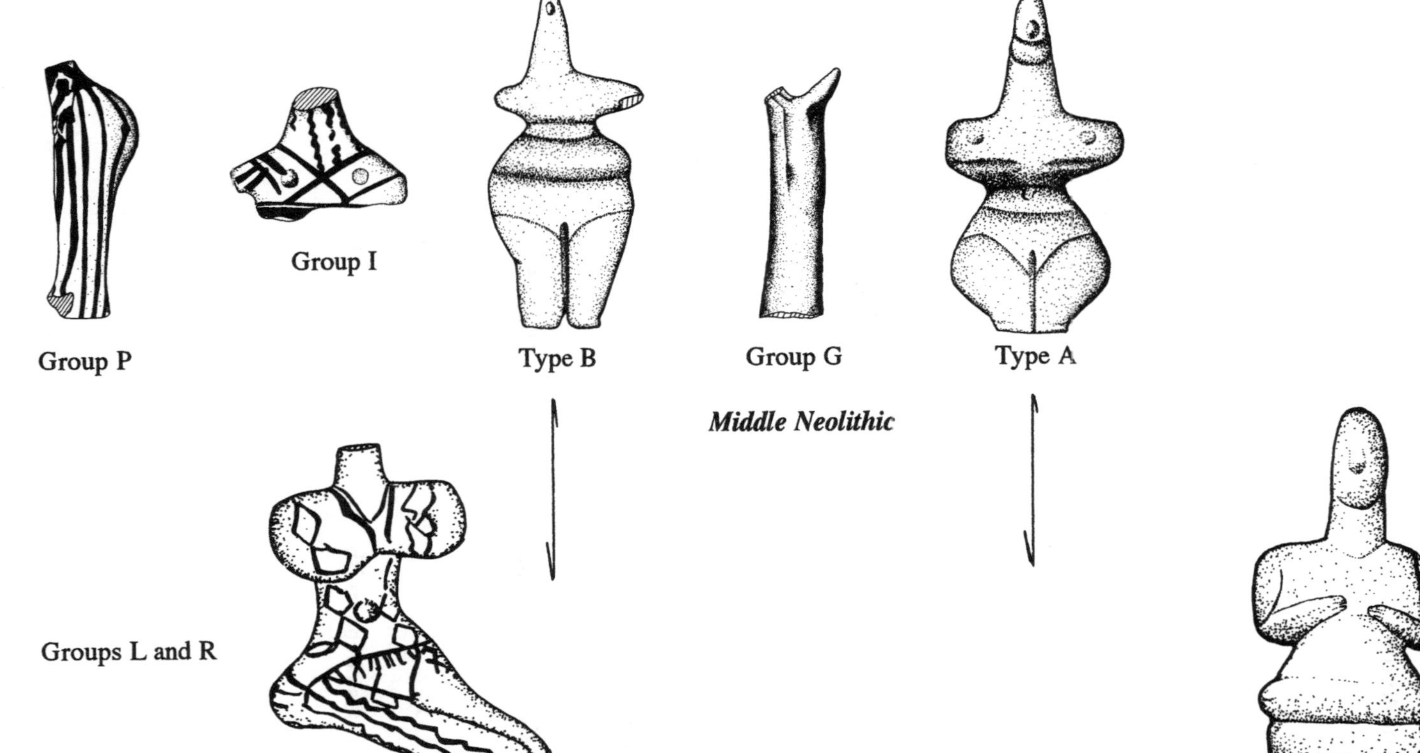
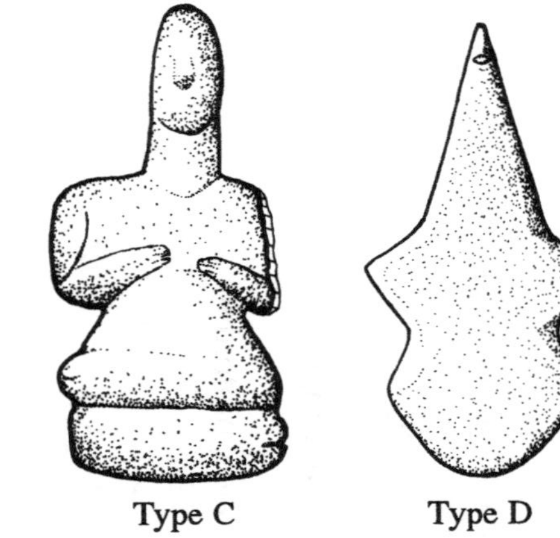

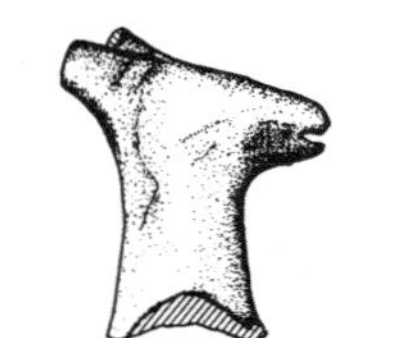
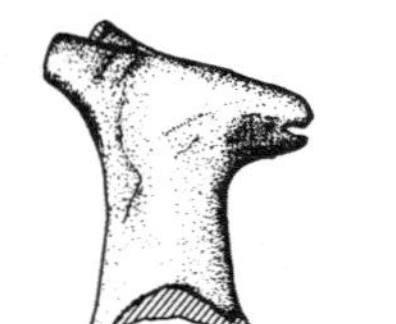
MAINLAND, KEA, AND AEGINA
CYCLADES
Group P
Group I
Type B
Group G
Type A
Middle Neolithic
Groups L and R
Type C
Type D
Late Neolithic
Group A
Group D
Group I
zoomorphic
Final Neolithic

TABLE 5

MAJOR TYPES AND GROUPS OF FIGURINES FROM SOUTHERN GREECE[a]

Class	*Brief Description*	*Examples/Date* [b]
Type A	full-bodied female, standing; arms folded horizontally across chest/abdomen; conical head; featureless face, protruding nose	NM 3927; Aeg. 1, 2 **MN or LN**
Type B	similar to Type A, except arms extend outward as stumps	NM 3930, 3932 **MN or LN**
Type C	similar to Type A, except seated, with legs drawn up and crossed	Patissia; Naxos; Amorgos; Saliagos 5[c]; MF 8504 **LN**
Type D	flat, violin-shaped figurine; featureless	Saliagos 1, 2[d], 3 **LN**
Group A	crude, cylindrically shaped figure; coil encircles middle	P 13926; Kephala 160 **FN**
Group D	triangularly shaped head, similar to EC II idols	P 25864; Kephala 128, 202 **FN**
Group G	cylindrical, featureless head, with ear-like protrusions	FC 30, 31 **MN**

Group I	flat, stumpy-armed torso, with pellet breasts	FC 4, 112; Kephala 127, 196, 197, 198; Kitsos; Asea 1, 4; MF 8065, 8543 **MN** and **FN** (two variants; 1 **LN** example)
Group L	decorated torso, with arms curled to breasts	FC 118, 28 **LN**
Group P	leg, protruding buttock, incised or painted pubic triangle; smoothed medial surface; scar or incisions indicating hands/fingers; linear decoration	FC 68, 124; Asea 2, 3; L7.46; Akratas 1021, 985; MF 4386, 68-94, 68-95, 68-96 **MN**
Group R	seated figure, legs extended outward, perpendicular to torso	FC 118, 57; MF 76-89 **LN**
Zoomorphic		FC 41, 88, 177; Nea Makri 1; Asea 5, 6, 7; MF 77-112, 3269, 8545, 13144, 68-103, 9915, 13145 **MN, LN, FN, or EH** (predominantly **LN or FN**)

[a] based on cluster analysis, Talalay 1983a
[b] See Figure 1 and Appendix F for examples; for catalogue numbers, NM=Koufovouno; MF=Corinth; P=Agora; FC=Franchthi; L=Lerna
[c] equivalent to Group N: lower body fragment, legs drawn up and crossed
[d] equivalent to Group F: conical head, featureless except for horizontal slit

DISCUSSION OF REGIONAL STYLES

Inferences drawn from various classes of data, including pottery and lithics, suggest that Franchthi was not a completely autonomous, isolated, and self-sufficient village, removed from intersettlement contact (Vitelli 1974, forthcoming; Runnels 1981, 1983, 1985; Cullen 1985a-b; Jacobsen 1984b; van Andel and Runnels 1987). To the contrary, the inhabitants of Franchthi apparently engaged in (probably shifting) social and economic relations with other communities throughout the Neolithic, although the precise nature and mechanism of those interactions are poorly understood. Ongoing communication with other communities could certainly have influenced both the style and use of figurines at the cave.[50]

Although archaeologists commonly regard stylistic similarities and differences in material culture as indications of interaction, problems of analysis loom large. Methodological and theoretical guidelines for measuring and understanding interaction among spatially distinct populations are still fairly coarse (Schortman 1989:52–53). Factors motivating intervillage communications and the consequences of such behaviors are difficult to isolate, as are the scale and frequency of contacts (Renfrew and Cherry 1986:vii).

Ethnographic reports suggest that stylistic conformities and nonconformities among villages are generated by a range of intentions. Neighboring settlements with ongoing communication may choose to underscore *differences* in their artifactual assemblages when those communities compete for limited resources (e.g., food, land, authority). Those differences effectively serve to mark the social or ethnic identity of each group. On the other hand, neighboring groups that share a symbiotic relationship may choose to underscore stylistic *similarities*. Those similarities signal the groups' affiliation. Distant villages which maintain social or economic bonds also may deliberately produce stylistically similar objects in order to reinforce their connections and symbolically minimize the geographic separation (Hodder 1978, 1979, 1981; Cullen 1985b:79). Cullen correctly warns that, in citing stylistic similarity as evidence to support interrelationships among communities, the archaeologist should consider the context in which the variation occurs, especially the degree of social differentiation and competition within and between societies; the geographic proximity of craftsmen/craftswomen; the visibility of the goods in question; the manner in which the goods are produced, distributed, and used; and the likelihood that the particular artifactual language is deliberately manipulated to support or deny social boundaries (1985b:79).

With those caveats in mind, the following pages explore intersite variability among figurines reported from EN through FN sites in Greece.

Early Neolithic

Despite substantial EN occupational debris at certain sites (e.g., Franchthi, Lerna, Corinth, Nea Makri), the first thousand years of settled village life in southern Greece is almost devoid of figurines. There are only three extant examples, all of them from Franchthi: FC 190, a clay torso; FC 11, a clay head assigned an EN/MN transitional date; and FC 122, the nearly complete left buttock, which is tentatively assigned an EN date on the basis of northern Greek comparanda. The dearth of figurines in southern Greece stands in marked contrast to regions farther north, especially Thessaly, where many of the published examples are dated EN (Table 6).

Parallels for the three Franchthi images are few and predominantly restricted to Thessaly and sites in the Northern Sporades. Long, cylindrical heads, generally comparable to FC 11, span the Early through Late phases. The form, however, is so simple that figurine-makers at spatially distinct villages could have created these heads independently. Consequently, the search for comparanda may not be meaningful.

Parallels for FC 190 are also problematic. The inserted shell head of FC 190 is, to my knowledge, unique, although "acrolithic" heads appear in Thessaly (Wace and Thompson 1912:Figures 25, 28g) and Macedonia (Areti Hondroyianni-Metoki, pers. comm. 1992), chiefly in contexts contemporary with the Final Neolithic of southern Greece.

While a number of (mostly EN) examples of simple, frontal torsos generally comparable to FC 190 are reported from Thessaly (e.g., Hourmouziadis 1973:Plates 13, 21, 23), the asymmetrical position of the arms on FC 190 is unusual. In addition, if FC 190 was intended to represent only the upper half of the human form, it appears to be anomalous among EN figurines.

Finally, FC 122, the possible half-buttocks from Franchthi, is generally similar to pieces found at Sesklo, Ayios Petros, and Karamoular. The examples from Sesklo are reported as Preceramic and EN, that from Ayios Petros as late EN or early MN, and the example from Karamoular as a surface find (Theocharis 1973:Plate XXII:4d; Wijnen 1982:Figures 14:12, 14:19; Efstratiou 1985:Figure 69:4, Plate 36d).

In sum, the occurrence of EN figurines at Franchthi appears to be anomalous for southern Greece. No other excavations in the Peloponnese, Attica, and the Cyclades have exposed EN figurines, nor have recent intensive surveys, such as the Argolid Exploration Project and the Nemea Valley Archaeological Project.

In contrast, surface reconnaissance and excavations in northern Greece have produced over 250 EN figurines. The regional differences raise obvious questions. Is the restricted production of figurines in the Peloponnese (and surrounding areas) related to problems of archaeological preservation and excavation bias, or were figurines simply not part of the material culture among these settlements? With such meager data, the answers are necessarily equivocal. On the one hand, evidence suggests that insufficient firing techniques may have severely reduced the chances of long-term survival for EN figurines in the south. FC 190 yielded a Mohs of 2.0 (Appendix C) after it had been bathed in a solution of Polyvinyl Acetate (P.V.A. acts to harden and preserve certain materials). The original hardness of the piece, therefore, may have been even lower. Possible explanations for such readings include low or short-term firings, or baking by the sun rather than in a kiln or equivalent device. While it is dangerous to draw conclusions based on evidence from a single example, the rarity of EN figurines (at least at Franchthi, if not elsewhere in the Peloponnese) may be partially due to the original firing or drying conditions.[51]

On the other hand, if we argue that the problem is not one of archaeological preservation, then other explanations are required to account for the scarcity of EN figurines in southern Greece. Part of the answer may lie in understanding the nature of EN settlements in the Peloponnese and the extent to which those communities may have differed from those farther north.

Current archaeological evidence reveals a concentration of sites at the beginning of the sixth millennium in Thessaly and western Macedonia (e.g., Nea Nikomedeia, Argissa, Prodromos, Otzaki). Thessalian sites favored the low ground of inland basins, river valleys, and their adjacent foothills, and, once established, appear to have spread across the landscape, ultimately creating a dense pattern of villages. In contrast, the beginnings of the Neolithic in the Peloponnese appear, perhaps, more halting. Early settlements, which are few, small, and often distant from one another, favored coastal rather than inland locations and, unlike their northern counterparts, failed to spread out to fill the available space. Halstead (1981) and others (e.g., van Andel and Runnels 1988) argue that the apparent dearth of early sites in southern Greece is due to the fact that, agriculturally, the region was not an appealing place to settle. It was drier, less fertile, and subject to greater seasonal variation in precipitation than the north. More than likely, Peloponnesian villages could support only small populations by growing cereals and pulses on restricted, spring-watered meadows or on

TABLE 6

NORTHERN GREEK SITES WITH NEOLITHIC FIGURINES[a]

Site	*Total*	*EN*	*MN*	*LN*	*Date Unknown or Unreported*
Prodromos	246[b]	186		11	49
Sesklo	142	16?	13	24?	89
Sitagroi	228	predominantly LN			
Achilleion	199	53	146?		
Ayios Petros	50	predominantly MN			
Otzaki	28	7		1	20
Karamoular	18		1		17
Dimini	17/49[c]	predominantly LN			
Tsani Magoula	15		3		12
Tsangli	14/45[c]	1	12		1
Phthiotic Thebes	11/21[c]			11	
Nessonis	10	2	1	1	6
Magoulitsa	10	7			3
Pyrasos	9		1		8
Soufli Magoula	9	3	2		4
Pazaraki	7		6		1
Nea Nikomedeia	11+	predominantly EN			
Dikili Tash	"numerous"	predominantly MN and LN			
Plateia Zarkou	10			8	2
Zerelia	4/20[c]		3		1
Olynthos	3			3?	
Chasan Magoula	3				3

Site	*Total*	*EN*	*MN*	*LN*	*Date Unknown or Unreported*
Pharsala	2		1		1
Krannon	2				2
Paradeisos	7			7	
Velestino	2				2
Topouslar	2				2
Vyrsi Tirnavos	2				2
Daudza	2	1			1
Magoula Syrmou	2			2	
Dendraki	2			2	
Sophades	1			1	
Phalanni	1		1		
Domeniko	1			1	
Myrini	1	1			
Rachmani	1/19[c]			1	
Gediki	1				1

[a] Numbers are based on Tsountas 1908; Wace and Thompson 1912; Rodden 1962, 1964, 1965; Daux 1962, 1968; Deshayes 1970; Hourmouziadis 1973; Gimbutas 1974b, 1986; Gimbutas et al. 1989; Galles 1982; Gallis 1985; Efstratiou 1985; and Hellstrom 1987. It is often difficult to determine from published data the date of northern Greek figurines. Some reports are preliminary; others do not catalogue figures individually. Also, chronological vocabulary is not consistent among reports. For the purposes of this table, figures reported from Proto-Sesklo, Aceramic, or Early Pottery contexts were labeled EN, those from Sesklo contexts MN, and those from Larissa, Rachmani, or Dimini phases were subsumed under LN (although Rachmani phase figurines are more correctly FN).

[b] Some totals may be inflated. Because not all the images are illustrated or described, it is impossible to check whether some may be more correctly categorized as miscellaneous objects. In addition, comparison of the raw numbers may be misleading, since it was impossible to compare the amount of earth removed from each site.

[c] The larger numbers indicate the counts reported by Wace and Thompson (1912). In some cases, marked discrepancies exist between these and those listed by Hourmouziadis (1973). Perhaps some figures recovered near the turn of the century have been lost, reassigned later dates, or discounted as bona fide figurine fragments.

the (now submerged) coastal plains (van Andel and Runnels 1988:236). Noting that many of the southern Greek sites seem well situated to maintain trade and contacts throughout the southern Aegean, van Andel and Runnels propose that an impulse for external contacts, not the traditionally assumed search for land, motivated the initial selection of site locations in the Peloponnese (1987:73).

If van Andel and Runnels are correct, then from the beginning of the Neolithic northern and southern Greek settlements reflected different kinds of communities. The former represented a mosaic of agriculturally-based villages situated close to arable land. The latter derived their *raison d'être* from key positions along nodes of a burgeoning exchange network. If such assumptions are valid, could these differences have affected the use and output of anthropomorphic images? Could the ostensible permanence and stability of EN communities in the north have encouraged the production of figurines, while the more tenuous existence and possibly sporadic occupation of villages in the south have precluded the use of such images? Until we gain a better understanding of the functions of these early figurines, such queries must remain unanswered. But one cannot help suspecting that if fundamental economic differences characterized EN (and perhaps later) settlements in northern and southern Greece, then these differences may have directly affected the contrasting output of figurines in both areas. For reasons we have yet to comprehend, the nature of EN settlements in southern Greece does not seem to have been conducive to the production of figurines.

Middle Neolithic

Unlike EN settlers, the MN inhabitants of southern Greece manufactured more than just the isolated few anthropomorphic images, although the numbers are still very modest. Thirty-four specimens are unequivocally MN, and an additional sixteen are assigned to either the Middle or Late phases (Table 7). Almost all of the definite MN examples are modeled from clay, and as a group they are confined principally to the northeastern Peloponnese, including the sites of Franchthi, Lerna, Asea, Corinth, Nemea, and Akratas. The MN or LN images, many of which are carved from stone, derive from a wider geographic area, encompassing Franchthi, Athens, Eleusis, Corinth, Tiryns, Mycenae, Koufovouno, Aegina, Alepotrypa, and Malthi.

Although these figures can be divided into several distinct typological classes, they also share a number of common features. Painted and incised decorations appear frequently; no examples of shell or bone exist; the sex is invariably female; posture is largely restricted to standing examples with flat, frontal torsos; arms are symmetrically positioned, lying either across the chest or extending outward; and the legs are always depicted in the same position (e.g., they are never crossed or portrayed in divergent poses).

These conformities notwithstanding, cluster analysis helped to distinguish five typological classes (Figure 3): (1, 2) the closely related Types A and B (full-bodied, standing, stone females) from Koufovouno and Aegina (FS 101, the stone head from Franchthi, may also belong with this type); (2) Group G (cylindrical and featureless heads with ear-like protrusions), exclusive to Franchthi; (3) Group I (flat, stumpy-armed torsos with pellet breasts) found at Corinth and Asea; and (4) Group P (split-leg figurines) from Franchthi, Lerna, Corinth, Nemea, Asea, and Akratas (see Table 5 for a list of figures within each of these groups or types).

Both Group P and the choice of decoration on MN figurines (see below), indicate that Franchthi's closest ties were with Lerna, Nemea, Asea, and Corinth.[52] These similarities can hardly be accidental, and the efforts on the part of figurine-makers at those sites to produce comparable images were likely prompted by a number of factors. Because we have yet to understand fully the

TABLE 7

MIDDLE NEOLITHIC FIGURINES FROM SOUTHERN GREECE[a]

MN		*MN or LN*	
Akratas	985	Aegina	1
	1021		2
Asea	1	Agora	AS 148
	2	(Athens)	S 1097
	3		
	4	Akratas	992
			1020
Corinth	MF 4386		
	MF 6730	Corinth	S 786
	MF 68-94		
	MF 68-95	Koufovouno	NM 3927
	MF 68-96		NM 3928
	MF 70-24		NM 3930
	MF 8065		NM 3931
	MF 8797		NM 3932
	MF 9948		
	MF 13704	Lerna	L5.162
			(unpublished)
Franchthi	FC 12		
	FC 30	Malthi	1
	FC 31		
	FC 42	Mycenae	1
	FC 68		
	FC 117	Tiryns	1
	FC 124		
	FC 167		
	FC 177		
	FC 208		
	FP 173		
Lerna	L7.46		
	L6.100		
	L5.388 (unpublished)		
	L6.58 (unpublished)		
	L7.48 (unpublished)		
	L7.316 (unpublished)		
Nemea	S702.2.1		

[a] See Appendix F for illustrations of published examples.

function of these images or the social organization of the region, we cannot precisely identify the forces motivating this stylistic homogeneity. What we can suggest, however, are general reasons why alliances or bonds (which might be symbolically expressed by conformity in material culture) would be beneficial. It is unlikely that any of the villages would have fared well if completely isolated and self-reliant: populations were relatively small, and food sources may have been scarce periodically. Exchange and movement of both people and goods could have alleviated certain stresses (Halstead and O'Shea 1989). As several studies suggest (Vitelli 1974, forthcoming; Jacobsen 1981, 1984b; Cullen 1985a-b; Talalay 1987), bonds among villages may have been maintained via transhumance, exogamous marriage policies, trading alliances, superlocal commitments in times of crisis, and nonresidential ties among clans or lineages. Any one of these mechanisms (or combinations thereof) would have facilitated communication among figurine-makers.[53]

While stylistic homogeneity among images from the northeastern Peloponnese is clearly evident, each site also exhibits some degree of individualism. Cluster analysis indicates that not all MN images fall neatly into one group or another. At Franchthi, for example, five pieces (FC 12, 42, 117, 167, 208) qualify as anomalous, though this may be partially due to sample size. The evidence suggests, therefore, that although regional conformity was deemed important, some nonconformity was also encouraged. Indeed, specific forms or decorations may have been viewed as emblematic of certain villages, and a Franchthiote might have been able (or even expected) to distinguish among figures produced at his/her village and elsewhere.

Two of the more interesting clusters generated by the computer are the related stone figurines from Koufovouno and Aegina (Types A [n=3] and B [n=2]). Both types span the Middle and Late Neolithic. All of the examples from Koufovouno, and probably one of the Aegina figures, exhibit nearly identical sets of proportions. The artist(s) apparently adhered to ratios in which the height of the figure was two times the width of the arms and four times the width at the waist (Table 8; Talalay 1981, 1983a:129).

TABLE 8

HEIGHT:ARM:WAIST MEASUREMENTS OF COMPLETE STONE FIGURINES FROM SOUTHERN GREECE (RATIOS 1:2:4)[a]

Figurine	*Height (cm)*	*Arm Stretch (cm)*	*Width at Waist (cm)*
NM 3927	7.1	3.7	1.8
NM 3930	7.6	4.0	1.9
NM 3932	6.9	3.2 (rt. arm truncated)	1.7
Aegina 2 (taken from photograph)	6.4	1.4	2.9

[a] The headless marble figurine from Alepotrypa (Appendix F) also has a waist which is approximately one-half the width of the arms. It was, however, taller than two times the arm stretch.

Although extensive research on the much admired stone "idols" of EC II has demonstrated that EBA figurines were planned according to a variety of mathematical canons, some quite complex (Getz-Preziosi 1972, 1977, 1987), the question of whether comparable "rules" for carving stone figurines existed prior to the Bronze Age has not been broached in the literature. The evidence from Koufovouno and Aegina suggests that perhaps a very simple sculptural plan was already employed by Middle or Late Neolithic artists. The existence of such practices should not be surprising, especially if they were seen as helping to eliminate mistakes on costly and valuable (e.g., imported) materials such as marble. What is unusual, however, is that the *same* mathematical canon seems to appear at two sites separated by a good deal of terrain and water (i.e., Aegina and Koufovouno). Exactly how we can account for the use of identical guidelines at these sites is open to discussion. A number of alternatives are possible: (1) individual artists may have produced the figurines at one site and subsequently distributed their pieces through some kind of exchange network; (2) one artist may have traveled periodically, peddling his or her work at one site or the other; (3) several artists from different villages may have communicated face-to-face at occasional (regional) gatherings or through exogamous marriage practices; or (4) the specifics of the canon could have circulated via a third party. Until a larger sample of intact figurines is available and characterization analyses on marble are more reliable, the discussion cannot be pursued very far. In the interim, we should not dismiss the possibility that certain stone figurines circulated among settlements as early as the Middle Neolithic.

There is, however, more convincing evidence that at least one MN figure found in southern Greece may have traveled some distance from its original place of manufacture. Excavations at Corinth exposed a fine example of an incised "rod-head" (MF 6730; Phelps 1987:Plate 33:1)—a type of figurine rarely found in the Peloponnese. Incised rod-heads are occasionally reported from Thessaly, Boeotia, and the Northern Sporades, but the majority have been found in the Balkans, especially Yugoslavia and Moldavia (see Nandris 1970). More importantly, the fabric and finish on the Corinthian rod-head are not characteristic of local production. The piece may, therefore, have been "imported," possibly from one of the sites farther north where rod-heads are common (Phelps 1987:234–235, 241).

Other, albeit tenuous, links with northern Greece[54] are suggested by two figurines from Franchthi, FC 42 and FP 173. FC 42, a painted torso with pendant breasts, has marked similarities to a piece from Sesklo (Tsountas 1908:Plate 33:5). The pieces share the same basic form, as well as the peculiar placement of the breasts. The rendering of the breasts, which diverges from normal perceptions of the human form, is unusual, and one wonders whether such an oddity arose independently at these two distant sites. Since both figures appear to be modeled from local clay, an argument for importation is improbable. While some form of intersite communication (or even the circulation of a common myth involving such a figure) would be a logical possibility, there is, to my knowledge, very little else in the material record at either site which suggests contact between the two settlements.[55] The similarity between the two figurines remains unexplained. Although it may simply reflect that an individual traveler made both figurines, we should not dismiss the evidence or label it coincidental. The similarity currently represents one of the few symbolic or material links between these two distant settlements.

Finally, FP 173, the "face-pot" from Franchthi, finds general parallels in northern and central Greece, rather than in the south. The best known face-pots are those from the EN site of Nea Nikomedeia (Theocharis 1973:Figures 219, 220). Other EN and MN examples are reported from Thespiae (unpublished), Achilleion (Gimbutas et al. 1989:Plate 7.13), and an unknown site in Thessaly (Hourmouziadis 1973:Plate 103).[56]

Late Neolithic

Excavation, survey, and chance finds in southern Greece have produced 37 figurines that are unequivocally LN, 16 that may be either MN or LN, 4 that are LN or FN, and 3 that are LN, FN, or possibly Early Helladic (EH) in date (Table 9). Six of the definite LN examples were unearthed at Franchthi.

By and large, LN figurines continue many of the patterns established in the preceding period: figurines are made of clay and stone (no other media are employed); sex, where determinable, is female; postures are similar to those of MN images; and an interest in embellishing figurines with paint or incision is maintained. There are, however, some significant differences. LN figurines seem to exhibit greater stylistic variability than their MN predecessors; the seated position with legs either drawn up and crossed or extending outwards appears for the first time; and zoomorphic figurines begin to occur at a number of sites.

In addition to Types A and B discussed above, six stylistic classes were distinguished with the help of cluster analysis. Type C and the related Group N are found at Patissia, Amorgos, Naxos, Corinth, Saliagos, and possibly Koufovouno. Type D and the related Group F are confined to Saliagos. Groups L and R are exclusive to Franchthi and Corinth.

Type C and Group N exhibit strong stylistic affinities with Types A and B. Although all four are probably variants of the same tradition, their geographic and chronological distributions differ. The seated figures (Type C and Group N), which are confined to the Late Neolithic[57], are distributed among the Cyclades, coastal sites in Attica, and the Corinthia. The earlier standing versions (Types A and B), which span the Middle through Late Neolithic, are found at Aegina, inland sites in the Peloponnese, and possibly the Argolid.

Two other LN classes relevant to this study are Groups L and R, both peculiar to Corinth and Franchthi. The six pieces in these groups (FC 28, FC 57, FC 118, MF 76-89, MF 77-111, MF 13360) exhibit not only similar postures, but nearly identical decorative elements. The incised lines on the back of MF 77-111 are conceptually the same as those painted on the back of FC 28; the "belt and skirt" design on FC 118 from Franchthi is strikingly similar to the design on MF 13360 from Corinth; and the unusual incisions across the lap of FC 57 are virtually identical to those painted on MF 76-89 from Corinth.

Stylistically, then, Franchthi's affinities during the Late Neolithic seem strongest with Corinth and suggest close social distance between the two villages. Indeed, some of the similarities in detail are so marked that face-to-face contact may have occurred among figurine-makers. At the very least, the makers had access to commonly shared images and designs. Why seemingly close bonds would have formed between Franchthi and Corinth in particular, and not, for example, between Franchthi and Lerna, requires further study.

Although the number of figurines from the Middle and Late Neolithic is roughly comparable (n=34 and 37, respectively), as is the number of sites (n=6 and 8, respectively), figures from the later phase appear to exhibit less stylistic uniformity and suggest a greater sense of experimentation among the makers. Despite inter- and intrasite variability among MN figurines, the overall repertoire is limited. Most MN examples depict simple standing images or schematized heads. In contrast, the LN sample includes two varieties of seated figures (cross- and straight-legged); two varieties of standing figures (straight-backed or bent forward); schematic and naturalistic heads; and zoomorphic pieces.

Conformities between northern and southern figurines are rare and, like the MN evidence, only hint at links between the two regions. Seated postures comparable to FC 118, MF 76-89, and MF 9944 appear in LN levels at Sitagroi (Gimbutas 1986:9.53, 9.143, 9.147), as do occasional similarities in decorative detail (e.g., cf. Corinth MF 6732 and Sitagroi 154 for possible "lumbar dimples"; FC 118 and Sitagroi 154 for belt with tassels; and FC 118 and Sitagroi 159 for chevrons at neck). In addition, the unusual pelleted hair on MF 8500 from Corinth is also found on a piece from Pyrasos (Theocharis 1973:Figure 40). By and large, however, the two regions seem to reflect divergent traditions.

TABLE 9

LATE NEOLITHIC FIGURINES FROM SOUTHERN GREECE[a]

LN		*MN or LN*	
Alepotrypa	2 3	See Table 6	
Amorgos	1	***LN or FN***	
Corinth	MF 6732 MF 68-103 MF 68-285 MF 70-36 MF 75-39 MF 76-89 MF 77-111 MF 77-112 MF 8500 MF 8504 MF 8505 MF 8506 MF 8543 MF 9900 MF 9915 MF 9944 MF 13360	Alepotrypa Corinth ***LN or FN or EH*** Corinth	1 MF 6741 MF 75-85 T 40 MF 1942 MF 3269 MF 13145
Eleusis	1		
Franchthi	FC 28 FC 57 FC 60 FC 101 FC 118 FS 101		
Naxos	1		
Patissia (Athens)	1		
Saliagos	1–8		

[a] See Appendix F for illustrations.

Final Neolithic

Excavations at various sites in southern Greece have produced 19 FN figurines, approximately half the number of LN examples (Table 10). Seven additional pieces (six from Corinth and one from Alepotrypa) may be LN, FN, or possibly EH (Table 9).

TABLE 10

FINAL NEOLITHIC FIGURINES FROM SOUTHERN GREECE[a]

FN			
Agora	P13926	Franchthi	FC 4
(Athens)	P25864		FC 41
			FC 88
Asea	7		FC 112
Corinth	MF 8545	Kitsos	1
	MF 9906		
	MF 13144		
		LN or FN or EH	
Kephala	96B		
	127		
	128	See Table 9	
	160		
	196		
	197		
	198		
	202		

[a]See Appendix F for illustrations.

While stylistic continuities between Middle and Late Neolithic figurines are arguable, FN preferences, for the most part, represent a clear departure from previous trends. Although the LN interest in modeling zoomorphic images continues, sexless and male (anthropomorphic) figures appear for the first time. Decoration, which was popular in the preceding two periods, is virtually absent.[58] Some basic shapes hark back to MN or LN forms (e.g., Type D and Group I), though the tendency is to produce cruder, more schematic images.

The departure from previous traditions is not without parallels among other classes of finds at Franchthi and other southern Greek sites. Discontinuities between the Late Neolithic and the Final Neolithic are noted in both pottery and lithics (Jacobsen 1976; van Andel and Runnels 1988). Vitelli suggests that, at least for the pottery, part of the shift may be attributed to changes in the economic base of ceramic production. Pottery manufacture may have "down-shifted" from part-time craft specialization in the Late Neolithic to modest household production in the Final Neolithic (Vitelli 1991).

In general, FN figurines in southern Greece exhibit less stylistic variability and greater inter- and intrasite homogeneity than was evident in the Late Neolithic. Four stylistic groups were isolated with the help of cluster analysis: (1) Group A (simple, undecorated, cylindrical figurines) from Franchthi, Kea, and the Agora; (2) Group D (prototypes for the classic EC II heads) found at Kea and the Agora; (3) Group I (flat, stumpy-armed, pellet-breasted torsos) excavated at Franchthi, Kitsos, Kephala, and possibly Corinth; and (4) zoomorphic images from Franchthi, Corinth, and Asea.

Few figures qualify as unique, and nearly all of the examples fit easily into one of the four groups. Indeed, the stylistic and morphological similarities among figurines, as well as the general coarseness of fabrics, are such that, at least from casual inspection, it is difficult to distinguish FN figurines manufactured at one site from those produced at another. The evidence suggests, therefore, not only that communication among villages was frequent, but that social factors encouraged figurine-makers to maintain a level of stylistic and symbolic conformity. Since several archaeologists have proposed a possible increase in herding and/or mobility among FN populations (Halstead 1981, 1987a-b; Cherry 1988), it is arguable that information about style could have flowed easily through communication channels established by herders.

Although the sample is extremely small, the FN site distribution seems to indicate that Franchthi's affinities with other sites may have shifted or expanded. While links with the northeastern Peloponnese can still be documented, strong similarities now occur with examples from Kitsos in southern Attica and the nearby island of Kea. As in the previous millennia, similarities between southern and northern Greek figurines are rare, suggesting limited, though continuing, communication between settlements in both regions.

Design Analysis

Although results of the cluster analysis presented in the previous sections included painted and incised decoration as an attribute, a more detailed discussion of design is warranted. Considered by some archaeologists as an active element of social relations (Shanks and Tilley 1987:139), design and style have been used to probe issues of social interaction, particularly at the regional scale (Hodder 1978, 1981, 1982; Plog 1980; Shanks and Tilley 1987).

Approximately 40 figurines from southern Greece are either painted or incised with lines which do not appear to represent anatomical details. As a group, the most coherent designs derive from Group P, the split-leg figurines. Eighteen of these figures are painted with a distinct composition, confined principally to chevrons, vertical lines, horizontal lines, and, infrequently, a series of dots and diagonal lines.

Chevrons occur almost exclusively on the back and sides (MF 4386, MF 68-94, MF 68-95, Akratas 985, L5.162, L7.48) and only once on the front of the legs (L7.46). These chevrons, which are usually vertically oriented, appear at Lerna, Corinth, and Akratas. No chevrons appear on examples recovered from either Franchthi or Asea. Vertical lines, usually running the entire length of the legs, are common and were chosen by the makers at all sites where split-legs occur: Corinth [MF 4386, MF 68-94, MF 68-95, MF 68-96], Asea [Asea 2], Akratas [Akratas 985, Akratas 1021], Lerna [L7.48, L7.316], Franchthi [FC 68, FC 124], and Nemea [S702.2.1). They occur on all three parts of the legs (i.e., the back, front, and sides). Horizontal and diagonal lines and dots are the least popular elements on split-leg figures, occurring only four times: once each on figurines from Asea, Akratas, Corinth, and Lerna. Like the vertical lines, they are not restricted to any particular part of the leg.

As a group, the designs on the split-leg figures form a limited and fairly uniform repertoire, both in terms of the individual elements and the overall composition or structure of those elements.

There is, however, a great deal of variety in the execution of the designs; the surety of the artists' lines, the spacing of the elements, and the general density of the pattern differ widely within and between sites. It is therefore difficult to argue which examples are closest stylistically and were possibly created by the same hand or the same group of figurine-makers.

Due to the fragmentary nature of the sample, the remaining design elements must be discussed as single attributes, not as parts of a composition. The four elements considered are rippling lines, crossing diagonal lines, diagonal lines with no apparent orientation, and concentric or stacked V-shaped elements. All of those elements were selected by figurine-makers at both Corinth and Franchthi.

Rippling lines occur on five examples: MF 8505, MF 68-285, FC 28, FC 118, and MF 8065. Except for the last piece, all are dated LN.

Crossing diagonal lines that form an X starting at the shoulders and terminating near the waist are found on one LN piece from Franchthi (FC 28) and two from Corinth. One of the Corinthian examples also dates to the Late Neolithic (MF 77-111); the other, to the Middle Neolithic (MF 8065).

The third design element selected at both sites is the series of diagonal lines in no apparent orientation. Makers from Franchthi used the design on two heads (FC 101, FC 117) and a torso (FC 208); a similar, though not quite identical, pattern appears on the neck and torso fragment from Corinth (MF 8797). All four pieces are Middle or Late Neolithic.

The final design occurring at both Franchthi and Corinth is that of the stacked or concentric V-shaped element pointing in various directions. That decoration appears on three MN figures (FC 42, FC 167, MF 8797).

A few design elements are peculiar to certain settlements. The solid triangles across the shoulders of an MN torso from Asea (Asea 1) are unique in the collection, as is the diamond network on the torso of FC 118. The concentric diamonds on the shoulder of NM 3928 (one of the complete stone specimens allegedly from Koufovouno) is not seen elsewhere in the Peloponnese, but does occur on a leg fragment (from either a vessel or a figurine) unearthed at Nea Makri (Theocharis 1956:Figure 42).

In sum, while the similarity in design on the split-leg examples would tend to link Lerna, Corinth, Asea, Akratas, Franchthi, and Nemea, decoration on other kinds of figurines is shared most often by Corinth and Franchthi during either the Middle or Late Neolithic. As discussed above, Groups L and R, both confined to LN, are also exclusive to Corinth and Franchthi. Interestingly, this apparently close interaction or contact between Corinth and Franchthi is also noted in Cullen's study on MN patterned fine wares (1985a).

Decoration as Evidence for Dress, Tattoo, and Scarification

Interpreting decoration on figurines is problematic, since the designs may have been intended to portray clothing, tattooing, scarification, or merely pleasing aesthetic patterns with no representational meaning. It is impossible to determine which of those intentions was in the mind of the makers. A study of scarification and tattooing among ethnographic societies does, however, provide food for thought. Curiously, and no doubt coincidentally, designs on some southern Greek figurines are similar to tribal markings illustrated in some ethnographic reports (e.g., Faris 1972:Plates 6, 21, 32, 37). This does not mean that one-to-one correlations must exist between specific designs on Neolithic figurines and more modern tattoos or scars. Nevertheless, the similarities should not be dismissed, and it is worthwhile examining the concepts behind scarification, tattooing, and body-painting. A striking example from the ethnographic record, showing body scarification mimicked on a figurine, is found among the Tabwa (Maurer and Roberts 1985:130).

Among most ethnographic societies, body-marking is based on taboos, rituals, and beliefs within the society (Hambly 1925; Teit 1930; Faris 1972; Ebin 1979). Permanent body markings, such as tattoos and cicatrizations (scarification), often indicate that the wearer has passed through some rite of passage, moving from one social status to another. Anyone familiar with specific body designs within a region can identify the wearer's rank in society or even his/her affiliation with a particular clan, group, or family. Nonpermanent markings, such as body paint, usually serve a different function from that of tattoos and scars. While the latter two techniques reflect permanent changes in status, body paint is used to symbolize more transient states or special occasions (Sieber 1972:93–94).

Tattooing, cicatrizing, and/or painting men and women at various stages throughout their lives are global phenomena. The tradition of tattooing, at least, may be a venerable one. A recent discovery in the Tyrolean Alps uncovered a frozen tattooed man, dated to approximately 2000 b.c. (Eijgenraam and Anderson 1991). We know from anthropological reports that tattooing, body-painting, and scarring often begin when a girl or boy is prepubescent. Markings are added at the onset of puberty, again when betrothal takes place, and at any point when significant events are approached or completed (Hambly 1925:30). For example, Plate 25a shows two stages of a woman's pre- and post-betrothal markings, while Plate 25b illustrates pre- and post-menses markings.

Markings can be quite elaborate, covering the entire body, or extremely simple and restricted to the upper arm, face, or abdomen. As a rule, those designs that are simple and confined to a specific part of the anatomy (e.g., facial scars) usually function as tribal or family markings (Hambly 1925:183).

Body decoration can also serve a host of other purposes—e.g., (1) identification marks that secure a place in the spirit world; (2) cures for pain; (3) protective signs for repelling evil; (4) good luck and love charms; (5) mechanisms for preserving youth; and (6) signs of mourning.

It would be unwise to assume that all the designs on the southern Greek figurines represent tattooing, scarification, or body paint; some decorations make sense as attempts to represent clothing or jewelry. To our twentieth-century eye, for example, the designs on FC 118 seem very like clothing. In fact, the diamond-shaped "vest" is similar to a knotted net dance-costume used by a tribe in Liberia (Sieber 1972:44), and the rippling lines on the figure's right side could portray a special one-sided skirt of grass or cloth. Equally reminiscent of clothing is the apparent fringed belt which encircles the figure. Comparable belts made of shell or bone are known among the Andaman Islanders (Fox 1878:Plate XII). Such belts may have been designed to make noise as the wearer moved. MF 13360 from Corinth shows a very similar skirt and belt, and possibly anklets or boots.

Interpreting some of the other decorations on the Neolithic figurines as clothing, however, is not as convincing. For example, the swirling designs on heads FC 101 and FC 117 do not seem to represent any kind of headgear. They could, however, be explained as imitations of facial painting or paintings on masks. Similarly, the double lines or incisions in the eye area of those two figures and also on MF 8500, Akratas 992, and MF 6730 can be compared with some of the facial scars and paintings among modern groups (Teit 1930:409). It may not be accidental that the creators of these five Neolithic heads chose both paint and incision: the incisions may reflect an attempt to imitate the process of scarification, while the paint may parallel the simple use of color to decorate the face.

The designs on the arms of NM 3928 also make little sense as clothing or jewelry. Rather, they may indicate some kind of simple body design like those among the Somali and the Galla (Plates 25c, d).

Along the same lines, patterns painted on the split-leg figurines find noticeable similarities to body paint used by the Nuba during ritual dances, ceremonies, and battles (see Faris 1972:Plates

6, 21, 32, 37). It is equally possible, however, that the makers of the split-leg examples were attempting to imitate some kind of skirts or leggings made of either painted fabric or woven textiles.

The designs on FC 42, Asea 1, FC 28, MF 8065, and FC 208 most clearly underscore the question of whether the artists were imitating body markings or clothing (or something altogether different?). The well-planned patterns on FC 42 could represent a cape and the top of a skirt (especially when viewed from the back), or an elaborate tattoo like one popular among the Motu (Plate 25b). Similarly, the unique patterns on Asea 1 might mimic designs that were painted onto or woven into cloth, or may reflect local designs in body-painting. Finally, straps or necklaces (cf. Sieber 1972:93) could have been intended by the paint on FC 28 and MF 8065. Alternatively, they may reflect ritual designs comparable to those used by the Nuba (Faris 1972:Plates 37, 38). Unfortunately, there is no way to settle these matters with certainty. Although distinctions among dress, tattoos, or scars cannot be made with any surety, the designs on the Neolithic images provide us with some idea of how the early inhabitants of southern Greece chose to decorate, ornament, and/or clothe their bodies.

DISCUSSION OF USE AND MEANING BY REGION

Like Franchthi, the other settlements in southern Greece do not provide data which allow for clear inferences about the use and meaning of Neolithic figurines. In fact, only three sites—Lerna, Saliagos, and Kephala—have produced evidence which is at all useful. The data from sites farther north, however, are more extensive and raise questions about the possible existence of both domestic and communal cults throughout northern Greece and the Balkans. In particular, remains from several Vinča sites suggest that, at least during the fifth and fourth millennia, a few sites may have functioned as regional ritual centers (J. Chapman 1981).

The evidence from southern Greece is first discussed in as much detail as the scanty data allow. A very brief overview of Balkan and northern Greek evidence follows.

Southern Greece

Lerna. Most of the Lerna figures reportedly come from rubbish pits or heaps located close to habitation areas (E. Banks, pers. comm. 1978). Since specific information about their contents is unpublished, it is impossible to evaluate the exact nature of those deposits.

The only figure which seems to be linked with a possible structure is L6.100, the finest image unearthed at Lerna. While no report of the figure's exact findspot has been published, a general description of the building levels associated with the piece is available. The strata reveal several moderate-sized, rectangular structures, containing a few hearths, a large quantity of millstones, pottery, and an assortment of stone and bone implements (Caskey and Eliot 1956:170–171). The general context seems to suggest domestic activities, possibly associated with eating and grinding.

Though explanations for the uses of the Lerna figures cannot be inferred from contextual information, the evidence, meager as it is, is consistent. All of the MN and LN figurines are found near (or, in one case, inside) domestic structures, therefore suggesting associations with activities performed in or near the living quarters. Moreover, if the pits were indeed used for rubbish, then some of the images were likely viewed as possessing limited power. Once they served their purpose(s), these figures were consigned to the garbage.

Saliagos. The figurines from Saliagos, all LN, were found in several different contexts. Excavators uncovered one inside structure G—a curious, circular, two-course stone building with a diameter of approximately 4 m. The area enclosed by the walls was floored with carefully laid stones, which had been renewed on several separate occasions. One of the floor renewals, blackened by fire, contained patches of burnt material, including grains of barley and emmer wheat, but almost no potsherds. Since the excavators believe that structure G was too small for habitation, yet too large for drying grain, they tentatively suggest that it served as a storage silo for grain (Evans and Renfrew 1968:18).

Not far from structure G, the excavators uncovered a hearth area, together with a great concentration of pottery (Evans and Renfrew 1968:18). From this deposit came the complete, violin-shaped figurine and an anthropomorphic pendant of red stone. Exactly what activities were performed around the fire is difficult to reconstruct from the limited information available, but given the quantity and type of pottery, it is likely that cooking and eating were the major events. Whether the vessels, the pendant, the figurine, and the hearth represent remains from a casual gathering or from a special meal or event cannot be established.

The best-known of the figurines, the "Fat Lady of Saliagos" (Saliagos 5), was found in the uppermost stratum at the site. Not associated directly with any features or finds of importance, the image lay near a large building complex that was enclosed by a perimeter wall of approximately 15 x 17 m. Unfortunately, the functions of the buildings are unclear, although some of the walls may represent foundations for living quarters, and others were likely cellars or storerooms (Evans and Renfrew 1968:22). Given the proximity of the figure to these built structures, it is arguable that the "Fat Lady" was connected with activities which transpired within or near the complex.

The remaining figures from Saliagos derive from unstratified deposits removed from the main areas of excavation. These deposits yield few recognizable structures or features and a scanty collection of finds.

Even from this meager evidence, a few patterns are detectable at Saliagos. Clearly, the images occur in a variety of contexts, but rarely (if ever) in association with other figurines. Like Franchthi and Lerna, a single piece appears to have been sufficient for a given activity. Moreover, nearly all the figures were found in areas peripheral to the main sections of habitation, or at least in areas where building remains are least dense. Except for the crude terra-cotta torso, none of the figures actually occur *within* any of the built structures. If the functional significances of the various buildings were better understood, the lack of figurines within them might prove instructive. Were figurines associated only with activities performed outside the buildings? Was it considered inappropriate to house an anthropomorphic image within certain structures? Would a figure lose its efficacy or power if placed in an improper location? There are, as yet, no answers to these questions.

Kephala. Unlike the evidence from Saliagos, Lerna, and Franchthi, the figurines from Kephala are not usually associated with habitation debris. Instead they are found near graves built within the limits of a formal cemetery immediately downslope from the small (FN) settlement. Prominently situated at the base of a headland, the cemetery was quite visible to anyone ascending to the village. Natural and man-made demarcations (i.e., clefts, built walls) confine the burial area, and stone platforms seem to have stood above a number of burials. All of these markers would have created a burial area that was visible even to the casual passer-by.

Although burials occur throughout the Neolithic of southern Greece, none contain figurines. Interments are documented in EN contexts at Lerna and Franchthi, MN levels at Lerna, Franchthi, and Ayioryitika, and LN and/or FN contexts at Lerna, Franchthi, the Agora, Kitsos Cave, and Alepotrypa. In none of those cases are figurines found with the dead. Kephala therefore reflects a unique situation: it is the only example in the Neolithic of southern Greece where figurines appear to have intentional sepulchral purposes.[59] Moreover, Kephala represents the earliest example in that region of a formal disposal area for the dead.

A key to understanding the function of those figurines may be found by exploring motivations for building formal, extramural cemeteries. Spatially distinct but dispersed intramural interments typify most of Neolithic Greece (Jacobsen and Cullen 1981), and the departure from such practices requires discussion.

Ethnographic data suggest that scattered burials in small villages point to a primary concern at death with individuality and personal social identity (R. Chapman 1981). Collective or corporate identities are not overtly, visibly, and publicly symbolized after disposition as they might be in a cemetery, where intentionally confined associations with other (often related) identities are made explicit. Non-cemetery interments, however, do not imply that membership in a family, subgroup, clan, sodality, or the like was unimportant during the lifetime of the deceased. Rather, separate and scattered burials in a community suggest that such ties are not drawn to the attention of the survivors by placing related groups within discrete, well-marked areas.

On the other hand, formally grouped interments explicitly, deliberately, and publicly identify *some kind* of collective or corporate identity, be it familial, political, administrative, or economic (cf. Hodder 1982:198). Cross-cultural studies reveal that such collective statements serve a variety of functions: as territorial foci, symbols of community cohesion, and visible references to ancestral authority (Saxe 1970; Binford 1971; Bloch 1971).

Research conducted by Saxe (1970) and Goldstein (1976) on the importance of cemeteries as references to ancestral power may have relevance to Kephala. Both Saxe and Goldstein argue that a corporate group seeking to legitimize its use and/or control of scarce but crucial resources may opt to ritualize or formalize that relationship through the maintenance of a permanent, specialized, and bounded disposal area for the dead. As Goldstein writes, "this corporate control is most likely to be attained and/or legitimized by means of lineal descent from the dead, either in terms of an actual lineage or in the form of a strong established tradition of the critical resources passing from parent to offspring" (Goldstein 1976:61). For sedentary agriculturalists, where there is continuous production and cooperation, together with permanent ties to fixed resources, descent (which provides for group membership and renews relationships of production) becomes a major concern. In such contexts ancestor cults and various kinds of historicized genealogies develop (Meillassoux 1973:194, 198; R. Chapman 1981:73).

If we accept the proposal that the Kephala cemetery was intentionally designed to broadcast the cohesion and power of a corporate group staking its claim to the use of critical resources, several questions emerge: who composed the group, where (and what) were the resources, and what do figurines have to do with the argument?

As regards the last question, the anthropological literature often cites the placement of figurines in and around burials. A large majority of these images are reported as ancestor images, or symbols which house the power of the deceased and are believed to exert strong prohibiting forces within society.[60] Many groups go to great lengths to win the benediction and approval of the departed spirit and to ensure ongoing ties with the deceased. This preoccupation with ancestral links holds not only social but economic importance; the transfer of goods or resources from one generation to the next is legitimized through these bonds. Ancestor images therefore act as important symbols within society, rendering explicit individual or group claims to control that is chartered by descent.

In view of Goldstein's and Saxe's arguments and the ethnographic evidence concerning figurines associated with burials, it would seem that both the Kephala cemetery and its figurines were communicating the same message: those related to the deceased were legitimizing their control over local assets through explicit recognition of ancestry.

The cemetery appears to have been occupied for approximately 150 years, during which time 65 skeletons were placed in 40 graves. Many of the graves were constructed side by side, others built directly above or overlapping one another. Although fragmentary walls may reflect rudimentary attempts at internal organization, there is little evidence of efforts made to distinguish groups or clusters of burials. The proximity of the cemetery to the settlement, however, suggests that this was the final resting place for the local villagers, which presumably encompassed several extended families. All age cohorts are represented: 21 adult males, 25 adult females, 5 adults of undetermined sex, 9 children, and 5 infants. Given this spread, it is likely that all members of society were disposed of by one of the methods popular at the site (i.e., cist graves, built graves, or jar burials).

Precisely which resources were of concern to this kin-based group is not clear. Perceptions of critical resources vary significantly from one culture to another, but Neolithic local assets might have included possession of arable land in an otherwise infertile area; shoreline, fishing, or grazing rights; restricted access to raw materials; control over a geographically strategic position; or special knowledge or technical means for producing valued goods (Brown 1981:27). Kea has limited resources, any of which may have been the subject of local tension or competition. Recent explorations on the island report the existence of very fine marble, though it is less abundant and often less pure than that from Parian or Naxian sources (Fitton 1984:35). In addition, Kephala is perched above an excellent and easily defensible harbor where strong winds prevail (Coleman 1977). Finally, the existence of slag at the site suggests that copper was probably worked at the settlement, although no local sources have yet been identified. Copper may also have been smelted at Paoura, a neighboring site contemporary with Kephala (Coleman 1977:108).[61]

Restricted access to local sources of marble, control over a good harbor, or, perhaps, special knowledge or means for working copper may have been critical to the ongoing survival and success of small FN settlements in the Cyclades. Rights to these resources certainly became instrumental in the emergence of ranked societies in the Greek Bronze Age. Kephala may, in fact, be more closely aligned with the ethos of the Bronze Age than with the seemingly egalitarian system of the Stone Age. While there is, as yet, no way to determine whether any of these resources was a source of internal or external competition, the recent survey of northern Kea identified three possible FN sites (Cherry et al. 1991). Since the island is fairly small and the resources limited, competition for local assets may have generated tension. If that was the case, the establishment of a formal cemetery which legitimized the claim of those associated with it to critical resources may well have been an important strategy for the FN settlers on the island.

Clearly, the evidence from southern Greece does not provide simple and well-defined answers to the questions of how, where, and why small figurines were used in the Neolithic. The data are, however, suggestive. An obvious and important point is that figures tend to occur singly (i.e., not in groups of figurines) and in a variety of contexts, most of which reflect domestic activities. The conclusions drawn in this volume point to at least five uses: (1) as dolls or toys (Franchthi Cave: EN, MN, LN); (2) as contractual devices or tokens of identification (Franchthi, Lerna, Asea, Corinth, Nemea, Akratas: MN); (3) as items of sympathetic magic associated with the success of the herd and animal fertility (Franchthi, Corinth, Asea: LN, FN); (4) as ritual or magical items associated with cereal agriculture (Saliagos: LN); and (5) as ancestor images used to legitimize claims to critical resources (Kephala: FN). The contexts and interpretations offered are far from homogeneous and emphasize the premise initially brought out by Ucko: archaeologists should avoid simplifying the function of Neolithic figurines. They likely served a variety of purposes which may have changed over the millennia.

Northern Greece and the Balkans

While the evidence from southern Greece indicates that figurines could have been linked to beliefs in superhuman powers (i.e., ancestor worship, guardians of the herd and cereal agriculture), the remains from northern Greece and the Balkans underscore more emphatically the association between figurines and beliefs in unseen and transcendent forces. Though the data do not establish, as Gimbutas asserts, the existence and worship of a fully developed pantheon, the material remains do suggest that throughout the regions of northern Greece and the Balkans a considerable degree of ritual[62] control may have existed (Whittle 1985:64).

Several archaeologists who propose that Neolithic figurines of southeastern Europe and northern Greece represent deities, votives, or votaries argue that the superhuman forces recognized by the Neolithic celebrants likely functioned on at least two separate but overlapping levels: domestic and communal (J. Chapman 1981; Whittle 1985; see Renfrew 1985:21–22 for a discussion of the distinction between domestic and communal ritual. Gimbutas's distinctions among deities are more specific: separate powers or concerns are the domain of distinct goddesses or gods, who appear to function on both the domestic and communal levels[63]). Domestic cults are usually suggested by concentrations of anthropomorphic and/or zoomorphic images within "ordinary" dwellings, or by images clustered together within foundation deposits beneath "ordinary" house floors. The general assumption is that these images served as protective spirits, guaranteeing the successful operation of household activities and/or safeguarding the inhabitants of a particular dwelling (J. Chapman 1981:75).

While the supporting evidence for domestic cults is ambiguous, the existence of communal cults appears to rest on more compelling evidence. By definition, communal cults involve the participation of an official acting on behalf of the community, usually, though not necessarily, within a communally recognized sacred area (Renfrew 1985:21–22). Though few in number, excavations in both the Balkans and northern Greece have uncovered seemingly "out-of-the-ordinary" structures, which contain not only collections of figurines, but occasionally some "unusual" artifacts. These "shrines" or "cult houses" (cf. n. 47) are considered liminal areas where all (or some) of the community periodically gather for public religious display. These special areas are distinct from domestic interiors with a ritual component (Whittle 1985:152). It is not entirely clear, however, whether distinctly different forces were revered or placated within the two different areas. Certainly, similar types of figurines seem to occur in both contexts, suggesting some degree of overlap.

J. Chapman suggests that religious ritual may not have been confined to rites performed within select shrines or domestic corners, but on an even larger, regional scale. He offers the intriguing possibility that entire sites like Potporanj, Turdaş, and Vinča, with figurine collections ranging from 500 to 2000, may have functioned as regional religious centers, serving (controlling?) several satellite communities within a catchment area (1981:74–75).

It is worthwhile summarizing some of the evidence used to support the existence of domestic, communal, and regional cults, though discussions in the literature are flawed by a number of untested assumptions, a lack of agreement on the definition of cult or ritual, and little detailed reporting on the exact arrangement and contexts of figurines and so-called ritual paraphernalia.

The presence of a domestic cult is usually based on the occurrence of a few figurines concentrated within one part of, or close to, a dwelling. Often, that is the sole criterion on which the conclusion is based, though occasionally a case is considered strengthened if "unusual" (e.g., "altars," "libation vessels") or particularly fine pieces of pottery, stone, or lithics are found in proximity to the images. At Achilleion, for example, EN and MN figurines are found in groups within "rubbish pits" near houses, or close to ovens and hearths placed both within dwellings or in adjacent courtyards (Gimbutas et al. 1989). As many as 14 figurines have been reported together (Gimbutas et al. 1989:217). The associated finds vary, but generally consist of querns, spatulas, ladles, grinding stones, pestles, a variety of lithics and, occasionally, some unusual pottery. For the most part, the associated finds suggest that daily household activities, especially food preparation, took place within the areas near the figurines. Although Gimbutas does not make a clear distinction between domestic and communal deities, she does point out that in certain phases at Achilleion specific types of goddesses occur only in the courtyards, while other types predominate within the houses (Gimbutas et al. 1989:215).

Evidence from the early excavations at Rachmani (Wace and Thompson 1912:39–41) also fits the pattern of figurine concentrations within seemingly unexceptional household contexts. House Q, associated with FN occupation debris, contained four complete terra-cotta figurines, two possible figurine fragments, several millstones, bone points, celts, ceramic vessels, and the remains of lentils and figs. The structure also contained a small raised platform and a possible hearth. An earlier Thessalian structure, House T at Tsangli, yielded six MN (?) figurines, several celts, bone points, pestles, whorls, and a heavy concentration of well-made Middle Neolithic pottery (Wace and Thompson 1912:115–117, 123, 124). Again, the finds suggest a variety of domestic activities—in this case, sewing, spinning, and grinding. If the figurines do, indeed, represent some kind of transcendent powers, they are not separated from the usual household equipment and seem to be part of the domestic landscape.

A more unusual collection of figurines in an otherwise unremarkable dwelling was recently unearthed at Plateia Zarkou in northern Greece. The find consisted of a small clay house model containing eight figurines, carefully positioned within a pit beneath the floor of a house (Gallis 1985). Although the model is unique in Neolithic Greece, its context beneath the house floor has good parallels farther north (see Makkay 1983 for a summary of foundation deposits in Neolithic houses). Gallis interprets the model as an offering, perhaps made when the house was first built, designed to safeguard the house and its inhabitants. Interestingly, he suggests that the eight figures carefully placed within the model are not necessarily deities, but may represent the extended nuclear family residing in the structure.

Chapman reports comparable contexts for figurines found at Early and Late Vinča sites throughout the Balkans (J. Chapman 1981:Table 26). Stapari and Varos produced figurines in foundation deposits, Selevac yielded an anthropomorphic image in a residential storage jar full of grain, and both Medvednjak and Zorlenţu Mare had figurines or incised human images associated with what appear to be objects related to household textile production.

Although the evidence is sparse, it is certainly arguable that the images found in these contexts could represent protective household "genii" or powers akin to the much later *lares* and *penates* of Roman times. If that conclusion is correct, several questions arise. Why are these domestic cults so widespread geographically? Which households opted to, or perhaps were allowed to, have such images? Who within the basic residential units decided when, how often, or by whom figurines were made? Did individual images or collections circulate among houses, families, kin groups, or sodalities? Were actual ceremonies performed with these objects, or did the images remain stationary in designated spots in or near the house? In essence, how did these domestic cults function and who was in charge?

Unfortunately, answers to those questions are not possible given the current data. Provocative answers emerge, however, when comparable queries are posed against the data supporting the presence of communal or regional cults.

A limited number of sites in Thessaly and southeastern Europe contain buildings that have been labeled shrines or temples, primarily on the basis of their contents and, to a lesser extent, on their size and layout. As Whittle points out, though, there are considerable problems with definition (1985:152). Other than the so-called Nea Nikomedeia shrine (see n. 47), structures that seem clearly out-of-the-ordinary are reported from fifth and fourth millennium sites in Bulgaria, several sites in the Ukraine, and a number of Vinča settlements.

At Ovcarovo, for example, a rather undistinguished building contained, adjacent to an oven, a small, decorated model of a house interior; within one meter of the oven were 27 miniature "cult" objects, including 4 female figurines, several tables, cylinders, and pots (Whittle 1985:153). The evidence at Sabatinovka II, in the western Ukraine, is even more striking. A substantial (70 m^2) structure produced (among other things) a bone figurine at the entrance; a large oven, positioned at the middle of the building, with a figurine near its base; and, opposite the entrance, a long, raised platform on which rested 16 clay figurines, all seated on horn-backed stools (Gimbutas 1974:72–73). Excavations at Kolmijschchina, also in the Ukraine, uncovered a comparable scene: an oven with an adjacent raised platform, 70 cm in diameter, on or near which were placed 24 figurines (Gimbutas 1974:73–74). There is also evidence at Tirpeşţi, in northeastern Romania, of 34 figurines and fragments of miniature clay tables and chairs, all concentrated within a confined area, though not associated with a specific building (Whittle 1985:152). Rozsokhuvatka in Bulgaria recently yielded an unusual two-story building with a pottery workshop on the ground floor and an alleged shrine on the first floor, containing a clay altar, figurines, building models, and a loom (Gimbutas 1980). Finally, several buildings at Vinča sites contain remains of life-size clay "bucrania," which are, perhaps, suggestive of shrines, though the buildings housing the bucrania are unremarkable (J. Chapman 1981:73).

Even on this slim evidence, one can argue that by approximately 5000 b.c. (uncalibrated) special nonresidential buildings had become integrated into village planning of select communities throughout the Balkans. The constellation of objects and features associated with the structures invariably includes platforms, hearths or ovens, figurines, miniature tables, and model chairs. Although comparable artifacts are also reported in "ordinary" houses, it is primarily in these so-called shrines that the objects appear in such abundance, or were deliberately placed in one focal area of the structure. As discussed by Renfrew (1985), the occurrence of special places, with special equipment, focal areas, and a redundancy of symbols, suggests the existence of liminal zones where religious ritual was enacted. It may be premature, however, to assume that all such special places were reserved exclusively for religious rites. The structures and associated artifacts may, in fact, have served multiple purposes, being part temple and part civic center. The rituals or public displays enacted may have been both sacred and profane, ranging from the installation of a village "chief" and the recognition of an elder to the initiation of various age grades and the placation or reverence of a given deity.

As mentioned above, public rituals, particularly those of a religious nature, were not necessarily restricted to a few shrines within select communal structures. J. Chapman (1981) has proposed that entire sites possibly functioned as regional ritual centers, which serviced smaller neighboring villages. His argument rests, at least in part, on proving that the high concentration of ritual paraphernalia at certain Vinča sites is not directly proportional to the size of the area excavated. The Vinča culture, which has produced the highest known density of figurines in fifth and fourth millennium Europe, has also produced, relatively speaking, exceptionally large sites (e.g., the area of Potporanj is estimated at 100 ha and that of Turdaş at 65 ha). A direct linear relationship between excavation size and figurine totals could account for the high number of figures at those sites. Chapman's preliminary analysis indicates, however, that no such linear relationship exists: sites of identical excavation areas can produce figurine totals ranging from 0–210. Equally important, Chapman calculates that sites with extremely high figurine frequencies often lie near communities with low figurine frequencies (1981:74–75). Although his report does not examine the relationship between these sites in much detail, he clearly implies that these centers exerted a force on neighboring villages, providing some kind of ritual leadership, if not control, throughout the area. Exactly how these possible regional centers functioned has not been adequately addressed. We have yet to understand, for example, the frequency of group gatherings, the selection process entailed in designating a ritual leader, the precise content of the ceremonies, and the role of figurine-makers or caretakers at places like Vinča or Potporanj.[64]

Probably by the fifth (and certainly by the fourth) millennium, parts of the Balkans appear to have witnessed not only a gradual increase in ritual objects and shrines and the possible emergence of religious centers, but a marked growth in settlement size and movement or expansion into more varied ecological zones (Whittle 1985:71). There are measurable differences in site size and an increased use of possible defensive structures or (symbolic?) boundary markers, which may emphasize the special nature of certain communities (Whittle 1985:146).

According to Whittle, as settlements grew (whether through nucleation and/or general population increase), so did tensions, the control of food production, and the control of ritual activities and ritual paraphernalia (1985:155–156). The role of ritual leadership and the symbols associated with it became the focus of intra- and intercommunity competition. In terms of the figurines, Whittle speculates that "as far as it can be discerned at all the actual content of ritual as derived from subjective interpretation of figurines seems to remain focused on such contrasts as people–nature and female–male and other themes such as birth and fertility. It is possible that this in some way symbolises a general concern with increased conflict within and between communities for social leadership and control of production. Ritual activity would thus have been the means of alleviating social tension, as well as one of its foci" (1985:156). Chapman adopts a similar perspective, stating that, at least for the Vinča culture, both basic domestic activities and higher-level ritual activities may have been governed by a ritually-prescribed code of conduct, subject to modification by a priest or village leader. Such leaders assumed the key role in ritual and used cult activities to cement their positions. For Chapman, the distinction between ritual and nonritual behavior is irrelevant, since the whole Vinča social fabric was steeped in cult behavior and society was dominated by ritual control (1981:77).

While the evidence is not such that either Whittle or Chapman can identify the precise role of figurines in Balkan or northern Greek society (although Gimbutas believes the data do lend themselves to such observations), there is tantalizing evidence that figurines were not only intimately tied to ritual behavior associated with beliefs in transcendent powers, but that control of these images was a source of competition, at least on the communal and regional levels. Exactly how one became a "ritual leader" (if such a position can be said to have existed) cannot be determined. It is equally difficult to know whether the manufacture and possession of figurines was a source of social tension on the domestic level. The fact that only certain houses contained figurines may suggest that ownership or guardianship of the images was restricted, though exactly who was involved in the decision-making on the household level remains a question.

As the evidence in the previous chapters indicates, there is nothing in southern Greece to suggest that figurine production was ever conducted on such a massive scale or that these seemingly modest objects were the source of intense competition. That at least some anthropomorphic and zoomorphic images from southern Greece were linked to sympathetic magic or beliefs in superhuman powers is entirely possible. As in the Balkans, some of these beliefs were likely directed at safeguarding hearth, home, and herd. Ritual behavior in southern Greece, however, seems anything but formalized or regionally organized, and the existence of ritual leaders is totally unsupportable. While there is a tendency in the literature to assume a continuity of religious behavior or beliefs from the Balkans to the Peloponnese, the data do not corroborate such an assumption. It would be wrong to view figurine usage and meaning in southern Greece as a faint echo of the Balkans. Indeed, it seems more plausible to conclude that the two regions found very different uses for their anthropomorphic and zoomorphic images.

CHAPTER SEVEN
Conclusion

Although the optimism characterizing the early days of the "New Archaeology" has waned in recent years, the conviction that archaeologists can infer a broad spectrum of behaviors and beliefs from material remains still pervades the literature. That optimism inspired many of the questions asked in this study. A dissonant note, however, sounds throughout the volume: despite claims to the contrary, archaeologists are still a long way from understanding prehistoric figurines. The future of figurine studies depends on new, thoughtful discussions of procedure, method, and theory, and on a willingness to discard long-cherished assumptions in the field. While this final chapter does not propose a "grand scheme" for future investigation, it does point to directions in which I believe research should move. Before turning to those possibilities, a brief review of the previous chapters is presented.

SUMMARY

Underlying much of the discussion in the preceding pages is the assumption that Neolithic figurines should not be defined as a unifunctional class of objects. It seems more productive to approach prehistoric figurines as a group of artifacts embodying a complex blend of behavioral and cognitive concerns and a multiplicity of uses and meanings. Like the anthropomorphic and zoomorphic images crafted by artists in modern nonliterate and nonindustrialized societies, prehistoric figurines inhabited a multi-dimensional world in which a series of options were available to their makers. The final products that archaeologists so carefully measure, draw, photograph, and analyze reflect a spectrum of stylistic, technological, economic, and ideological choices consciously and unconsciously made by ancient craftsmen/craftswomen. On a more substantive level, such assumptions mean not only that archaeologists should adopt varied approaches to analyzing these objects, but that they should guard against reductionist interpretations. The various "types" or "groups" of figurines isolated by Aegean prehistorians likely had a range of functions. Some may have been seen as possessing superhuman, magical, or curative powers; others may have served as social or instructional devices, broadcasting an array of information; and still others may have acted simply as toys. Much to the frustration of archaeologists, Neolithic figures probably moved in and out of such categories during their life-spans.

Although not stressed in this study, it was also observed that within a given community different age cohorts and genders may have attached subtly different meanings to groups of images. Such subtleties, however, do not leave indelible marks in the archaeological record, and, at least for the moment, archaeologists must be satisfied with attempting to isolate the "dominant" reading of anthropomorphic and zoomorphic images produced by early nonliterate societies.

This study has not endorsed the belief in a pan-Mediterranean religion, populated by a pantheon visibly manifested by both anthropomorphic and zoomorphic images. That a common and overarching, though not necessarily very formalized, religious system bound together Greece, Anatolia, and the Balkans is entirely possible. The existence of such a shared ideational system, however, has yet to be demonstrated. Certainly, the seeming homogeneity of both human and animal images throughout "Old Europe" is hardly sufficient evidence, especially if one argues, as I have here, that only some of these images may represent tangible forms of such superhuman powers.

The interpretation and analysis of the Franchthi figurines presented in this volume has proceeded with these biases either implicitly or explicitly in mind. Like other villages in southern Greece, Franchthi produced a small sample of figurines. This need not imply that anthropomorphic and zoomorphic images were considered culturally unimportant; however, it does pose obvious problems. In contrast, several settlements in Thessaly, Macedonia, and the Balkans have produced hundreds of Neolithic images. While it is not easy to identify the underlying causes of such regional differentiation, it is more than likely that northern and southern Greek villages, as well as communities in southeastern Europe, were not politically, socially, and economically comparable. As Runnels and van Andel argue (1987), Neolithic communities in Thessaly and the Peloponnese likely arose for different reasons. If we can gain a greater understanding of those differences, the reasons for such small samples of figurines in southern Greece may become clearer.

Despite the frustrations of dealing with meager samples, analysis of the Franchthi figurines has yielded several conclusions. Technically and artistically, the manufacture of these artifacts appears embedded in the much larger-scaled production of ceramic vessels. Within the Middle Neolithic, Late Neolithic, and Final Neolithic, the clay fabrics, surface treatments, color, paint, and decoration of pottery and figurines were nearly identical. If potter and figurine-maker were not one and the same, the two probably worked in concert (likely on the household level), routinely exchanging materials and ideas. The overlapping production of these objects was probably motivated by several factors, not the least of which was the ease with which the figurine-maker could borrow small lumps of prepared clay, tools, or paints from the potter. Ceramic vessels and figurines, however, also may have been linked by symbolic factors. Both classes of artifacts were possibly associated with a common symbol: the human form. Precisely why potters and figurine-makers chose to forge such a link is not known.

Although Franchthi figurine-makers maintained a degree of individualism in the form and design of their images, communications were ongoing or sufficiently regular to ensure stylistic homogeneity among sites. During the Middle and Late Neolithic, Franchthi's ties were clearly with villages in the northeastern Peloponnese. The closest social distance, as measured by similarities in style, is recorded for Franchthi and Corinth. In fact, some designs and small details are remarkably similar and may suggest face-to-face contact among figurine-makers. Parallel conclusions are drawn in a study of MN fine wares which involved a much larger sample, subjected to several tests (Cullen 1985a-b). Cullen notes that "the Urfirnis samples from Franchthi and Corinth are strikingly comparable in virtually all categories of measurement. . . " (1985a:340).

Exactly why a Franchthi–Corinth link should develop and seemingly be stronger than, for example, a Franchthi–Lerna bond is not readily understood. Franchthi is closer to Lerna by both sea and land. However, our current perceptions of distance in that region may be based on factors different from those of the Neolithic inhabitants. The nature and purpose of interactions, not simply the time and distance between sites, likely dictated the degree of energy one was willing to expend traveling from one settlement to another. Travel between more distant sites may also have provided "intervening" opportunities to the traveler—acquiring a better understanding of the surrounding areas, engaging in small-scale collecting of local resources, visiting settlements along the way, or even encountering other travelers who might prove socially or politically useful in the future.

(Intervening opportunities can also reduce the perceived advantage of traveling to more distant locations [see Cullen 1985a:347–348].)

The striking stylistic similarities of MN pottery throughout the northeastern Peloponnese have prompted both Vitelli (1974) and Cullen (1985) to speculate that village potters, most of whom likely were women, moved within a regional system of exogamy. Relocation of women from one community to another provided the opportunity for close interaction and instruction among potters, both of which seem necessary to explain the regional homogeneity of Urfirnis (Cullen 1985a:351). Moreover, the sophisticated technological processes involved in the production of this fine ware may have required personal instruction (Vitelli 1984b:126).

If women did circulate between Franchthi and Corinth (as well as other villages), they would bring with them more than just their knowledge of and expertise in ceramic technology. Their "cognitive baggage" would have included a broad range of knowledge or information about the symbolic expressions of their community, such as the shape and design of human or animal figurines, the role such images played in village life, the "rules" of ownership and display, and the like. If, indeed, some of the decorative elements on the figurines were intended to mimic tattoos or scars marking age groups, ritual status, or "clan" membership, it is possible that at least some of the figurines served as models to instruct village newcomers or young initiates in the proper symbolic dimension of body decoration. Such emblematic badges would render an individual immediately recognizable to his or her cohorts. The similar decorative schemes on both Franchthi and Corinthian figurines may indicate that allied or related members of these two settlements decorated their bodies with comparable designs.

The cluster analysis run on the southern Greek collection reveals that, while Late Neolithic figurines exhibit stylistic continuities with those from the Middle Neolithic, Final Neolithic figures depart from earlier trends, both geographically and stylistically. For reasons that are not clear, Franchthi's affinities appear to have moved northward and eastward: FN stylistic conformities are not confined to villages in the northeastern Peloponnese, and similarities are documented principally among figurines from Franchthi, Kitsos, Kephala, and Athens. The similarities among these fairly crude images, which, unlike MN and LN examples, do not usually include decoration, are marked. As in the two previous periods, efforts were made to maintain symbolic homogeneity among certain villages. Again, while we can isolate such links, we can only speculate on the factors behind intervillage communication processes, perhaps transhumance, exogamy, and/or annual celebrations or meetings.

Despite the existence of a stone-carving tradition at Franchthi, figurines were rarely manufactured from materials other than clay. Clay may have been seen as less expensive, more readily available, or symbolically more appropriate than stone for figurines. The one marble head recovered from the site (FS 101: LN), is comparable to MN and LN specimens excavated or reported from Saliagos, Aegina, and Koufovouno. It is currently impossible to determine whether the similarities among these pieces resulted from the existence of an exchange network through which stone figurines circulated, or the existence of communication channels through which stylistic information flowed. If the latter, the information may have included guidelines for a possible canon of proportions.

Occasional, though striking, similarities between northern and southern Greek figurines are observed. Although these parallels could simply be coincidental, they equally could signal indirect and direct contacts among settlements in regions such as the Argolid, Thessaly, and Macedonia. Current evidence increasingly suggests that, despite rough terrains and significant distances, raw materials, valued objects, and people moved hundreds of miles during the Neolithic. For example, Melian obsidian is known from numerous settlements throughout mainland Greece (Torrence 1986); honey-colored flint, whose source may be the Balkans, occurs in small percentages at several sites throughout the mainland (Perlès 1989); and *local* raw materials for chipped stone tools appear to be the minority at many Neolithic communities (Perlès 1989). Neolithic settlements were also obtaining *Spondylus* (either as a raw material or as jewelry), marble, emery, andesite, and possibly copper from distant sources (Runnels 1983; van Andel and Runnels 1988; Perlès 1989). Long-distance transport was not limited to goods and raw materials. Broodbank and Strasser (1991) argue that, during the sixth millennium, maritime transfers of both people and domesticates in sufficient numbers to establish a founder group likely took place from the Greek mainland to the island of Crete.

Given the seemingly extensive mobility of individuals or groups during the Neolithic, it is entirely possible that traders, adventurers, and craftsmen/craftswomen ventured from their home villages and brought with them knowledge (or now lost examples?) of their figurines. Contact need not have been direct; either the figurines themselves or verbal descriptions of images may have transferred from settlement to settlement in a kind of "down-the-line" system. The question that remains, however, is why either individuals or groups from settlements as distant as Sesklo and Franchthi would choose to produce similar figurines. A clearer idea of the extent and nature of contact between northern and southern Greek sites, as well as a more fine-grained understanding of the functions and meanings of the figurines, is required before we can offer reasonable speculation on the factors motivating such phenomena.

In terms of use, the images from Franchthi appear to be varied. I have suggested, albeit on slim evidence, that figurines were employed as dolls during the Early Neolithic and continued to be used as toys until the Late Neolithic. Other uses are more restricted chronologically. The split-leg figurines, which are confined to the Middle Neolithic, may have functioned as contractual or identifying tokens, serving as an effective form of visual communication in a preliterate society. The magical use of animal images to ensure the health and fertility of local herds appears at Franchthi only during the Final Neolithic (though the same uses may occur earlier at other sites).

Neolithic settlements that, broadly speaking, neighbor Franchthi also appear to have used their figurines for a range of purposes. Some functions are shared by several communities. The MN split-leg figurines appear at Corinth, Lerna, Asea, Akratas, and Nemea, suggesting that these sites were linked into a superlocal network. LN and FN animal images used as items of sympathetic magic also occur at several sites in southern Greece, including Asea, Corinth, and possibly Nea Makri. As discussed above, the appearance of these images during the latter half of the Neolithic may be associated with shifts in herding strategies. Kephala, however, seems to yield primarily ancestor images which were placed in or above the burials clustered in the local FN cemetery. The cemetery and figurines could have served as mutually reinforcing symbols: both laying claim through ancestral rights to local resources. Finally, excavations at Saliagos exposed one LN figurine possibly related to the storing of grain. Found in what may have been a granary, the figure might have been used magically to ensure the success of local harvests.

None of the figures exposed in Franchthi Cave or on Paralia can be associated with ideas of an afterlife or with cult practices involving the worship of specific deities. This is not to deny the existence of belief by the Franchthiotes in "superhuman beings." Indeed, most cultures past and present worship higher, unseen powers which demand reverence or obedience. In many societies one's destiny may depend on placating such powers. Archaeologically, however, there is nothing associated with the figurines at Franchthi—no special places, no unusual paraphernalia, no remains of feasting, no special investment of wealth in equipment, architecture, or offerings, no suggestive symbols—to imply the practice of sacred ritual at the site.

Not surprisingly, isolating the symbolic dimensions of these Neolithic figurines proved the most elusive aspect of this study. Only the half- or segmented bodies gave rise to specific discussion of meaning. This curious symbol occurs in several forms at Franchthi, including the half-body pendants, the seemingly complete disembodied figures (FC 122, FC 190), and the half-skirt design on FC 118. The repetition of a presumably single concept in different forms and at different times is hardly accidental. We can only guess at the meaning of such a visual code. However, as ethnographic reports suggest, many societies view the body, or its connected parts, as templates for organizing their view of the world. Perhaps the Franchthiotes employed such conceptual frameworks in their own zeitgeist.

AVENUES FOR FUTURE RESEARCH

More than other classes of data, figurines tend to inspire unbridled speculation. While some of the speculation in the literature has proven stimulating, it may ultimately impede our progress in understanding these prehistoric images. At this stage in our research, energies are best expended in: (1) designing more rigorous analytical approaches to the data; (2) devising appropriate analytical vocabularies; (3) creating a serviceable pool of ethnographic analogies which are detailed enough to be useful for and applicable to archaeological research; and (4) gaining a deeper understanding of how nonverbal, symbolic systems communicate.

In attempting to devise better theoretical and methodological frameworks, we should initially clarify the ways in which figurines overlap or diverge from other material remains in the archaeological record. At least as a first step, we need to evaluate the peculiarities and limitations of this particular class of objects and the extent to which we can borrow analytical approaches from other subfields within archaeology.

Much can be gained, for example, by employing frameworks used to study other types of artifacts. Some of these are obvious. Analysis of design on a regional scale has provided understanding of intersite communication on a level unparalleled by early ceramic studies. Comparable lines of inquiry are feasible for figurines. Unfortunately, well-conceived design analysis of prehistoric figurines rarely appears in the literature. Hesitancy on the part of figurine specialists may stem, in part, from the lack of large and reliable samples. As I hope this study shows, however, even small samples repay careful investigation of design on a regional scale.

Characterization studies of materials such as clay and stone have been used successfully on various classes of artifacts. Archaeometric tests can at least partially answer questions regarding the possible sources of raw materials and the local production and distribution of artifacts. Again, studies of Neolithic figurines rarely adopt such approaches, despite their potential value.

Experimental archaeology also holds promise for the study of figurines. By replicating as closely as possible the steps involved in the creation of these images, we may gain better insights into length of time invested in producing different kinds of figurines, the level of talent required, the tools used by the makers, and, as this study shows, even something about the cognitive schemes of the makers.

Some of the future avenues of research for prehistoric figurines, therefore, entail treading old paths successfully explored by other subfields within archaeology. The more difficult objective is devising approaches for understanding the multiplicity of the objects' uses and meanings. Past research has shown that we cannot jump from the objects to reasonable interpretations until we have some solid middle range theory and a more refined analytical vocabulary. Nor can we continue to offer interpretations that isolate figurines from their social and cultural contexts. While I believe that a larger pool of ethnographic analogies that can be operationalized for the archaeological record would be useful, such parallels will not answer the larger question of how silent discourse works in nonliterate societies like those of the Aegean Neolithic.

One avenue of research which may hold potential is the investigation of the human body as a symbol (see Douglas 1970). Anthropomorphic figurines represent a very special kind of nonverbal message because of their subject matter—the human form. A highly structured organism, the body probably served as our first and most natural instrument of expression (Mauss 1973), and the ability to recognize, utilize, and depict the body as an ordered set of symbols may represent a kind of intellectual rubicon in the development of symbolic expression. Moreover, this capacity probably reflects an evolving sense of self-perception, particularly an understanding of the symmetry, balance, order, and divisions of the body's structure. Admittedly, how cultures view the human form and how those views are encoded in the material remains of a group are enormously complicated issues. I believe, however, that carefully forging our way through the thicket of such ideas may prove rewarding.

Another admittedly difficult quarry to stalk, but one which may reward investigation, is that of gender ideology. A recent study on the evolution of gender inequality in prehistoric Italy raises intriguing questions about the different kinds of inequalities which probably existed in that region (Robb 1991). Using a variety of human images, including figurines, petroglyphs, cave paintings, and stelae, Robb attempts to trace the emergence of gender stratification, sexual identity, and the foundation of the Iron Age military (male-based) aristocracy. Although neither the Stone Age nor the Bronze Age material from Greece readily lends itself to a comparable study, future researchers may find ways to explore the role of gender inequality (or simply gender roles) in prehistoric Greece without falling into the trap of assuming that a predominance of female figurines necessarily reflects either a Mother Goddess-based religion or a matriarchal society. The seeming preponderance of female images in a corpus of prehistoric figurines is not necessarily a *direct* reflection of either ideology or social organization. Indeed, recent studies on the nature of symbol stress that symbols, especially religious ones, do not "simply prescribe or transcribe social status. . .Gender-related symbols, in their full complexity, may refer to gender in ways that affirm or reverse it, support or question it; or they may, in their basic meaning, have little at all to do with male and female roles" (Bynum et al 1986:2). For prehistorians, such observations may sound nihilistic, suggesting that symbolic expression is so hopelessly complex that the disentangling of meanings is impossible. To the contrary, we should take such comments as a positive reminder—a kind of intellectual prodding—that our interpretations of figurines will remain simplistic if we look only for direct relationships between seemingly gender-related symbols and their meanings.

Archaeology will always engender multiple pasts produced in accordance with ethnic, cultural, social, and political views and beliefs (Shanks and Tilley 1987:245). The pluralism in figurine interpretations, therefore, is no surprise. While multiple approaches to any given problem are essentially healthy, very few of those which characterized figurine research in the past have been directed by solid theory. I hope this study will encourage some new rigor in the field of figurine studies, or at the very least, some renewed dialogue.

Appendixes

APPENDIX A
Findspots of Franchthi Figurines

This catalogue describes the findspot of each figurine. For each image the following information is noted:

(a) the excavation unit (see Jacobsen and Farrand 1987:7, 16) from which the figure was recovered;

(b) the nature and extent of disturbance (e.g., postdepositional pit-digging) and contamination[65] within that excavation unit and, where relevant, contiguous areas (e.g., crosscut units);

(c) the archaeological features associated with the unit from which the figurine came and, where relevant, contiguous units (features are *not* listed for excavation units which contain modern cultural material);

(d) the finds associated with the unit from which the figurine came and, where relevant, contiguous units (finds are *not* listed for units which contain modern cultural material)

(e) the range of dates of pottery found in each excavation unit and the date assigned to the unit on the basis of the wares (the date reflects the latest wares found within the excavation unit).

The catalogue is arranged according to excavated trenches (see Jacobsen and Farrand:1987) in the following order: A, F, FA, G, H (all in the cave), and L5, O5, P5, and Q5 (all on Paralia). A table summarizing features and finds associated with the Franchthi figurines (Table 11) appears at the end of the appendix.

CAVE

Trench A

The entire Neolithic sequence in Trench A was excavated in the initial (test) season of 1967. All pottery was "lotted"[66], and only a small percentage of the more interesting or diagnostic sherds were saved and inventoried.

FC 11

a. A:31
b. no modern contamination; mixed ceramic deposit suggests postdepositional disturbance
c. small pit with ash and carbonized matter (possible source of disturbance)
d. inventoried finds: FP 55, 59, 60, 61, 63: MN, LN sherds
   FS 76: endscraper with possible sickle gloss
   FV 4: bracelet fragment *(Spondylus gaederopus)*
e. pottery lotted and thrown; notebook records MN, LN, coarse, and undiagnostic sherds
   unit dated to: **LN**

FC 12

a. A:53
b. no modern contamination; disturbed
c. ash and carbonized matter throughout; unit below (A:54) contains possible oven or hearth
d. inventoried finds: FP 24–27: MN sherds
   FB 39: tip of bone point
e. pottery lotted and thrown; notebook records MN, coarse, and undiagnostic sherds
   unit dated to: **MN**

Trench F

Trench F was cleared of surface contamination and topsoil in the initial (test) season of 1967 and was then expanded in 1968 to include FF1. Most of the pottery was lotted and thrown.

FC 4

a. F:4
b. topsoil; modern contamination/disturbance
c. —
d. —
e. contaminated; pottery lotted and thrown; notebook records MN, LN, FN, and modern sherds

FC 28

a. FF1:5
b. topsoil; modern contamination/disturbance
c. —
d. —
e. contaminated; pottery thrown; notebook records MN, LN, FN (?), and modern sherds

Trench FA

Trench FA was begun in 1969 and was excavated under the same trench supervisor in 1971, 1973, and 1974. It provides the deepest and best-stratified ceramic sequence at the site. The upper units (i.e., above FAN:59 and FAS:59) were subject to extensive post-Neolithic disturbances.

FC 88

a. FAN:59
b. no modern contamination; possibly disturbed by activities in FAN:62, which partly underlies FAN:59–61 and contains modern cultural material
c. possible hearth surrounded by circle of stones; shallow depression near hearth
d. inventoried finds: FS 258 and 261: grinding/hammerstones
   FC 91 and 92: biconical whorls (clay)
   noninventoried: a number of "typical" FN stone tools (Perlès, pers. comm. 1982)

e. majority of sherds are FN; small percentage Urf; all small in size and poorly preserved; some LN present
unit dated to: **FN**

FC 101

a. FAN:114
b. no modern contamination
c. charcoal-flecked stratum; possible hearth in unit beneath (FAN:115); appears to be stratigraphically associated with FAS:115 and FAN:115.
d. inventoried finds: FAN:114: FS 283: double awl (honey flint)
FAS:115: FV 109: stone/shell bead
FV 375: columbella bead
FB 375: worked bone fragment
Fr 29: skull fragment and molar tooth root of young adult, possibly male
Fr 29A: five pieces of skull vault, child under 5 years
FAN:115: no finds inventoried
e. pottery includes: MN, LN
unit dated to: **late MN or early LN** (transitional unit? [Vitelli, pers. comm. 1990])
radiocarbon date from FAN:114: 6690 ± 80 B.P., 4740 b.c.

FC 112

a. FAS:68
b. no modern contamination; mixed ceramic deposit suggests postdepositional disturbance
c. possible hearth or ash pit
d. inventoried finds: FV 29: cerithium (part of possible necklace; over 70 pierced examples found in units FAS:61, 63, 65, 68, 70)
FC 106: clay whorl
e. pottery includes small percentage MN; LN, FN
unit dated to: **FN** (no FN sherds diagnostic of early or late phases of FN [Vitelli, pers. comm. 1990])

FC 118

a. FAS:103
b. no modern contamination; mixed ceramic deposit suggests postdepositional disturbance; FAS:103 crosscut with FAS:109
c. possible hearth; stones suggesting part of wall or partition
d. inventoried finds: FAS:103: FV 59: stone bead
FV 575: shell bead
FB 299: burnt bone point fragment
noninventoried: millstone?; two worked bone points; sliced bone fragment (0.028 m/dia.); five large whole land snails (not evident in units above or below)
inventoried finds: FAS:109: FB 305: bone point
FB 306: bone point
e. pottery includes MN, LN

unit dated to: **LN** (middle of phase [Vitelli, pers. comm. 1990]); radiocarbon date from FAS:102 (which is directly above FAS:103, and contains MN and LN sherds) 8410 ± 90 B.P., 6460 b.c.

FC 124

a. FAS:123
b. no modern contamination
c. possible hearth
d. inventoried finds: FAS:123: FS 465, 466: quern fragments
FAS:124: (immediately below FAS:123) contains bottom half of hearth exposed in FAS:123
FS 463: fragment of chisel-ended head (honey flint)
FS 467: quern fragment
FS 462: stone bead
FR 133: lower pm1 of 25–30-year-old
FR 134: phalanx of neonate
e. pottery includes MN (some possible LN?)
unit dated to: **MN**

Trench G

Trench GG1, located against the cave wall near the present entrance to the cave, is marked by deep disturbance. Vitelli observes that, although post-Neolithic material is present in nearly every unit that produced pottery, the same basic ceramic sequence which characterizes other trenches in the cave is present in GG1. She argues, therefore, that the post-Neolithic disturbance must have been confined to relatively small areas crosscut during excavation (Vitelli, forthcoming). Most of the pottery is MN, with little evidence of LN; some FN is present.

FC 30

a. G1:3
b. modern contamination
c. —
d. —
e. contaminated; notebook records MN, LN, FN, and modern sherds

FC 31

a. G1:5
b. modern contamination
c. —
d. —
e. contaminated; notebook records MN, LN, FN (?), and modern sherds

FS 101

a. G1:19
b. possible modern contamination (1 possible modern sherd out of 1000+ sample)

c. —
d. inventoried finds: FS 99: soapstone ornament
FS 105: stone ornament or pin head
FS 110: grinding/hammerstone
FS 127: perforated sphere/weight
FS 128: grinding/hammerstone
FS 129: unfinished serpentinite celt
FS 173: grinding/hammerstone
FB 95, 138, 139: bone point fragments
FC 43: fragmentary sling bullet?
e. bulk of pottery is MN (early); also includes EN, LN, FN, and possible modern

Trench H

Trench H is located on a central cone near the present entrance to the cave. Excavations in H began in 1968, those in H1 during 1969. Both H1A and H1B are characterized by deep contamination; Units H1A:78 and above contain modern cultural material. H2 is located between HH1 and the rockfall at the cave entrance. A wall constructed of rough stones (possibly a windbreak) was discovered in H2 at ca. 1 m depth, and possibly accounts for some of the disturbance in the area.

FC 41

a. H:21
b. modern contamination
c. —
d. —
e. contaminated; pottery includes MN, LN, FN, Myc. (?), Roman, and modern sherds

FC 42

a. H:21
b. modern contamination
c. —
d. —
e. contaminated; pottery includes MN, LN, FN, Myc. (?), Roman, and modern sherds

FC 57

a. H1:18
b. modern contamination
c. —
d. —
e. contaminated; pottery includes MN, LN, and modern sherds

FC 60

a. H1:27

b. modern contamination
c. —
d. —
e. contaminated; pottery includes EN (?), MN, LN, and modern sherds

FC 68

a. H1:51 (figurine fell out of scarp wall)
b. modern contamination
c. —
d. —
e. contaminated; pottery includes MN, LN, FN, Myc. (?), and modern sherds

FP 173

a. H1A:78
b. modern contamination; marks borderline of deep disturbance and contamination in H1A; H1A:80, unit immediately below H1A:78, contains early phase of MN
c. —
d. —
e. notebook records EN, MN, possible LN, and modern sherds

FC 122

a. H2B:59
b. no modern contamination; mixed ceramic deposit suggests disturbance
c. —
d. —
e. pottery includes MN, LN, FN
unit dated to **FN**

PARALIA

Outside the shelter of the cave, excavations opened seven trenches along the modern shoreline (Paralia): L5, O5, P5, Q4, Q5, Q6, and QR. The areas revealed substantial building activity (mostly in the form of walls) and several burials. The occupational debris is confined to a deep sequence of EN activity, substantial MN remains, no LN to speak of, and a certain amount of material from the Final Neolithic.

Trench L5

FC 208

a. L5:69
b. no modern contamination; mixed ceramic deposit suggests postdepositional disturbance
c. —
d. —

e. pottery includes mostly MN, with some FN, all in poor condition
unit dated to **FN**

Trench O

FC 167

a. O5NE:27
b. no modern contamination; redeposited dump or fill?
c. —
d. —
e. pottery includes EN, MN
unit dated to **MN**

Trench P

FC 177

a. P5:31
b. no modern contamination; redeposited dump or fill?
c. —
d. —
e. pottery includes MN, some possible FN
unit dated to **FN**

Trench Q

FC 190

a. Q5S:186
b. no modern contamination
c. —
d. inventoried finds: FC 188: part of pierced disc (whorl?)
FS 747: talc pendant or bead fragment
FR 80: basal phalanx of adult left toe
noninventoried: 6 flint drills
units above and below (Q5S:185, 187) include pierced clay discs (whorls?), beads, and flint drills
e. pottery includes EN, MN
unit dated to **transitional EN/MN phase** (Vitelli, pers. comm. 1990)

FC 117

a. Q6NE section
b. section taken along beach wall

c. not available
d. not available
e. not available

TABLE 11

FEATURES AND FINDS ASSOCIATED WITH FRANCHTHI FIGURINES

Figurine	Location	Features	Ground Stone	Chipped Stone	Bead/pendant	Whorl	Worked Bone	Human Bone	Varia	Excavation Unit	Figurine Date
FC 190	Paralia			various	pendant/bead fragment	whorl?		phalanx	flint drills	Q5S:186	EN
FC 11	cave	ash pit or hearth		various					shell bracelet	A:31	EN/MN
FC 12	cave	ash pit or hearth?		various			bone point			A:53	MN
FC 117	Paralia			various						Q6NE section	MN early?
FC 124	cave	ash pit or hearth	quern fragments	various	assoc. unit = stone bead			assoc. unit = molar/phalanx		FAS:123	MN
FC 167	Paralia			various						O5NE:27	MN early?
FC 177	Paralia			various						P5:31	MN
FC 208	Paralia			various						L5:69	MN
FC 101	cave	possible hearth		various	assoc. unit = beads		assoc. unit = worked bone	assoc. unit = skull/tooth frag.		FAN:114	LN
FC 118	cave	ash pit or hearth	millstone?	various	stone/shell beads		bone points		whole land snails	FAS:103	LN
FS 101	cave	possible hearth	celt; grinder/ hammerstones	various	stone ornaments	whorl?	bone points		sling bullet?	G1:19	LN
FC 88	cave	ash pit or hearth; hole	grinder/ hammerstone	various		whorls				FAN:59	FN
FC 112	cave	ash pit or hearth?		various	shell necklace fragments	whorls				FAS:68	FN
FC 122	cave			various						H2B:59	EN?

APPENDIX B
Hardness Ratings of Clay Bodies from Franchthi (Mohs Hardness Scale)

Early Neolithic

FC 190: 2.0
FC 122: 4.0
Average: 3.0. Range: 2.0–4.0

Early Neolithic/Middle Neolithic Transitional

FC 11: 4.0

Middle Neolithic

FC 12: 4.0
FC 30: 5.0
FC 31: 4.0
FC 42: 4.5
FC 68: 5.0 (medial: 3.5)
FC 117: 3.0
FC 124: 5.0
FC 167: 4.0
FP 173: 3.5 (average of ext.: 3.0; int.: 4.0)
FC 177: 2.0
FC 208: 3.0
Average: 3.9. Range: 2.0–5.0

Late Neolithic

FC 28: 4.0
FC 57: 4.0
FC 60: 3.0
FC 101: 5.0
FC 118: 6.0
Average: 4.4. Range: 3.0–6.0

Final Neolithic

FC 4: 4.0
FC 41: 3.0
FC 88: 3.0
FC 112: 3.0
Average: 3.2. Range: 3.0–4.0

APPENDIX C
Color Values of Figurines from Franchthi (Munsell Soil Color Charts)

Catalogue Number	*Surface Color*	*Decoration*
Early Neolithic		
FC 190	7.5YR 4/0 dark gray	
FC 122	7.5YR 3/0 very dark gray & 7.5YR 5/2 brown	
Early/Middle Transitional		
FC 11	5YR 5/4 reddish brown & 5YR 3/1 very dark gray	
Middle Neolithic		
FC 12	5YR 6/4 light reddish brown	5YR 3/1 very dark gray
FC 30	2.5YR 3/0 very dark gray	
FC 31	2.5YR 6/6 light red & 2.5YR 5/6 red	
FC 42	5YR 7/4 pink	10R 4/6 red

FC 68	5YR 6/6 reddish yellow medial surface: 2.5YR 6/6 light red	2.5YR 4/8 red & 2.5YR 3/2 dusky red
FC 117	7.5YR 6/4 light brown	2.5YR 5/6 red & 2.5YR 3/0 very dark gray
FC 124	2.5YR 5/8 red	2.5YR 3/4 dark reddish brown
FC 167	7.5YR 6/4 light brown	10R 5/8 red
FP 173	ext.: 5YR 6/3 light reddish brown	10R 4/6 red
	int.: 5YR 5/1 gray	5YR 5/2 reddish gray & 5YR 5/3 reddish brown
FC 177	5YR 6/4 light reddish brown	5YR 3/1 very dark gray
FC 208	7.5YR 6/4 light brown	2.5YR 5/6 red
Late Neolithic		
FC 28	7.5YR 8/2 pinkish white	7.5YR 3/0 very dark gray
FC 57	5YR 6/6 reddish yellow & 2.5YR 4/0 dark gray	
FC 60	7.5YR 6/4 light brown	2.5YR 4/8 red
FC 101	5YR 4/1 dark gray	5YR 2.5/1 black
FC 118	7.5YR 6/4 light brown	7.5YR 3/0 very dark gray
Final Neolithic		
FC 4	10YR 2.5/2 very dark brown	
FC 41	2.5YR 5/6 red & 2.5YR 6/6 light red	

FC 88	5YR 5/3 reddish brown
FC 112	7.5YR 3/0 very dark gray & 7.5YR 5/4 brown

APPENDIX D
Possible Figurine Fragments

Figure	*Pottery Type*[a]	*Maximum Height (m)*	*Maximum Width (m)*	*Description and Plate Number*
FC 27	(FN) coarse ware	0.079	0.039	leg of fig. or vessel (Plate 22)
FC 29	(FN) coarse ware	0.062	0.034	leg of fig. or vessel (Plate 22)
FC 45	(FN) coarse ware	0.040 (diam.)	0.031	base of fig., cf. Coleman 1977: Plates 72:127, 73:160; or lid handle, cf. Coleman 1977: Plates 37M, 84AF (Plates 20, 21)
FC 97	(FN) coarse ware	0.052	0.016	clay coil (Plate 24)
FC 98	(FN) crusted ware	0.042	0.015	clay coil (Plate 24)
FC 114	(FN) coarse ware	0.031	0.036 (diam.)	see FC 45, above (Plates 20, 21)
FC 130	(EN) Lime	0.050	0.028	leg of fig. or vessel (Plate 22)
FC 131	(MN)	0.016	0.025	attached pubic triangle?, cf. FC 68 (Plate 24)
FC 170	(MN) patterned Urfirnis	0.018	0.014 (diam.)	neck of figurine? (Plate 24)
FC 175	(MN) coarse Urfirnis	0.047	0.028 (diam.)	leg of fig. or vessel (Plate 24)

FC 176	(FN) coarse ware	0.027	0.022	schematic, headless figurine (Plates 20, 21)
FC 178	(MN) patterned Urfirnis	0.030	0.047 (diam.)	neck and shoulders of fig.? (Plates 20, 21)
FC 180	(EN) Lime	0.019	0.018	see FC 130, above (Plate 22)
FC 181	(EN) Lime	0.037	0.019	see FC 130, above (Plate 22)
FC 191	(EN) Lime	0.035	0.018	see FC 130 above (Plate 24)
FC 194	MN/FN?	0.033	0.023	zoomorphic figure with two ears (Plate 24)
FC 195	(EN) Lime	0.066	0.028	see FC 130, above (Plate 22)
FC 202	(FN) crusted ware	0.034		clay coil (Plate 24)
FC 204	coarse ware?	0.048	0.036	zoomorphic figurine? (Plates 20, 21)
FP 80	(LN) matte paint paint? (Myc.)?	0.039	0.043	dish-like container, with figurines? cf. Erlenmeyer and Erlenmeyer: Plate XLIII:80 (Plate 23)
FB 82	bone	0.091	0.033	schematic figurine? (Plate 24)

[a] With the exception of EN Lime (see n. 6), the pottery types correspond with the traditional terminology first devised by Weinberg (1947) and later amplified by Jacobsen (1969, 1973b).

APPENDIX E
Coded Dimensions Used in Cluster Analysis

The cluster analysis was based on approximately 30 dimensions, each of which had several associated attributes. For example, Dimension C (Nose) had 10 entries, including: 0. not determinable; 1. absent; 2. rounded-to-oval protrusion or pellet in middle of face; 3. beak-like protrusion starting at or near top of forehead; 4. narrow and continuous projection protruding from middle of face, over top of head and down upper part of back of head; 5. small projection in middle of face; 6. large, bulbous protrusion in middle of face; 7. rounded snout of animal; 8. pointed snout of animal; 9. flat or pig-like snout of animal. A complete list of all the dimensions and their associated attributes can be found in Talalay 1983a:73–83. The matrices and dendrograms generated by the computer are also available in Talalay 1983a:272–294.

Coded Dimensions

A. Head and neck (general configuration)
B. Eyes
C. Nose
D. Nostrils
E. Mouth
F. Ears or "horns"
G. Hair
H. Cap
I. General posture or position of torso
J. General modeling of torso
K. Arms
L. Hands
M. Fingers
N. Breasts
O. Midriff/Stomach
P. Navel
Q. Back
R. Waist
S. Features on torso which do not represent naturally occurring and/or recognizable anatomical details
T. Position and articulation of leg(s)
U. Genitals

V. Buttocks
W. Feet (foot)
X. Toes
Y. Zoomorphic body shape
Z. Zoomorphic legs
AA. Zoomorphic tail
BB. Zoomorphic anus
CC. Surface Treatment
GG. Basic Decoration (painted and incised)
JJ. Sex

APPENDIX F
Published Figurines from Southern Greece

The following drawings are miniature versions of all published Neolithic figurines from southern Greece. These drawings provide the reader with an easily accessible visual record. No scale is provided, nor are any descriptions included. Where possible, the catalogue number given in the original publication is listed beneath the image, as is the approximate date of the piece (EN, MN, LN, FN), according to my assessment. The drawings are arranged alphabetically, by site. For more detailed drawings or photographs, the reader is directed to the following:

Aegina: Welter 1938:Figure 8, 1954:Figures 3–5; Thimme 1977:Plate 10.

Akratas: Phelps 1975:Figure 79.

Alepotrypa: Hauptmann 1971:Figures 52a, b; Papathanasopoulos 1971:Figure 19.

Amorgos: Weinberg 1951:Plate 2B; Thimme 1977:Plate 2.

Asea: Holmberg 1944:Figure 111, 6–12.

Athens (Agora): Immerwahr 1971:Plate 14; Broneer 1939:Figure 88.

Corinth: Phelps 1987.

Eleusis: Thimme 1977:Figure 31.

Kephala: Coleman 1977:Plates 26, 71–73.

Kitsos: Lambert 1974:Figure 21.

Koufovouno: Theocharis 1973:Plates 17, 200, 226; Wolters 1891:52.

Lerna: Caskey 1958:Plates 36d, e; Caskey and Eliot 1956.

Malthi: Valmin 1938:Plate xxv:46.

Mycenae: Diamant 1974b.

Naxos: Weinberg 1951:Plate 2C.

Nea Makri: Theocharis 1954:Figure 5.

Nemea: Cherry et al. 1988:Figure 9.

Patissia: Weinberg 1951:Plate 1C; Thimme 1977:Plate 5.

Saliagos: Evans and Renfrew 1968:Figures 75–78, Plates XLII–XLV; Renfrew 1986.

Tiryns: Müller 1976: Plate II:1 .

AEGINA

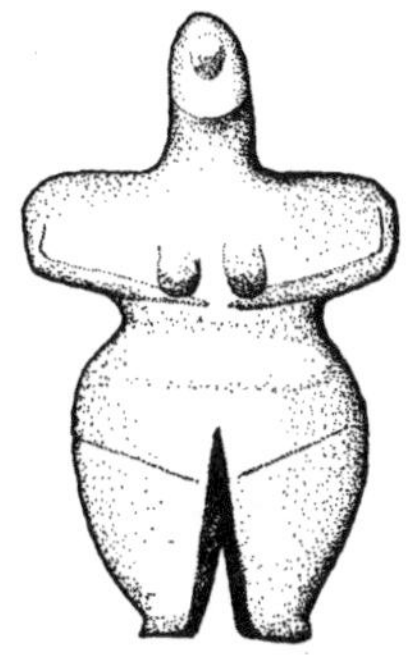

1: MN or LN

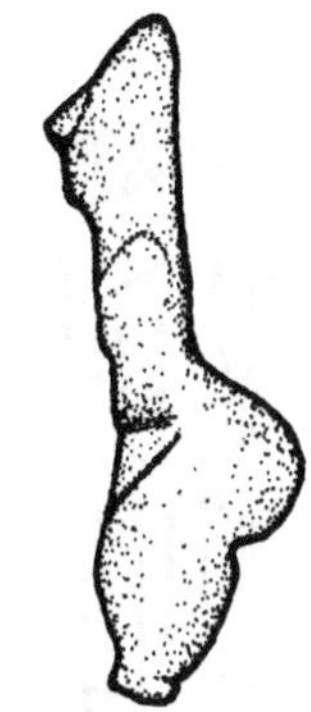
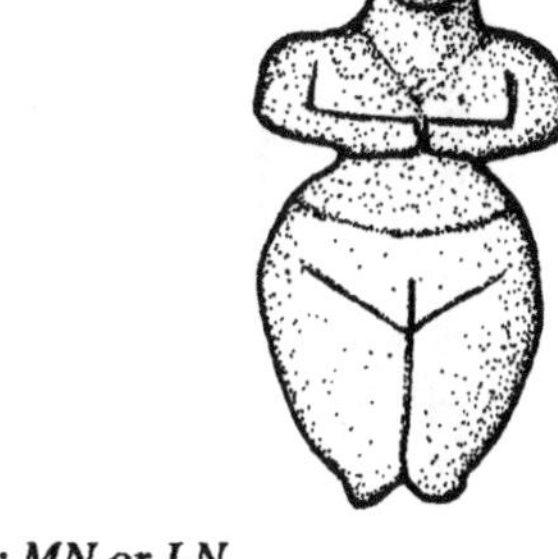

2: MN or LN

AGORA (ATHENS)

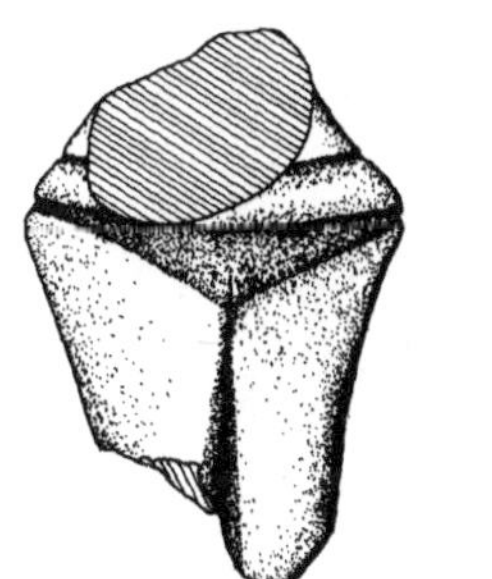
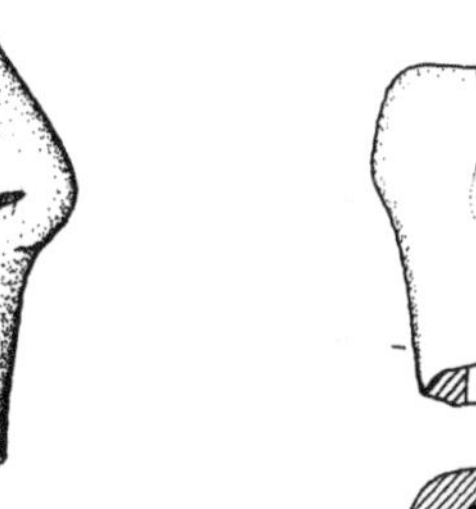

AS 148: MN or LN

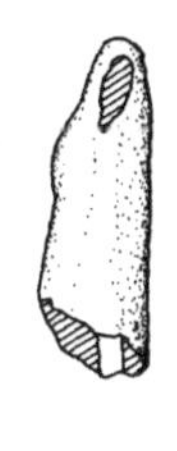

P25864: FN

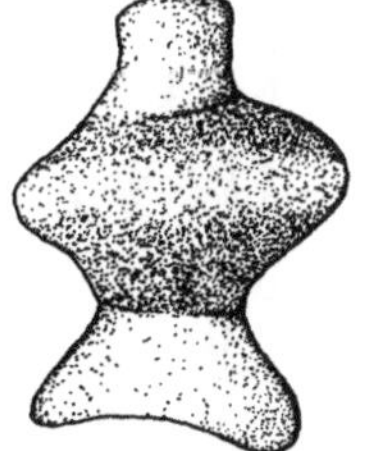
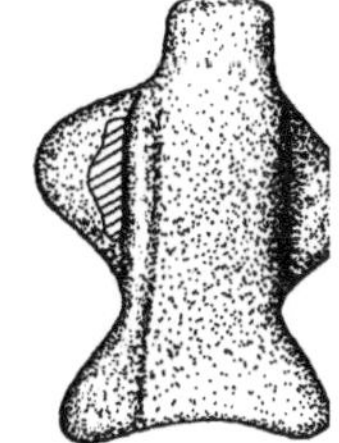

P13926: FN

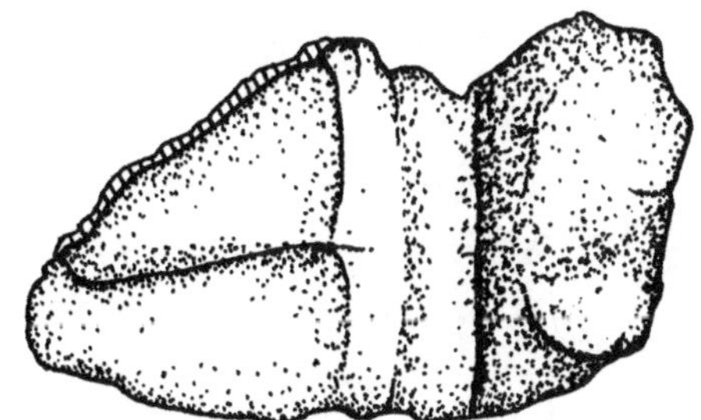
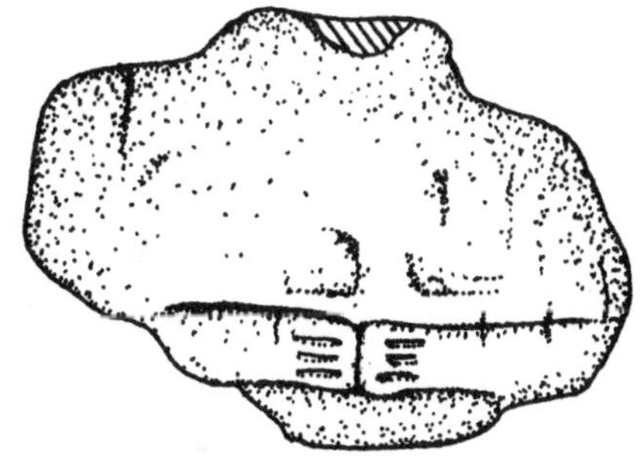

S1097: MN or LN

AKRATAS

Ak. 1021: MN

Ak. 985: MN

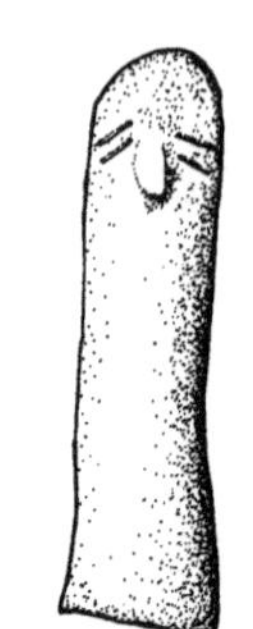

Ak. 992: MN or LN

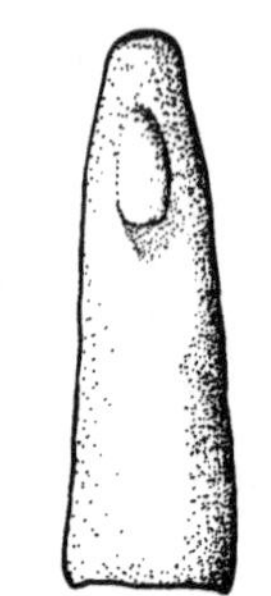

Ak. 1020: MN or LN

ALEPOTRYPA

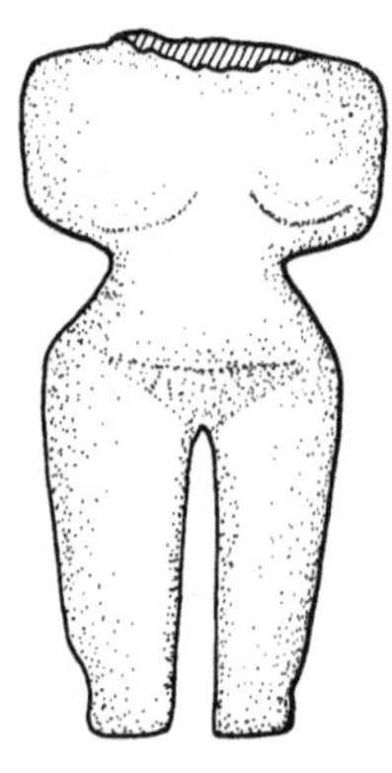

1: LN or FN

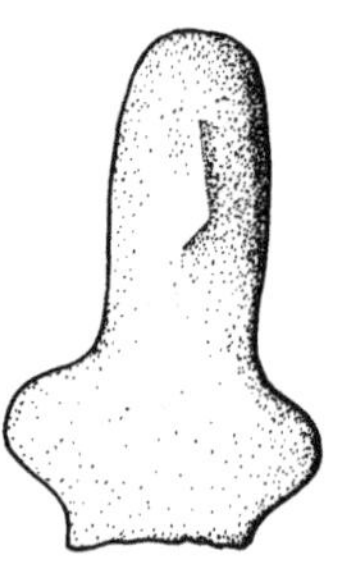

2: LN

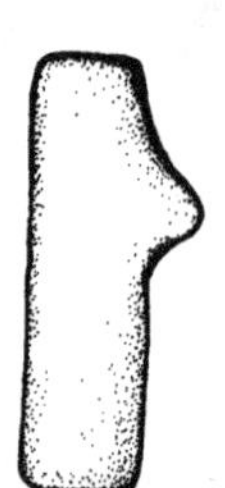

3: LN

AMORGOS

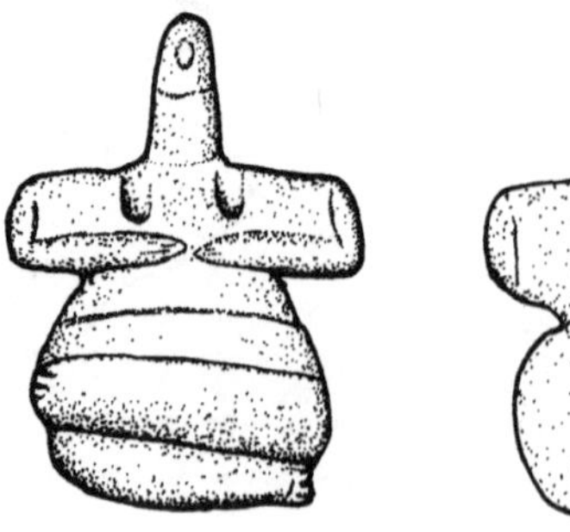

1: LN

ASEA

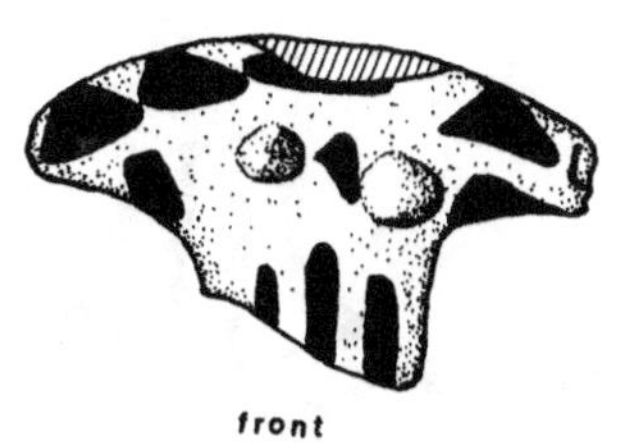

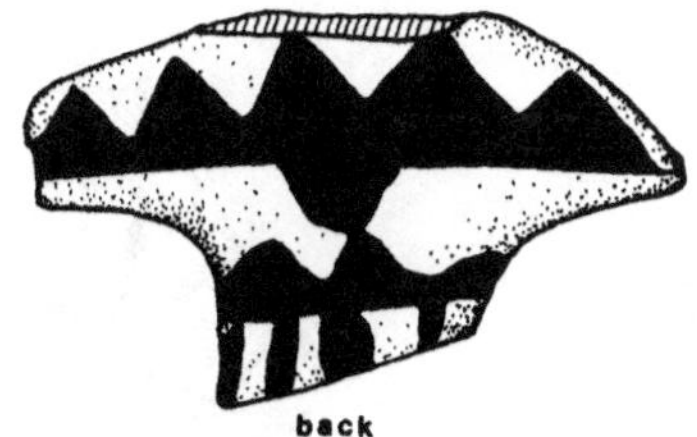

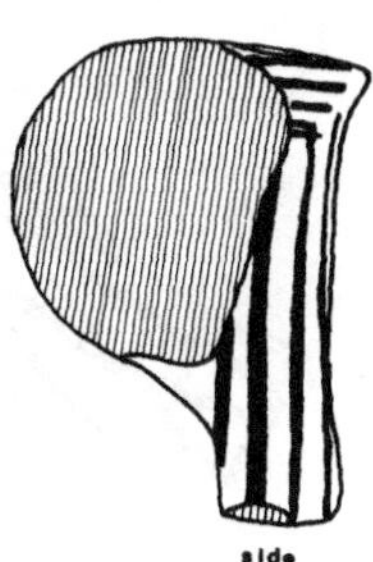

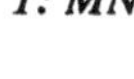

1: MN

2: MN

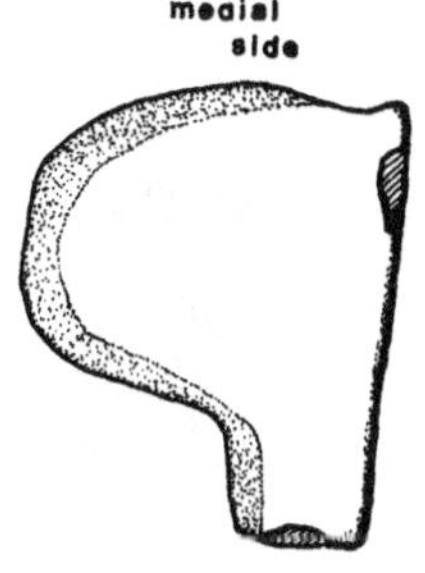

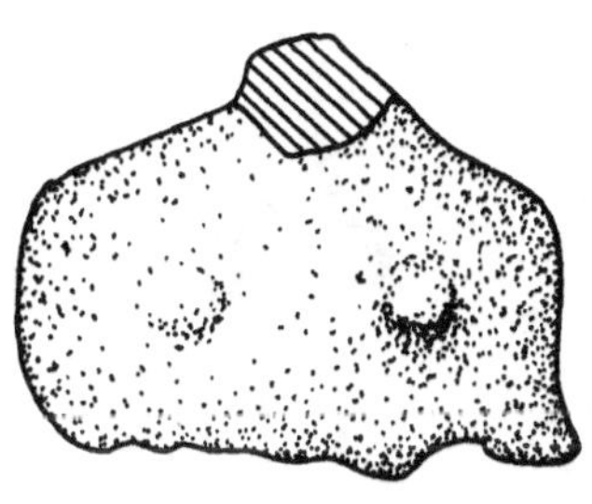

3: MN

4: MN

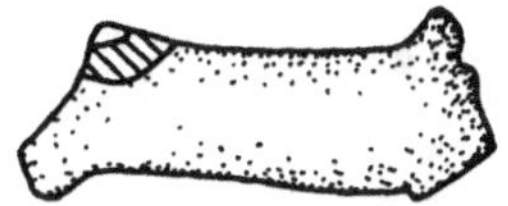

5: MN, LN, FN, or EH

6: MN, LN, FN or EH

7: FN

CORINTH

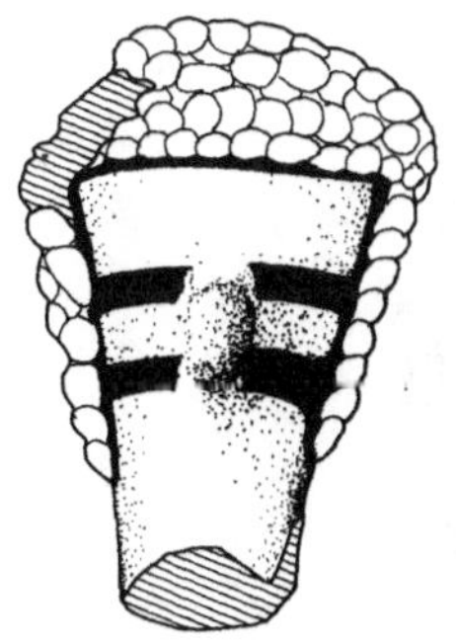

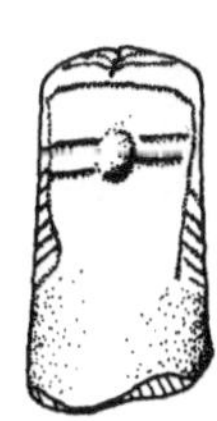

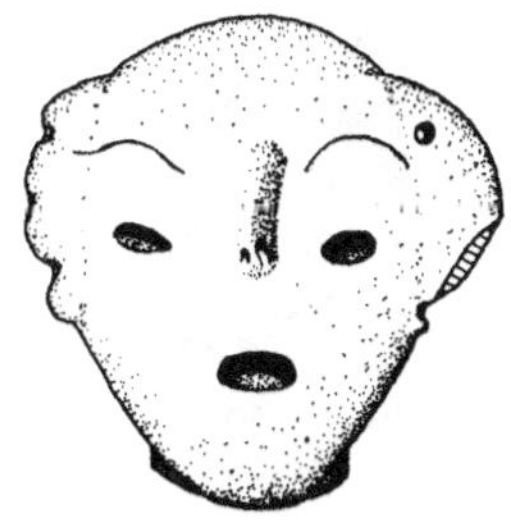

MF 8500: LN

MF 6730: MN

MF 1942: LN or EH

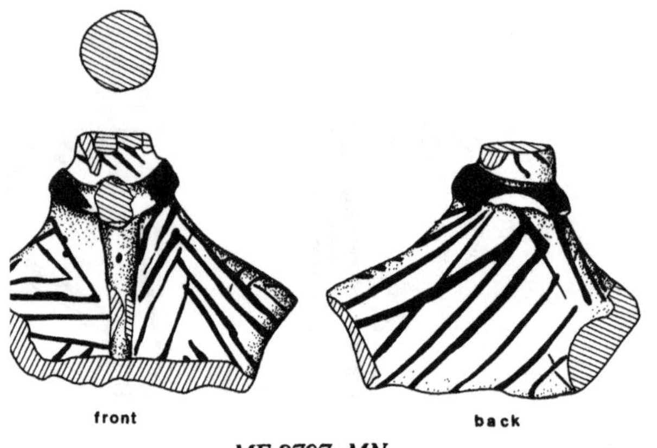

MF 8797: MN

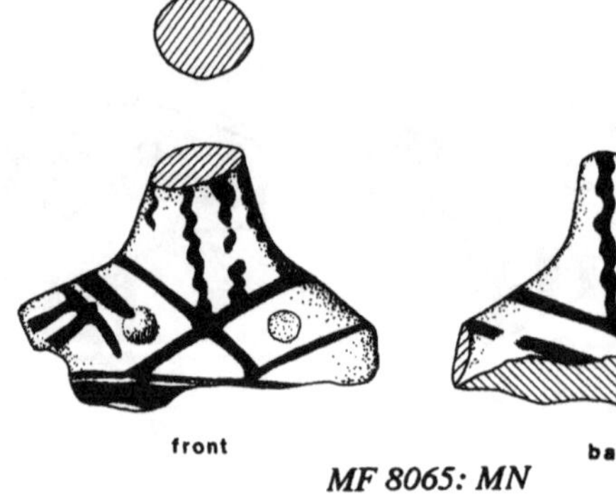

MF 8065: MN

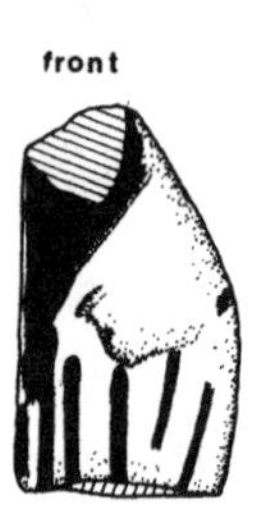

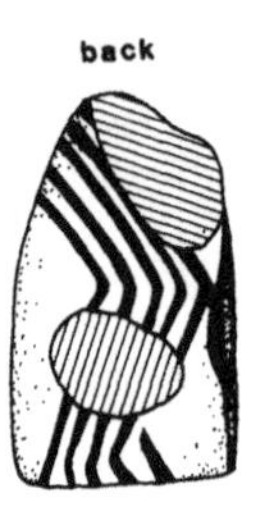

MF 4386: MN

MF 68-95: MN

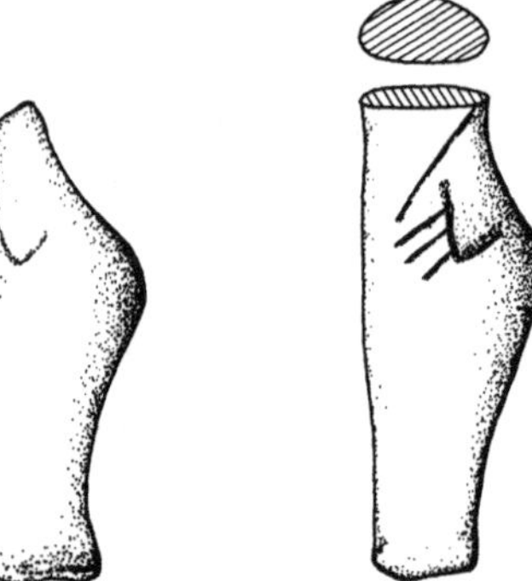

MF 9948: MN

MF 68-94: MN

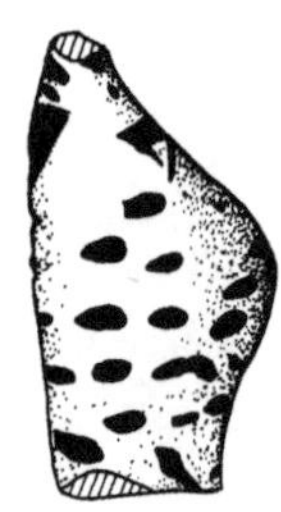

MF 70-24: MN

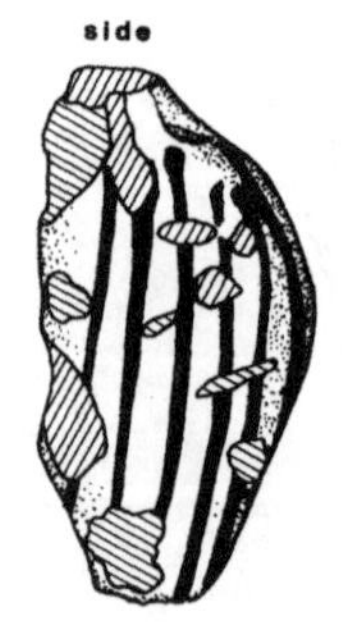

MF 68-96: MN

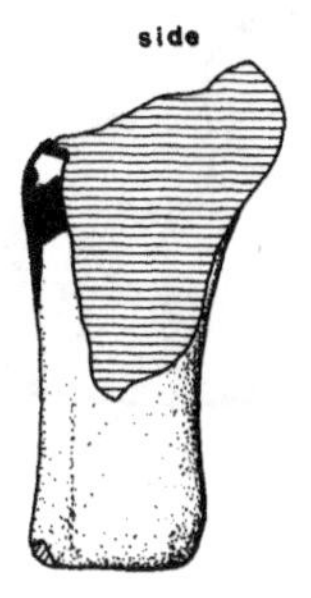

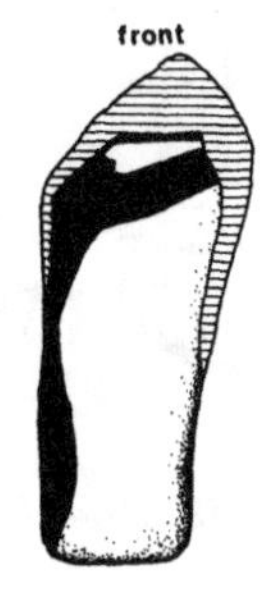

MF 70-36: LN

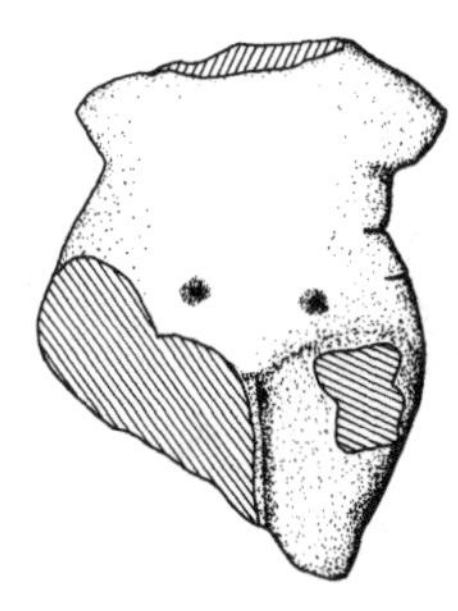
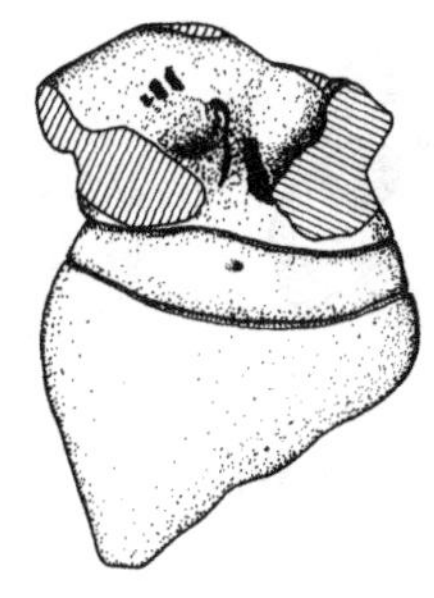
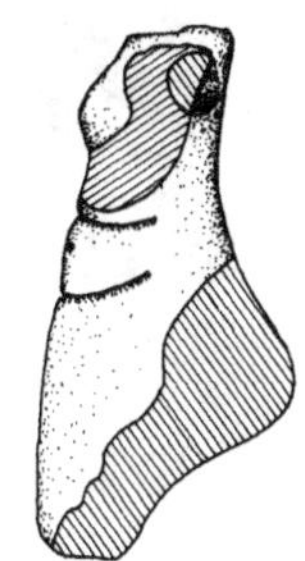

MF 6732: LN

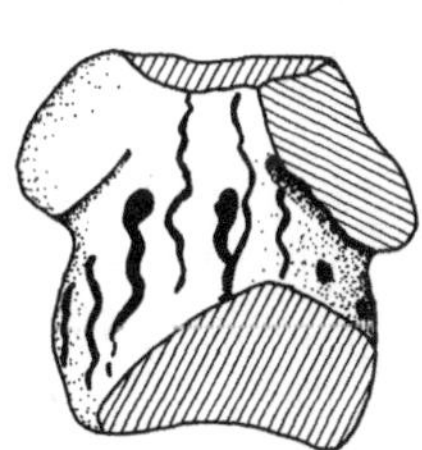

MF 68-285: LN

MF 75-39: LN

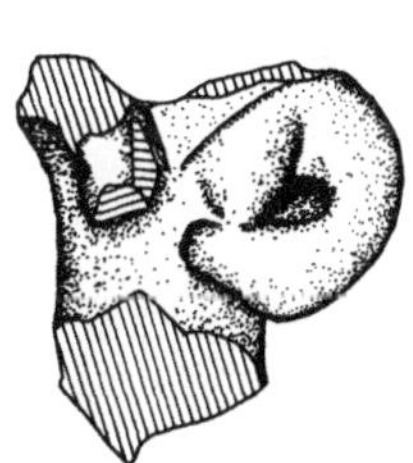
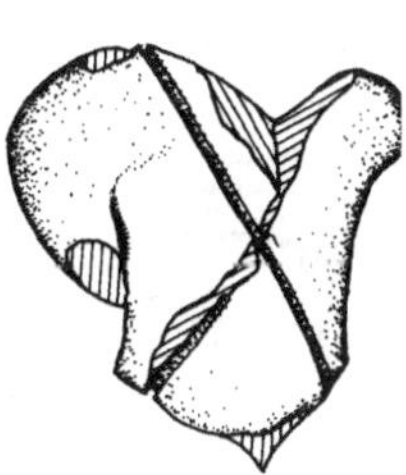

MF 77-111: LN

MF 13360: LN

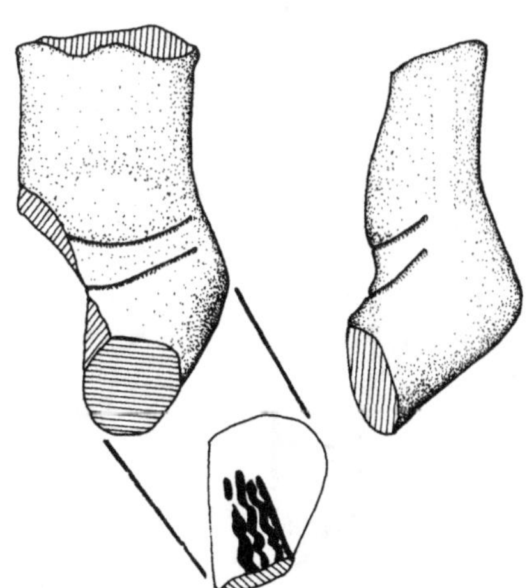

MF 8505: LN

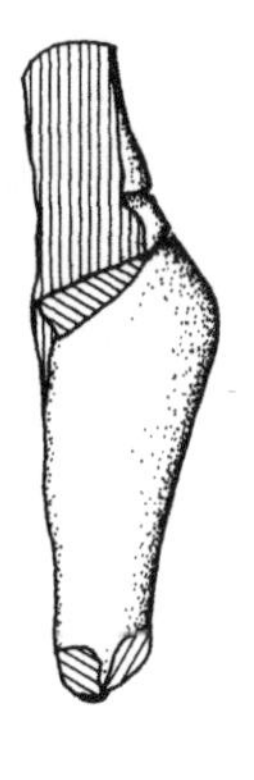
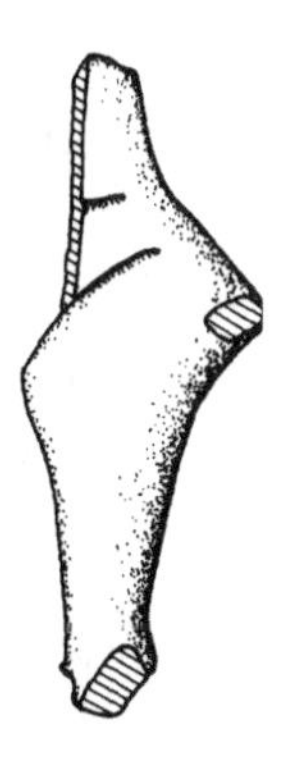

MF 8506: LN

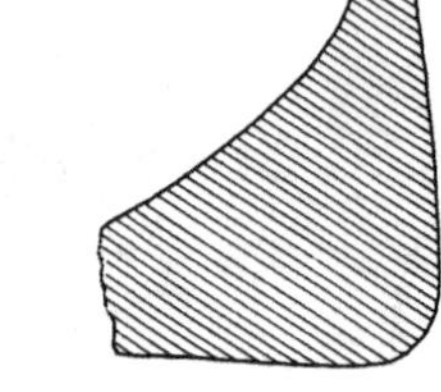

MF 9944: LN

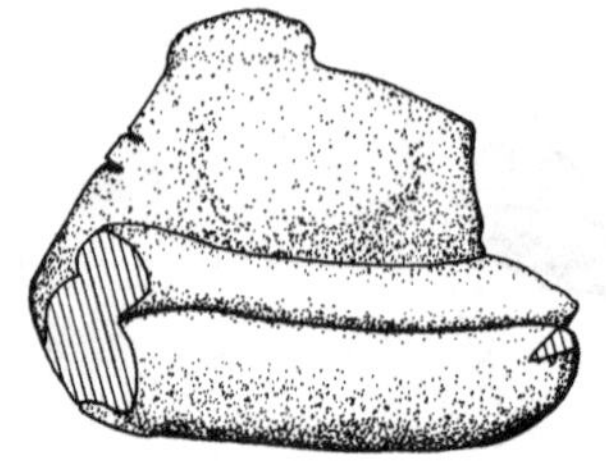
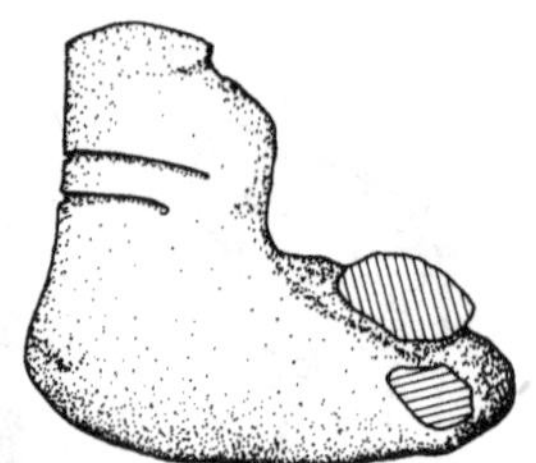

MF 8504: LN

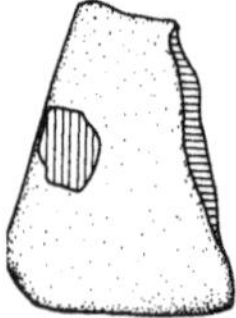

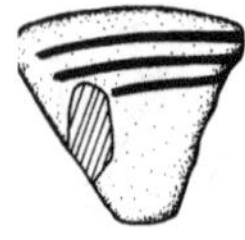

MF 76-89: LN

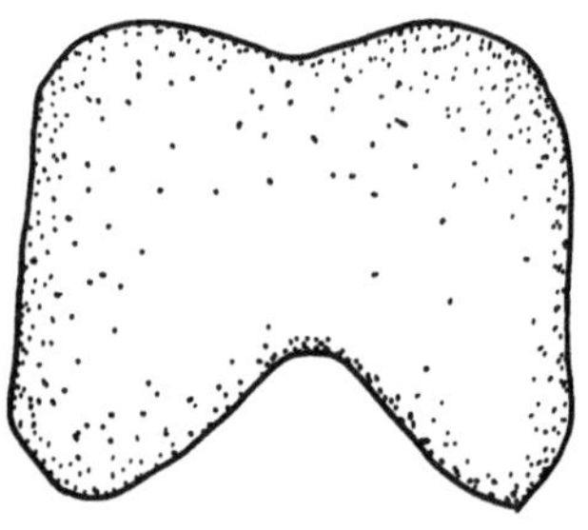

MF 6741: LN or FN

MF 13704: MN

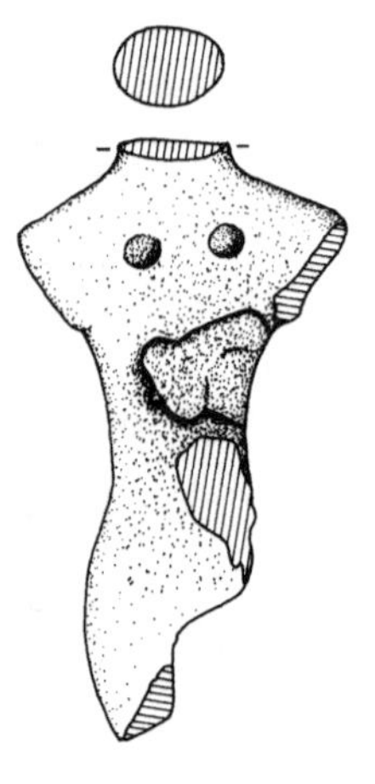

MF 8543: LN

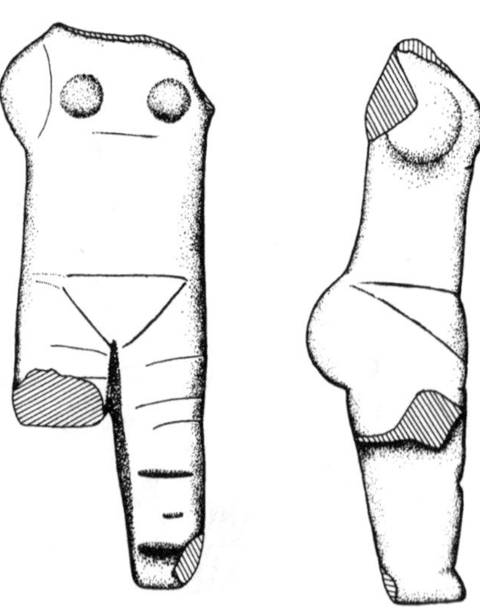

S 786: MN or LN

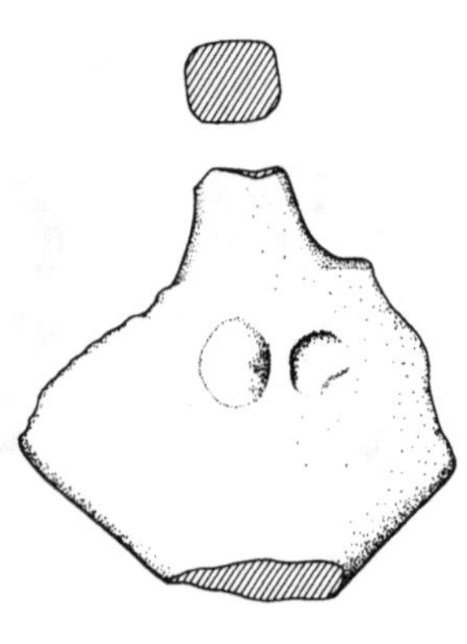

MF 75-85: LN or FN

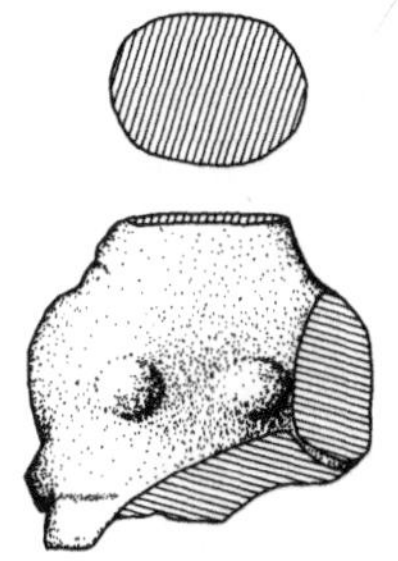
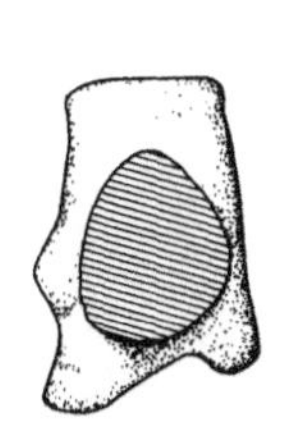

MF 9906: FN

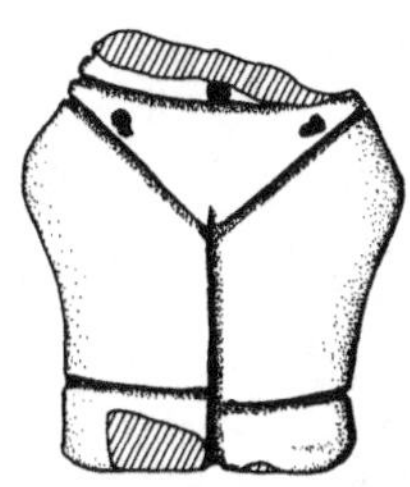
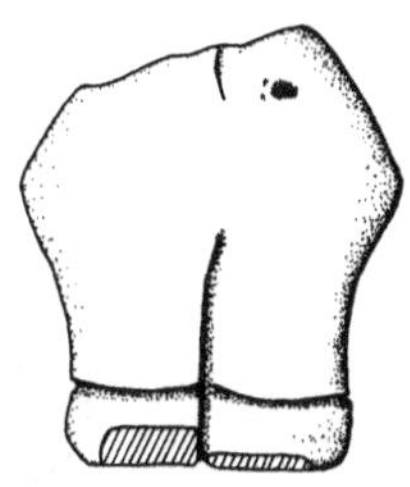

MF 9900: LN

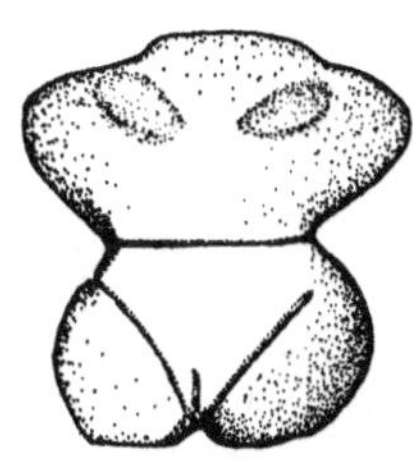

T40: LN or FN

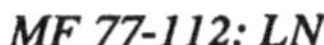

MF 77-112: LN

MF 3269: LN, FN, or EH

MF 8545: FN

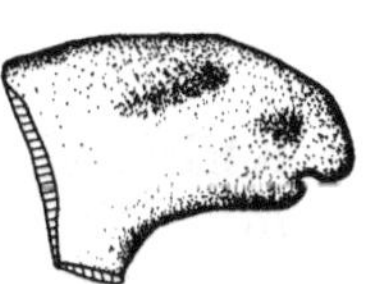

MF 13144: FN

MF 68-103: LN

MF 9915: LN

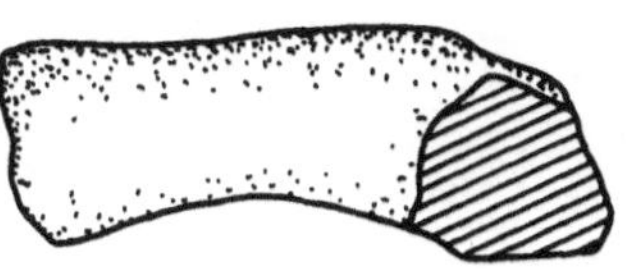

MF 13145: LN, FN, or EH

ELEUSIS

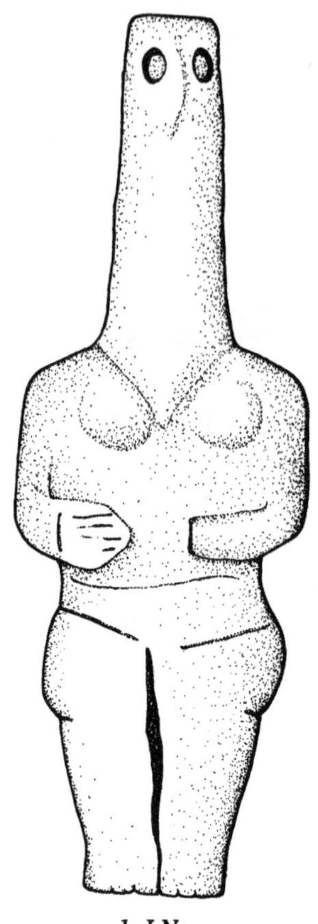

1: LN

KEPHALA
(all FN)

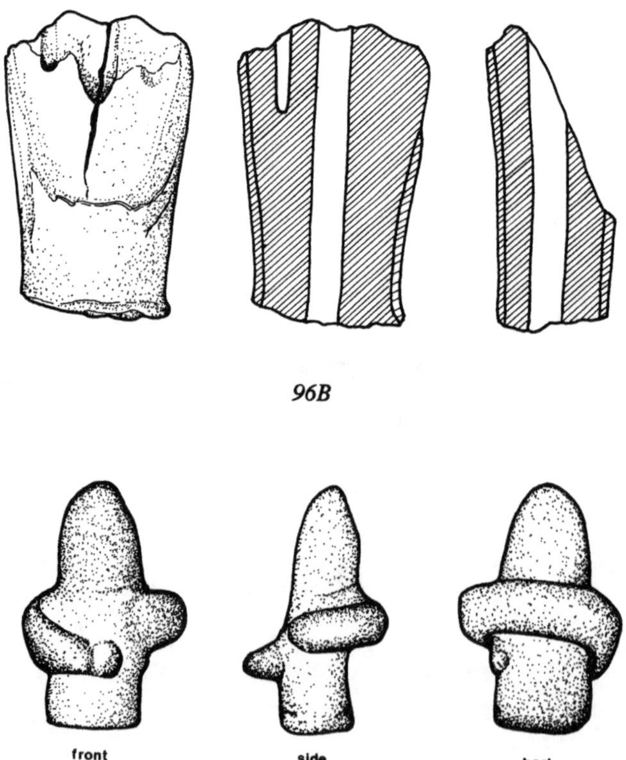

96B

front

side

196

197

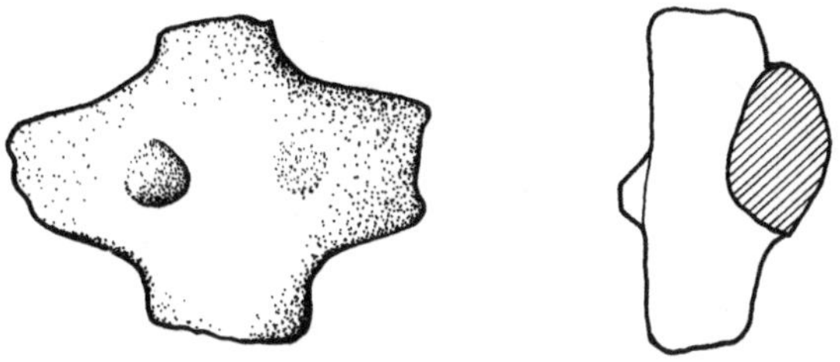

198

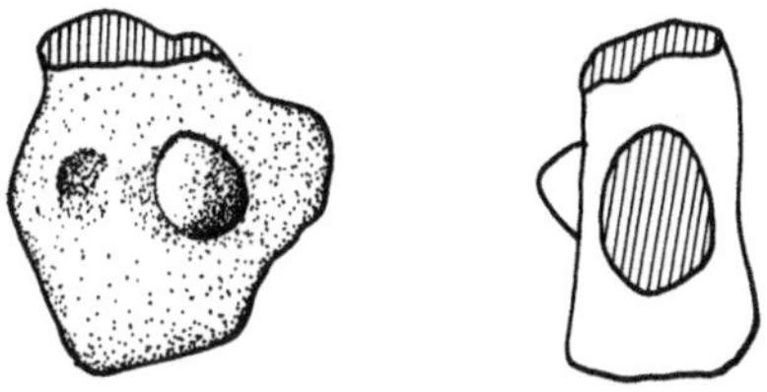

127

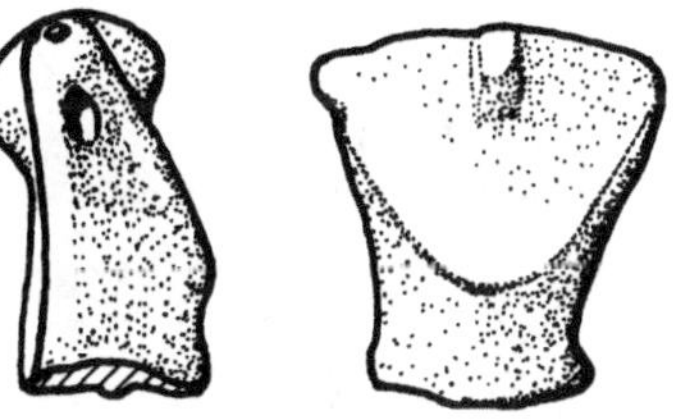

128

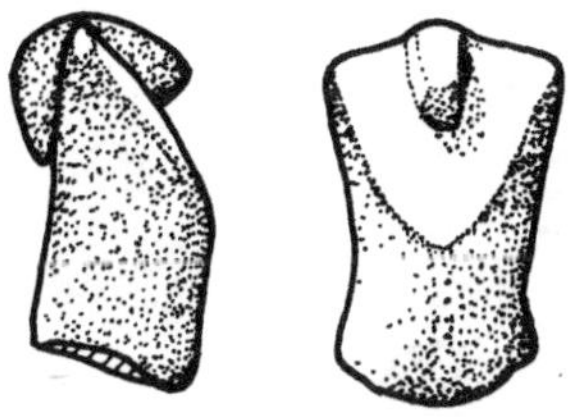

202

KITSOS

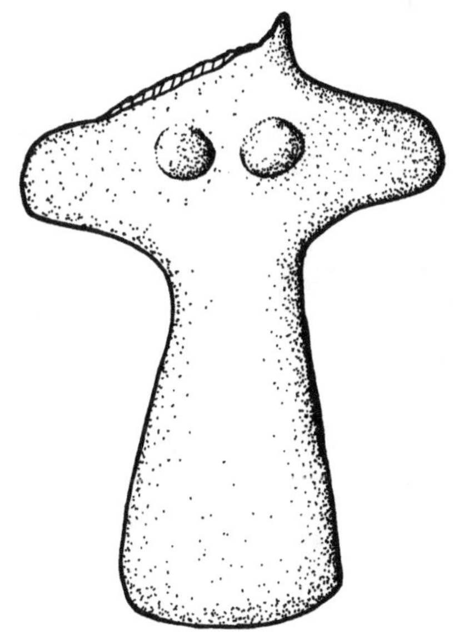

1:FN

KOUFOVOUNO
(all MN or LN)

NM 3928

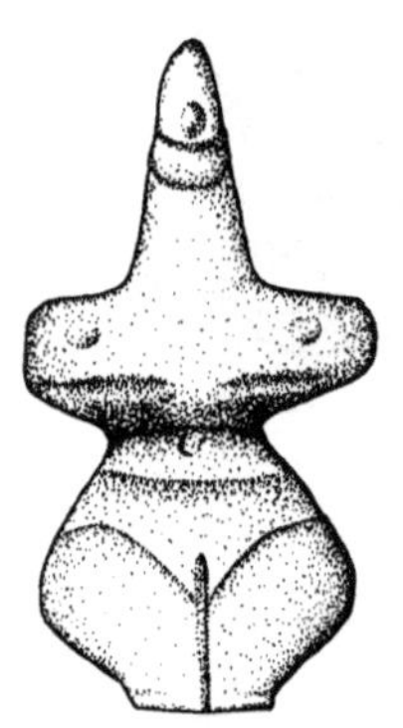

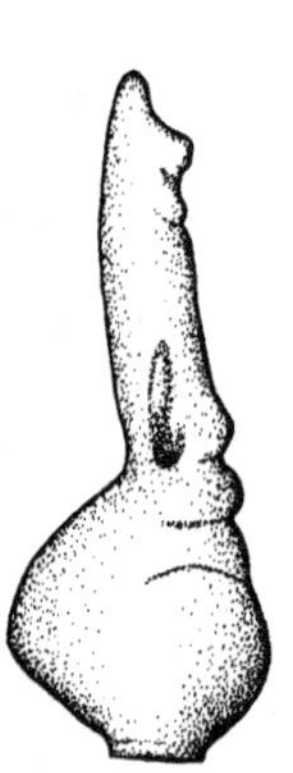

NM 3927

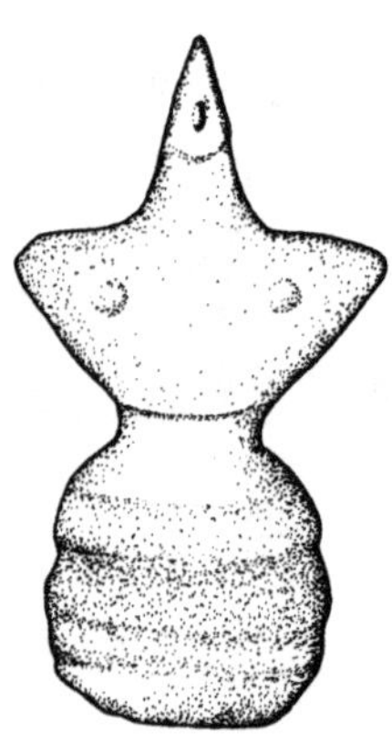

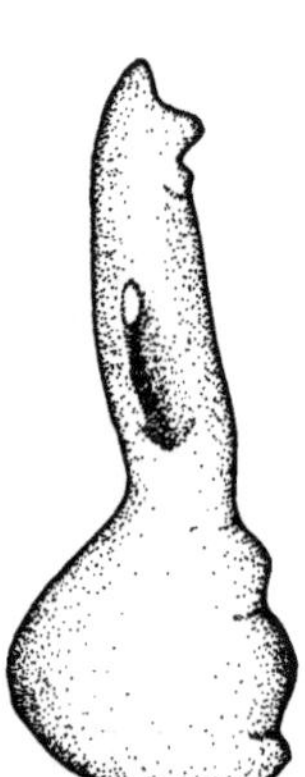

NM 3930

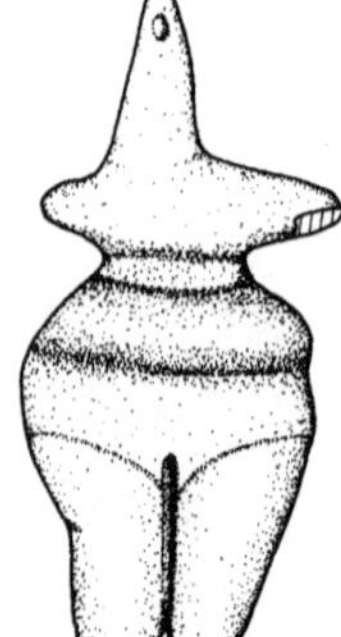

NM 3932

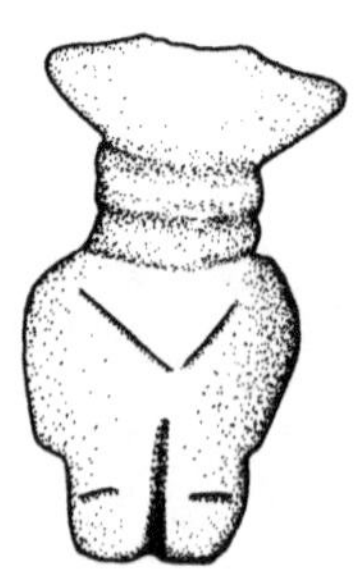

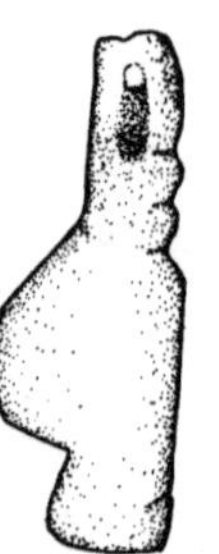

NM 3931

LERNA

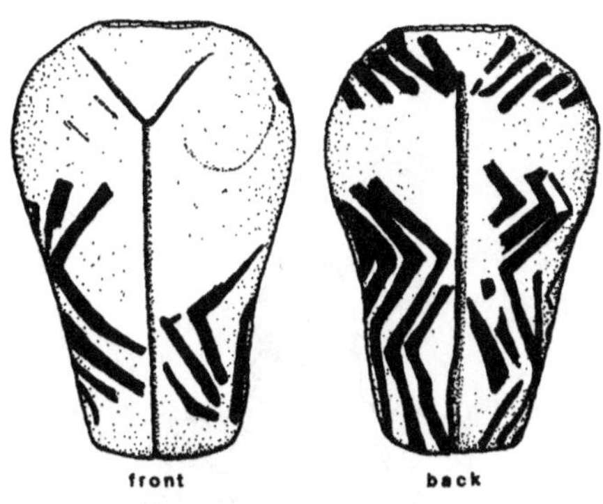

L7.46: MN

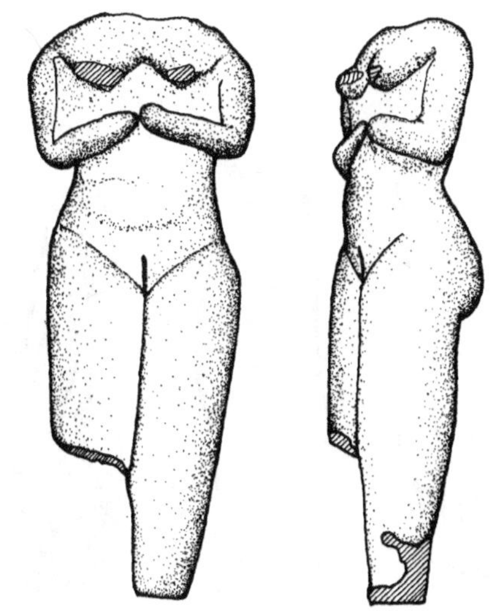

L6.100: MN

MALTHI

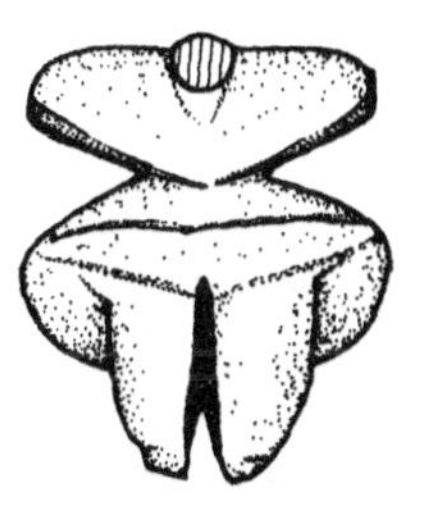

1: MN or LN

MYCENAE

1: MN or LN

NAXOS

1: LN

NEA MAKRI

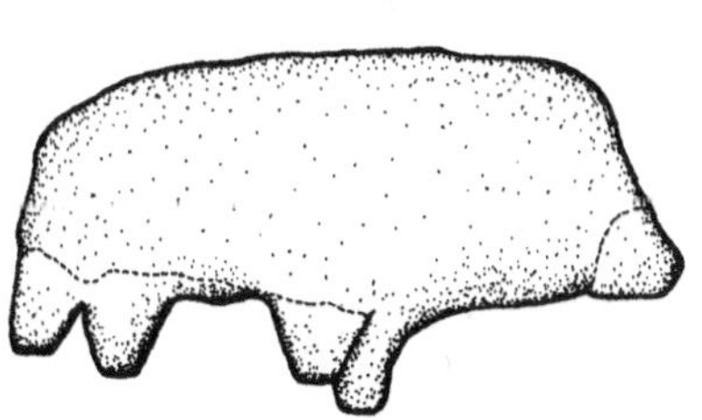

1: EN or LN

NEMEA

S702-2-1: MN

PATISSIA (ATHENS)

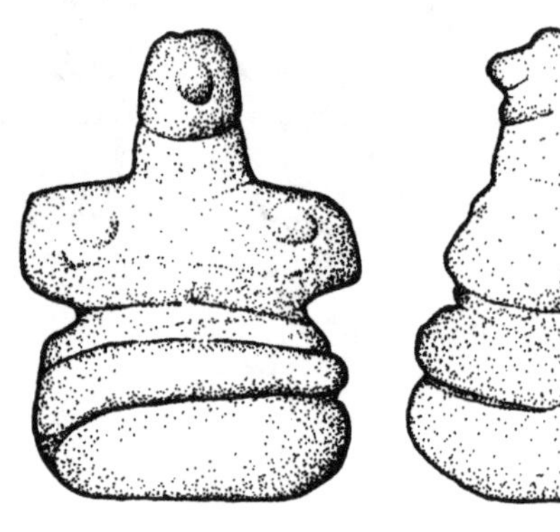

1: LN

SALIAGOS
(all LN)

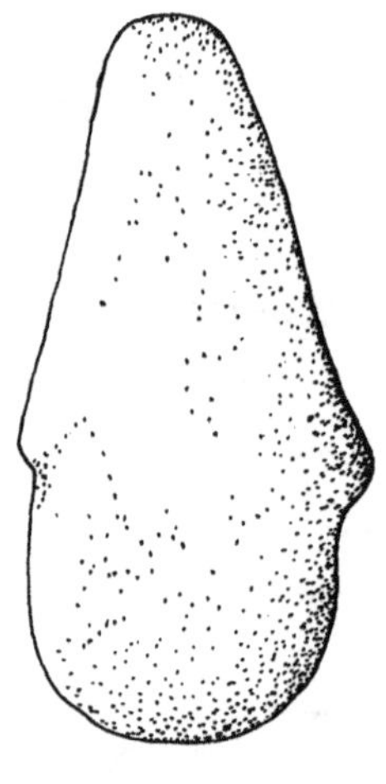

1

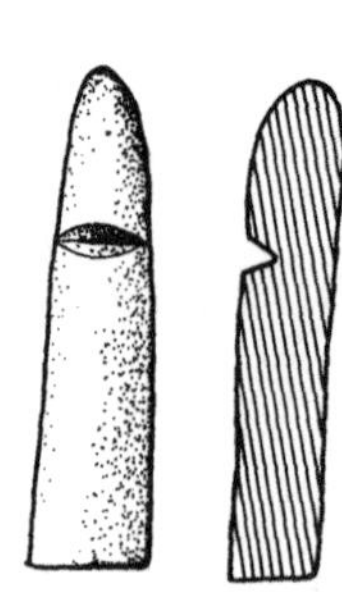

2

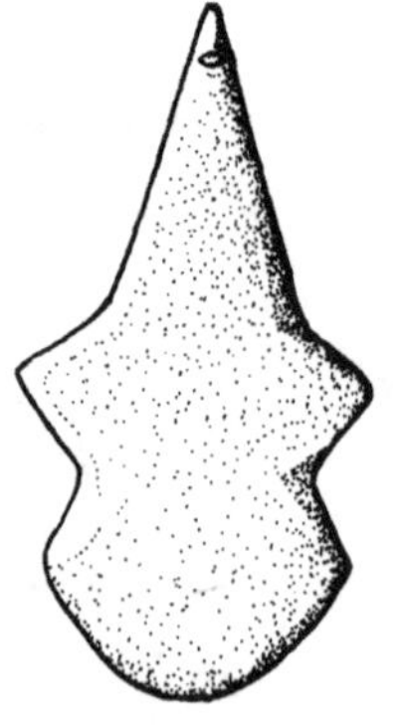

3

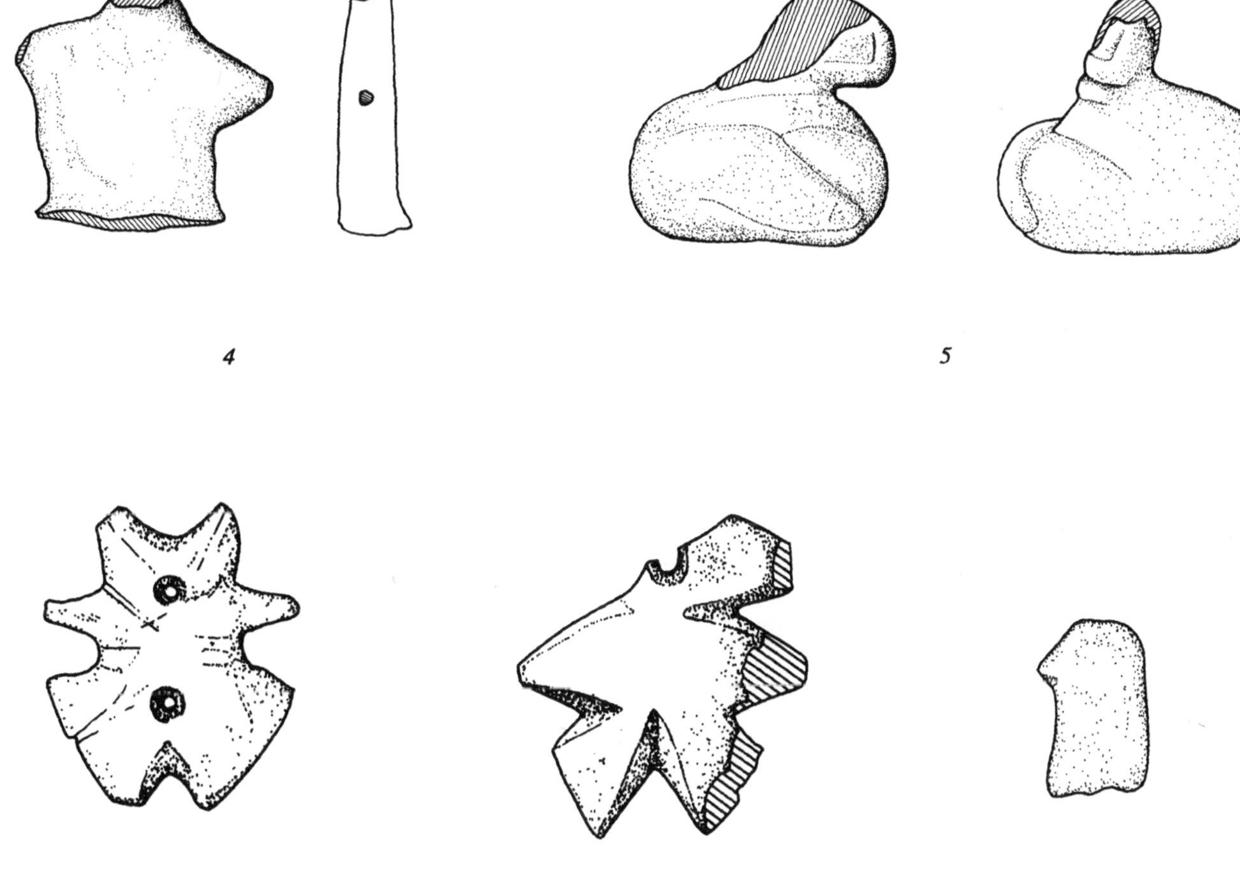

4 5

6 7 8

TIRYNS

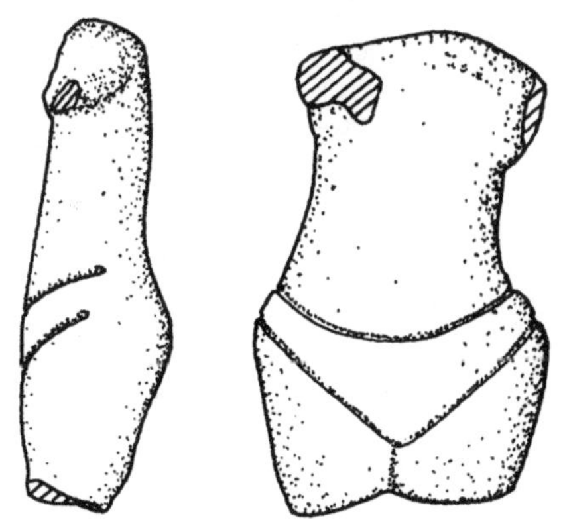

1: MN or LN

NOTES

1. Excavations were confined to the forepart of the cave, since the rear portion (about two-thirds of the interior) was filled with a small pool and massive breakdown from the roof (see Jacobsen and Farrand 1987).

2. Southern Greece is arbitrarily defined in this study as the Peloponnese, Attica, the Cyclades, and the islands of the Saronic Gulf.

3. No distinction is made between the terms "figurine" and "figure." They are used interchangeably throughout this study.

4. The decision to examine exhaustively the southern Greek corpus and give only summary treatment to northern Greek comparanda was based on several factors. A preliminary analysis of published figurines (which number well over 1000) from Thessaly, Macedonia, and Boeotia revealed that figurine production north of Attica often developed along lines different from those farther south. Moreover, I knew from several archaeologists working in the north that hundreds of Neolithic figurines were in private collections, and permission to see them might prove problematical. To investigate fully all the stylistic, contextual, and possibly functional differences among the figurines from the two regions did not seem feasible. The evidence provided in this volume will allow other scholars with more complete information on northern Greek collections to evaluate accurately where, when, and how northern and southern Greek figurines appear either to converge or diverge typologically, contextually, and functionally.

5. The 21 possible figurine fragments are not considered part of the sample proper but are relegated to Appendix D.

6. K. D. Vitelli, the ceramic specialist at Franchthi, is currently writing a major, final report on the ceramic sequence at the site (forthcoming; fascicle 8 of this series). Since her work is not yet published, I felt that adoption of her phasing and terminology would be more confusing than beneficial. I have, however, used one of her terms (No or Low Lime/Sandy) to describe two of the earliest figurines at the site (FC 11, FC 190), since the published descriptions of EN wares are fairly coarse. One of at least five varieties of ceramic biscuit identified by Vitelli, EN No (or Low) Lime/Sandy, was probably produced locally. Lime refers to $CaCO_3$, which was added as a temper to the raw clay by the potters. The most abundant EN biscuit at Franchthi is a Lime variety, which contains "sharply defined crystals of calcite, up to 2–3 mm in size, distributed irregularly throughout the biscuit" (Vitelli 1984a). No Lime/Sandy is the second most frequent biscuit in the EN assemblage.

7. Franchthi was excavated in "units." Each unit represents the smallest layer or area deemed by the excavators logically to limit manageable deposits during the sequence of excavating. Some units were predetermined spits or levels of a given thickness (usually 0.05 m); others were defined by changes in the color, texture, and nature of the soils, and still others by archaeological or architectural features visible at the time of excavation (see Jacobsen and Farrand 1987:7, 16).

8. During conversations with Dr. Vitelli, she informed me that three patterned Urfirnis figurines (FC 42, FC 117, FC 167) could be classified as early types within her MN sequence and that two FN figures (FC 4, FC 112) were made from clays not found in the early part of her FN sequence. These observations are noted in the catalogue (category F) as "Vitelli, pers. comm. 1990."

9. Very few Upper Palaeolithic sites have been excavated in Greece; none, including Franchthi, have produced figurines. The first appearance of a figurine at Franchthi postdates the earliest evidence for human occupation or visitation to the site by at least 15,000 years. While more than 300 so-called Venus types have been recovered at Upper Palaeolithic sites ranging from Spain to Siberia (Delporte 1979; Gamble 1982; Conkey 1983), most of the images date to the Gravettian and, therefore, essentially predate any archaeological evidence from Franchthi.

10. FC 122 was reported as clay in my Ph.D. dissertation (Talalay 1983a), but Vitelli has recently suggested that the piece may not, in fact, be made of clay. It is anomalous for Franchthi wares, and she believes it may be made of stone.

11. No shell figurines and only one example of a possible bone figurine (FB 82; see Appendix D) were recovered from Franchthi. Perhaps shell and bone, both of which are preserved fairly well at Franchthi, were reserved for other classes of artifacts (e.g., articles of personal adornment, specialized tools). Such preferences are documented cross-culturally. See McGhee 1977 for a study on the associations among various raw materials, classes of artifacts, and ideology in the Thule culture of Arctic Canada.

12. Occasionally, Neolithic sites in Greece have yielded a number of stone figurines. For example, five stone examples (and no clay pieces) reportedly came from the site of Koufovouno near Sparta. Phthiotic Thebes produced 11 LN marble examples and, to my knowledge, no clay images (Hourmouziadis 1973:27). The anthropological literature suggests that stone, unlike clay, often holds certain status among various societies cross-culturally. Instances of hierarchical significance attached to various raw materials are not uncommon among ethnographic societies today (Allison 1968:45; Biebuyck 1973:165; Greub 1988:88), and such preferences may have existed in antiquity.

13. Sexless figurines are recorded among a number of ethnographic collections. For example, most of the so-called "nkisi" figurines, a type of anthropomorphic image known over a wide region of west equatorial Africa, are intentionally designed as asexual. These protective spirits are used in a variety of rituals, including initiation rites and medical curing ceremonies (Greub 1988:38 ff.).

14. The half-body pendants, which are briefly discussed in this study, are reported in Jacobsen 1973b and Schaeffer 1977.

15. Other examples of deliberate breakage are occasionally reported in the literature on Stone Age figurines from the Mediterranean and the Near East. Several burials at Tell es-Sawwan (Level I) contained headless figurines. The excavators suggest that, while the figurines could have broken accidentally at the weak and narrow juncture of the neck, the fact that no separate heads were found in the graves suggests that the heads were intentionally broken off and removed prior to placing the figurines in the burials (Oates 1966:151). Recent reports from Kissonerga in Cyprus also suggest that figurines may have been broken prior to deposit in certain contexts (Peltenburg 1988, 1991).

16. Pat Getz-Preziosi has demonstrated that various ratios on EC II idols may be used to identify individual hands or master sculptors. Ucko's work on pin figures from predynastic Egypt suggests that ratios can be used to determine sex (Ucko 1968:174).

17. Ratios are recorded for the few complete stone figurines from southern Greece. The results suggest that similar canons may have been employed at widely separated sites (see Chapter 5).

18. See above, nn. 6 and 7.

19. Like the Munsell Soil Color Charts, the Mohs Scale is not an ideal system for measuring attributes of archaeological objects. Recent work in the New World has employed a method which is not only more precise than the Mohs Scale but appears better suited to the kinds of problems often encountered in archaeological research: indentation hardness testing (Simon and Coghlan 1989). This technique was not known to me until after the research for this volume was completed.

20. Recent excavations at a cave in Peru, where conditions allowed for remarkable preservation, produced a number of figurines with clothing and jewelry still intact. The figurines themselves often lacked marks that might indicate sex, although the clothes usually allowed for such determinations (Joyce Marcus, pers. comm. 1989).

Ethnographic evidence also supports the suggestion that the sex of a figurine may be signaled by distinct features which are culturally, not biologically, associated with sexual identification. For example, a number of ancestor and spirit figurines from Indonesia indicate sex by special kinds of hair knots, or earrings placed in one ear or the other. Certain gestures and postures may also reveal the sex of an image (Greub 1988:238).

21. Similar kinds of questions have been asked of the EBA stone figurines. See Oustinoff 1984 for an interesting experimental approach to the carving of EC II stone idols.

22. A torso from Thespiae in Boeotia is a good example of this technique (Bass 1959:Figure 1). Gimbutas has also reported on the additive process involved in manufacturing figurines from Achilleion (Gimbutas et al. 1989:171–174). In addition, examples from Servia (Ridley and Rhomiopoulou 1972; Ridley and Wardle 1979) and Nea Nikomedeia (Rodden 1962, 1964, 1965) were often constructed out of separate pieces, some of which were pegged or dowelled together.

23. Though probably not the only way to replicate this distinctive configuration, it does successfully reproduce the leg sockets visible on FC 42.

24. I would like to thank Dr. K. D. Vitelli for this discovery. She designed a clay figurine similar to FC 190, into which she stuck a shell head. Although rare, clay figurines with detachable stone heads (so-called acrolithic figurines) are known from northern Greece, primarily from the Late or Final Neolithic (see Wace and Thompson 1912:49, Figure 25; Tsountas 1908:Plates 34:1, 35:1).

25. Cone shells are often reported from Neolithic and Bronze Age contexts in Greece (Reese 1982). For a full study of marine molluscs from Franchthi Cave, see Shackleton 1988.

26. Small thumb-size depressions occur at the breaks on figures other than FC 208. Both FC 12 and FC 57 have slightly rounded concavities on their medial breaks, and FC 41 reveals a noticeable depression at the neck break. The purpose of these depressions is not known, and they need not all have served the same function.

Experiments conducted by students at Indiana University during a class on ancient technology revealed that figurine heads modeled separately and then attached to the body frequently became detached during the drying process. For reasons which are not completely clear, heads adhered best to the body when a small hole or depression was poked in the base of the neck prior to attachment (Vitelli, pers. comm. 1990).

27. In some cultures, the method by which an artifact is created holds great significance and may, in fact, be seen as more important than the final product (Crowley 1973:228; Fernandez 1973:212–214). This issue is touched upon by Broman in reference to the figurines from Jarmo (Broman 1958; Morales 1990). Broman argues that the more realistic anthropomorphic and zoomorphic images were "personal wishes," with the desire expressed in the *modeling* of the form. She suggests that a figure was "either dried, fired and kept until the wish was fulfilled, or was discarded after manufacture (before drying), squashed and other misshapen forms attesting to this latter practice and denoting perhaps some failure, inadequacy or else a short term wish fulfillment" (Broman 1958:74).

28. Clay appears in many creation myths as the substance from which the world's first inhabitants were modeled (Joyce 1988:383). The reasons for this choice are open to debate, though it may be related to the interest that certain cultures had in the transformative qualities of clay.

29. Pat Getz-Preziosi has argued convincingly that EC figurines were laid out according to a variety of canons, some quite complex (Getz-Preziosi 1972, 1977, 1987). The existence of compa-

rable canons prior to the Bronze Age is also possible (see Chapter 5; Talalay 1983a:129, 185; Talalay 1983b).

30. In her experiments on the manufacture of Cycladic figurines, Oustinoff has observed that obsidian blades work well not only for incising, but also for shaving. She writes that shaving with obsidian "is convenient for eliminating shallow abrasion marks and for removing stone from narrow or confined areas" (Oustinoff 1984:39).

31. The abrasive properties of emery (a form of corundum) are ideal for working stone. Some of the earliest evidence in Greece for the use of emery derives from the LN site of Saliagos, where excavations recovered more than 30 emery axes, most of which probably came from a Naxian source (Evans and Renfrew 1968:65–66; Oosterom 1968:99–100; Oustinoff 1984:39, 43, n. 3).

32. A recent definition of preindustrial economic specialists, which aims to be archaeologically operational, is offered by Abrams (1987:486). Specialists are "those individuals who fill socioeconomic positions within which the specific and primary role is to produce and supply goods and/or services designed to meet a specific demand created by individuals who themselves do not produce or supply such goods and/or services."

33. The Munsell readings for MN and LN figures also suggest some degree of control over production (see Appendix C). Surface colors or painted decorations on several of the MN examples are virtually identical or nearly the same. The LN figures show comparable similarities in surface color and paint.

34. Both Vitelli (1974) and Cullen (1985a-b) have suggested that during the Middle Neolithic the main potters at settlements in the northeastern Peloponnese were women. The ceramic homogeneity observed among a number of sites in that region has been tentatively attributed to exogamous practices; the circulation and relocation of women potters within such a system would have provided the necessary mechanisms for the instruction and interaction among potters from various villages. Movement of women among villages would have been occasioned not only by marriage, but by divorce or widowhood (David et al. 1988:368).

35. Firing clouds rarely appear on any of the Franchthi examples, or, for that matter, on any figurines from southern Greece. The absence of clouding indicates that the figurines were protected from direct contact with the fuel source (Shepard 1956:76), and it is possible that, prior to firing, they were placed in open-mouthed vessels. Such a procedure would protect these small images from larger vessels which might otherwise crush them. It would also make it easy to find the figurines after the firing was complete (see Vitelli 1974:23 on the stacking of Neolithic pots for firing).

36. The ultimate choice of the figurine-maker(s) within the Franchthi settlement was probably linked to the purpose of a given figurine. The anthropological literature reveals that in societies which do not usually employ permanent, full-time specialists, a variety of people may be selected or self-appointed to manufacture anthropomorphic or zoomorphic images. The choice often depends on the figurine's function.

Among the Bantu, for example, initiation figurines are manufactured by a fairly random selection of male and female adults (some being the parents of the initiates), who are appointed as overseers for the novices (Cory 1956:32). The figures' preparation, which is not associated with specific ceremonies, takes place in gay, casual gatherings. In contrast, initiation images used by both the Bemba and the Lega are carved by more restricted groups. Among the Bemba, figures are modeled by the mistress of ceremonies (usually a midwife with status in the community) and a few select helpers (Richards 1956:57). The Lega artists work in semi-secrecy, creating their figures in small, guarded hamlets away from the main villages (Biebuyck 1973:229). Navaho images, which are made for use in ceremonies designed to maintain and restore health, are created by either the "singer" who is hired to perform the ritual or by a member of the sick person's family, who carves the figure while the singer acts as overseer (Kelly et al. 1972:62). Finally, clay figurines used as dolls or toys are frequently reported in the ethnographic literature. These images may be produced by various people within the community, including children. According to Fortes, making clay figurines is a favorite diversion of small boys and adolescents among the Talensi. He notes, "many boys. . .take such delight in [modeling clay figures] that they devote the whole dry season to producing dozens of clay figures for themselves, brothers and sisters and friends. Gifted boys model extremely carefully." (Fortes 1938:60).

37. Imbedded within the definition of "use" are both active and passive implications. A figurine which sits on a shelf and whose very presence is considered effective in a given situation would be defined as having a passive usage. On the other hand, figurines which are manipulated and altered in any way during a rite or ceremony are more properly defined as having active usages. Prehistoric figurines probably served both active and passive roles in society.

38. Some meanings may be quite subtle and defy recovery by archaeologists, while others may be more openly expressed.

39. Ucko uses similar categories in his analysis of prehistoric figurines. His categories include: "1) features of the figurines themselves; 2) the archaeological contexts of the figurines; 3) relevant historic practices from the areas concerned as well as similar ethnographic practices" (Ucko 1968:427).

40. A number of these functions were initially discussed by Ucko in his pioneering works of the 1960s; the reader is directed to his Ph.D. dissertation and his book on anthropomorphic figurines.

41. This scenario does not preclude the possibility that some of the figurines found in these contexts (e.g., the split-leg example) served other functions as well. Ethnographic evidence demonstrates that figurines can have multiple uses, shifting from one to another as circumstances demand (Greub 1988:72).

42. Gimbutas has focused much of her thinking on deciphering the meaning of Neolithic figurines in "Old Europe" (Gimbutas 1982, 1986). While I do not agree with many of her conclusions and, indeed, wonder whether we can ever understand the "shorthanded allusiveness" (Gimbutas 1986:229) of these objects, she does provide a number of interesting and provocative insights. Moreover, she correctly stresses that these miniature forms are highly charged symbolic images and that more attention is often devoted to the "proper placement of fortifying and appropriate symbols" than to the realistic rendering of details of the human form (Gimbutas 1986:226). Gimbutas's statement about the figurines at Sitagroi may be applicable to other Neolithic sites as well: in the production of figurines "symbols took precedence over body portrayal" (1986:263).

43. Although archaeologists in the Mediterranean have yet to wrestle successfully with the complexity of sign systems—particularly how they are operationalized and how prehistorians might make inferences about the manifold meanings of symbols—there does exist an enormous body of interesting and provocative literature in anthropology that reveals important understandings about signs, symbols, and semiotics. Of particular interest are the writings of Clifford Geertz (1966), Victor Turner (1967, 1969, 1974, 1975), Mary Douglas (1970), Paul Ricoeur (1972), Foster and Brandes (1980), and Caroline Walker Bynum et al. (1986). While there is no general consensus in these works on the nature of symbol, they offer stimulating insights that Mediterranean prehistorians may be able to utilize at some point in their probings into the possible meanings of anthropomorphic images.

44. One of the most common postures found on Neolithic figurines throughout Greece is that of arms folded across the chest. Interestingly, this same position is repeatedly found in the human burials of the Greek Neolithic (Hourmouziadis 1973:211). Whether the repetition of nearly identical postures among both the figurines and the dead is connected in any way remains to be determined.

45. To my knowledge, the depiction of dismembered body parts is rarely part of the Neolithic repertoire farther north. The few exceptions appear at Sitagroi, Sesklo, and Karamoular. The example from Sitagroi portrays the lower part of a female (Gimbutas 1986:297, cat. no. 151, Figure 9.51, Plate LIV:4); the pieces from Sesklo and Karamoular are similar to FC 122, representing the lower half of the human form or possibly half a buttocks (Theocharis 1973:Plates XXII:4d, f; Wijnen 1982:Figures 14:12, 14:19).

46. Ethnographic reports suggest that left–right bodily divisions are more frequent than upper–lower divisions. See Needham 1973 for an interesting collection of essays on the importance of left–right symbols and dual classifications among cultures. See also Corballis 1980 and Ellen 1977.

47. The structure within which the five figurines were found also contained stone axes, several unusual clay vessels, hundreds of unworked blades, and clay rondels. Although Rodden (1964, 1965) and others have labeled the building a shrine, it may more correctly be viewed as a council house or civic structure for corporate activities. Ethnographic evidence suggests that village planning among small, nonindustrialized settlements frequently displays one or more distinctive structures surrounded by a number of smaller, plainer buildings (as is the case at Nea Nikomedeia). In many of those instances, the larger edifices represent men's clubhouses or the local headman's hut (Fraser 1968). The clubhouses serve social as well as economic and sacred functions, and the villagers gather there for sacred rites, ceremonies, and dancing, as well as to discuss important issues such as marriage, residence, and inheritance. The Nea Nikomedeia structure may have served a similar function, with the figurines serving in an array of special ceremonies.

48. Ideally, comparative studies should also include a precise definition of diversity in the archaeological record and a program for measuring and/or quantifying variability within and between collections. These issues are a matter of debate in the archaeological literature (see Leonard and Jones 1988).

49. Several classificatory systems for prehistoric figurines appear in the literature. One of the earliest is that of Clarence L. Hay in the early 1900s (unpublished), which was later revised and elaborated on by George C. Vaillant (1930). More recent endeavors include those of Parsons (1972), Drennan (1976), and Bartel (1981).

50. While Neolithic remains in Attica, the Peloponnese, and the Cyclades often display stylistic similarities, northern and southern Greek objects exhibit much less conformity. Ultimately, a detailed comparison between the figurines from the two regions would be valuable, but such an undertaking is beyond the scope of this study. References to northern Greece which appear in this chapter are made selectively and are based on published material, which represents a small percentage of the known sample.

It is important to bear in mind that regional studies in Greece are subject to bias. Our present knowledge of the Neolithic is based largely on sites chosen for excavation, not after detailed surveys established them as representative, but, in most cases, because of accidental discovery or promising surface finds (Efstratiou 1985:87). A regional study on the variability of Neolithic figurines inevitably is written within the shadow of that bias.

51. Sun-baking, rather than firing, figurines is not without ethnographic support. Certain African tribes today rely upon arid conditions to preserve clay images for as long as they are needed, obviating the necessity of firing (Vitelli, pers. comm. 1989). The dry climate in southern Greece during the summer months and the low level of precipitation throughout most other seasons would have provided good conditions for sun-baking during at least part of the year.

52. Not only are certain classes of MN figurines common throughout the northeastern Peloponnese, but a few isolated and curious attributes recur at select settlements. For example, the punctated pubis on FC 12 also appears on an example from site 702 near Nemea (Cherry et al.

1988:Figure 9); and the small, plastic pellet on the back of the same piece from Franchthi is duplicated on L6.100 from Lerna (Caskey 1958:Plate 36). Also, as discussed in the section on design, some of the painted decorations on MN figurines from Franchthi and Corinth are strikingly similar.

53. Although I have assumed that each site had its own figurine-makers who communicated with one another, it is also possible that the homogeneity among MN images is due to itinerant figurine-makers or to the circulation of the images themselves.

54. It is difficult to understand the nature of the bonds which may have linked Franchthi with settlements farther north. Although transhumance, exogamous marriage policies, trading alliances, and nonresidential sodalities may explain contacts and communication among communities in the northeastern Peloponnese, they seem unlikely explanations for villages like Franchthi and Sesklo, which are separated by substantial distance and difficult terrain, and show virtually no similarities in other classes of material remains. Explanations which stress intermittent or irregular forms of contact may be more suitable and should be sought.

55. No one, as far as I know, however, has conducted an exhaustive search for similarities between northern and southern Greek sites.

56. Face-pots are reported among several African tribes. The Suku of Zaire use them as drinking vessels. A sign of office, these pots serve as a symbol of transmission of authority (Greub 1988:80).

57. The LN dating of Type C is based on the fact that both the example from Saliagos (Sal. 5) and the fragment from Corinth (MF 8504) can be securely dated to the Late Neolithic. Moreover, limited exposures and/or surveys on Amorgos and Naxos, where other Type C examples were found, indicate that these islands were not visited or occupied before the later part of the Neolithic.

58. The seeming rarity of painted decoration on both the FN pottery and figurines of southern Greece may be misleading. FN potters were apparently partial to a thick, whitish paint that may have been applied *after* firing. Since the paint is fugitive, most of the original design may have flaked off over the millennia.

59. Given some ambiguities in the data, it is difficult to decide whether the figurines were originally intended as grave offerings or, like some of the other material remains in the cemetery, were part of the debris that must have been continually making its way downslope from the settlement (Coleman 1977:53). While both suggestions are defensible, the possible occurrence of figure 202 *within* grave 38 suggests that at least one of the figurines was purposely set alongside the deceased. Moreover, excavation reports make it clear that the offering of goods (mostly vessels) to the dead was indeed practiced at Kephala, albeit infrequently. The giving of figurines could certainly have been part of the practice. Finally, the only figurine possibly associated with the settlement (Coleman 1977:Figure 96B) is significantly larger than any of those recovered from the cemetery, suggesting that certain kinds of figurines were designed for sepulchral use and others for domestic use. Figurines are occasionally reported in cemeteries or burials farther north, such as the cremations at Plateia Zarkou (Gallis 1982).

60. Ancestor images are reported among a number of groups, including the Dogon, the Edo, the Hebbe (Ucko 1962:782–783), the Bambara (Plass 1956:16), the Bokota (Segy 1958:19), the Mumuye (Fagg 1977:29–30), the Fang (Greub 1988:34), and various groups of Indonesia (Greub 1988:178, 216, 238).

61. The source of the copper is not known, though Paros, Syros, and Lavrion have been proposed (Coleman 1977:108; see also Gale and Stos-Gale 1981 and Muhly 1985 for a general discussion on the development of Bronze Age metallurgy in the Aegean).

62. Neither "religion" nor "ritual" are well defined in the archaeological literature. To date, the most systematic and archaeologically useful discussion is that of Renfrew (1985:Chapter 1).

63. Gimbutas does point out, however, that representations of certain types of deities seem confined to household shrines, while other, distinctly different, goddesses are limited to the more public (?) courtyard platforms (Gimbutas et al. 1989:219–220).

64. J. Chapman proposes that figurine production at some Vinča sites was a craft for specialists: "Whilst household production is likely in small villages with little ritual specialisation, ritual centers such as Vinča, Turdaş, Potporanj, and Zorlenţu Mare are likely to have relied on part-time specialists. Similarly, the distinction between low-quality and well-finished figurines. . .is suggestive of different modes of production" (1981:119–120).

65. As used here, contamination refers to the existence of modern or twentieth-century cultural materials within a unit.

66. Lotting, which was by and large abandoned at Franchthi after the first season, consists of combining potsherds from stratigraphically adjacent units. An attendant decision was made to inventory the larger, better preserved, most representative, or most unusual sherds and discard the rest, which could represent 75–95% of the total (see Vitelli, forthcoming).

REFERENCES

Abrams, Elliot M.

1987 Economic Specialization and Construction Personnel in Classic Period Copan, Honduras. *American Antiquity* 52:485–499.

Acquaviva, Marcus Cláudio

1977 *Vodu: Religião e Magia Negra no Haiti e no Brasil.* 2d ed., rev. and enl. Aquarius, São Paulo.

Allison, Philip

1968 *African Stone Sculpture.* Praeger, New York.

Ascher, Robert

1961 Analogy in Archaeological Interpretation. *Southwestern Journal of Anthropology* 17:317–325.

Bartel, Brad

1981 Cultural Associations and Mechanisms of Change in Anthropomorphic Figurines during the Neolithic in the Eastern Mediterranean Basin. *World Archaeology* 13:73–86.

Bass, George

1959 Neolithic Figurines from Thespiai. *Hesperia* 28:344–349.

Béart, Charles

1955 Jeux et jouets de l'Ouest africain. *Mémoires de l'Institut français d'Afrique noire*, no. 42 (2 vols.).

Bent, J. Theodore

1884 Researches Among the Cyclades. *Journal of Hellenic Studies* 5:42–58.

Bergsma, Harold M.

1973 Tiv *Kuraiyol,* Body Protectors. *Africa* 43:147–152.

Biebuyck, Daniel P.

1973 *Lega Culture; Art, Initiation, and Moral Philosophy among a Central African People.* University of California Press, Berkeley.

Binford, Lewis R.

1971 Mortuary Practices: Their Study and Their Potential. In *Approaches to the Social Dimensions of Mortuary Practices*, edited by James A. Brown, pp. 6–29. Memoirs of the Society for American Archaeology, no. 25. The Society, Washington.

1972 Smudge Pits and Hide Smoking: The Use of Analogy in Archaeological Reasoning. In *An Archaeological Perspective*, edited by L. R. Binford, pp. 33–51. Seminar Press, New York.

Bintliff, John L.

1977 *Natural Environment and Human Settlement in Prehistoric Greece.* BAR Supplementary Series, vol. 28. British Archaeological Reports, Oxford.

Blacking, John (editor)

1977 *The Anthropology of the Body.* A.S.A. Monographs, vol. 15. Academic Press, New York.

Bloch, Maurice

1971 *Placing the Dead: Tombs, Ancestral Villages and Kinship Organization in Madagascar.* Seminar Press, London.

Broman, Vivian L.
1958 Jarmo Figurines. Master's thesis, Radcliffe College, Cambridge.
Broneer, Oscar
1939 A Mycenaean Fountain on the Athenian Acropolis. *Hesperia* 8:317–433.
Broodbank, Cyprian, and Thomas F. Strasser
1991 Migrant Farmers and the Neolithic Colonization of Crete. *Antiquity* 65:233–245.
Brown, J. A.
1981 The Search for Rank in Prehistoric Burials. In *The Archaeology of Death*, edited by R. Chapman, I. Kinnes, and K. Randsborg, pp. 25–37. Cambridge University Press, Cambridge.
Buck, P. H. (Te Rangi Hiroa)
1930 *Samoan Material Culture*. Bernice P. Bishop Museum Bulletin No. 75. The Museum, Honolulu.
Bynum, Caroline W., Stevan Harrel, and Paula Richman (editors)
1986 *Gender and Religion: On the Complexity of Symbols*. Beacon Press, Boston.
Cabrera, Lydia
1971 *El Monte, Igbo, Finda, Ewe, Orisha, Vititi Nfinda*. 3d ed. C. R., Miami, Florida.
Carrington Smith, Jill
1972 Evidence for Spinning and Weaving at Franchthi Cave. Manuscript on file, Program in Classical Archaeology, Indiana University, Bloomington.
Caskey, John L.
1958 Excavations at Lerna, 1957. *Hesperia* 27:125–144
Caskey, John L., and Mary Eliot
1956 A Neolithic Figurine from Lerna. *Hesperia* 25:174–77.
Chapman, J. C.
1981 *The Vinča Culture of South-East Europe*. 2 vols. BAR International Series, vol. 117. British Archaeological Reports, Oxford.
Chapman, R.
1981 The Emergence of Formal Disposal Areas and the 'Problem' of Megalithic Tombs in Prehistoric Europe. In *The Archaeology of Death*, edited by R. Chapman, I. Kinnes, and K. Randsborg, pp. 71–81. Cambridge University Press, Cambridge.
Cherry, John F.
1981 Pattern and Process in the Earliest Colonisation of the Mediterranean Islands. *Proceedings of the Prehistoric Society* 47:41–68.
1988 Pastoralism and the Role of Animals in the Pre- and Protohistoric Economies of the Aegean. In *Pastoral Economies in Classical Antiquity*, edited by C. R. Whittaker, pp. 6–34. Supplemental Volume 14. The Cambridge Philological Society, Cambridge.
Cherry, John F., Jack L. Davis, Anne Demitrack, Eleni Mantzourani, Thomas F. Strasser, and Lauren E. Talalay
1988 Archaeological Survey in an Artifact-Rich Landscape: A Middle Neolithic Example from Nemea, Greece. *American Journal of Archaeology* 92:159–176.
Cherry, John F., Jack L. Davis, Eleni Mantzourani
1991 *Landscape Archaeology as Long-Term History: Northern Keos in the Cycladic Islands*. Monumenta Archaeologica 16. Institute of Archaeology, University of California, Los Angeles.
Clarke, David
1973 Archaeology: The Loss of Innocence. *Antiquity* 47:6–18.
Coleman, John E.
1977 *Keos*. Vol. 1, *Kephala: A Late Neolithic Settlement and Cemetery*. The American School of Classical Studies, Princeton.

Conkey, Margaret W.

1983 On the Origins of Paleolithic Art: A Review and Some Critical Thoughts. In *The Mousterian Legacy: Human Biocultural Change in the Upper Pleistocene*, edited by E. Trinkaus, pp. 201–227. BAR International Series, vol. 164. British Archaeological Reports, Oxford.

Corballis, Michael C.

1980 Laterality and Myth. *American Psychologist* 35:284–295.

Cory, Hans

1956 *African Figurines: Their Ceremonial Use in Puberty Rites in Tanganyika*. Grove Press, New York.

Crowley, Daniel J.

1973 Aesthetic Value and Professionalism in African Art: Three Cases from the Katanga Chokwe. In *The Traditional Artist in African Societies*, edited by W. L. d'Azevedo, pp. 221–249. Indiana University Press, Bloomington.

Cullen, Tracey

1985a A Measure of Interaction among Neolithic Communities: Design Elements of Greek Urfirnis Pottery. Ph.D. dissertation, Program in Classical Archaeology, Indiana University, Bloomington.

1985b Social Implications of Ceramic Style in the Neolithic Peloponnese. In *Ancient Technology to Modern Science*, edited by W. D. Kingery, pp. 77–100. The American Ceramic Society, Columbus, Ohio.

Cullen, T., A. P. Grimanis, M. Vassilaki-Grimani, F. Pomoni-Papaioannou, and R. E. Jones

1984 Neolithic Urfirnis in the Northeastern Peloponnese: Physico-chemical and Design Analyses. Paper delivered at the First Southern European Conference on Archaeometery, Delphi, Greece.

Culwick, A. T., and G. M. Culwick

1934 Treatment of Fits by the Wambunga. *Man* 34:156.

1935 *Ubena of the Rivers*. G. Allen & Unwin, London.

Daux, Georges

1962 Dikili-Tach (Chronique des fouilles 1961). *Bulletin de correspondance hellénique* 86:912–933.

1968 Dikili Tach (Chronique des fouilles 1967). *Bulletin de correspondance hellénique* 92:1062–1077.

David, Nicholas, Judy Sterner, and Kodzo Gavua

1988 Why Pots are Decorated. *Current Anthropology* 29:365–389.

Decle, Lionel

1898 *Three Years in Savage Africa*. Methuen & Co., London.

Delporte, Henri

1979 *L'image de la femme dans l'art préhistorique*. Picard, Paris.

Deshayes, Jean

1970 Dikili Tash (Travaux de l'école française en 1969). *Bulletin de correspondance hellénique* 94:799–808.

Diamant, Steven R.

1974a The Later Village Farming Stage in Southern Greece. Ph.D. dissertation, Department of Classical Archaeology, University of Pennsylvania, Philadelphia.

1974b A Prehistoric Figurine from Mycenae. *Annual of the British School at Athens* 69:103–107.

Douglas, Mary T.

1970 *Natural Symbols: Explorations in Cosmology*. Barrie & Rockliff, The Cresset Press, London.

Drennan, Robert D.

1976 *Fábrica San José and Middle Formative Society in the Valley of Oaxaca.* Memoirs of the Museum of Anthropology No. 8, University of Michigan, Ann Arbor.

Dumarest, Noel

1919 *Notes on Cochiti, New Mexico.* Translated and edited by Elsie Clews Parsons. *Memoirs of the American Anthropological Association* 6:137–236. Published for the Association, Lancaster, Pa.

Durkheim, Émile

1915 *The Elementary Forms of the Religious Life: A Study in Religious Sociology.* Translated by J. W. Swain. G. Allen & Unwin, London.

Earthy, Emily Dora

1933 *Valenge Women of Portuguese East Africa.* Oxford University Press, London.

Ebin, Victoria

1979 *The Body Decorated.* Thames and Hudson, London

Efstratiou, Nikos

1985 *Agios Petros: A Neolithic Site in the Northern Sporades.* BAR International Series, vol. 241. British Archaeological Reports, Oxford.

Ehrenreich, Paul M. A.

1891 *Beiträge zur Völkerkunde Brasiliens.* Veröffentlichungen aus dem Königlichen Museum für Völkerkunde, vol. 2. W. Spemann, Berlin.

Eijgenraam, Felix, and Alun Anderson

1991 A Window on Life in the Bronze Age. *Science* 254:187–188.

Elisofon, Eliot, and William B. Fagg

1958 *The Sculpture of Africa.* Praeger, New York.

Ellen, Roy F.

1977 Anatomical Classification and the Semiotics of the Body. In *The Anthropology of the Body*, edited by John Blacking, pp. 343–374. Association of Social Anthropologists Monograph 15. Academic Press, New York.

Erlenmeyer, M. L., and H. Erlenmeyer

1960 Über Philister und Kreter. I. *Orientalia*, n.s. 29:121–150.

Evans, J. D., and C. Renfrew

1968 *Excavations at Saliagos near Antiparos.* British School of Archaeology at Athens, Supplementary Volume 5. Thames & Hudson, London.

Evans-Pritchard, E. E.

1937 Economic Life of the Nuer: Cattle. *Sudan Notes and Records* 20 (pt. 2): 209–245.

Fagg, William B.

1977 *The Tribal Image: Wooden Figure Sculpture of the World.* 2d ed. British Museum, Department of Ethnography, London.

Faris, James C.

1972 *Nuba Personal Art.* Duckworth, London.

Fernandez, James

1973 The Exposition and Imposition of Order: Artistic Expression in Fang Culture. In *The Traditional Artist in African Societies*, edited by W. L. d'Azevedo, pp. 194–220. Indiana University Press, Bloomington and Indianapolis.

Fewkes, J. Walter

1923 Clay Figurines Made by Navaho Children. *American Anthropologist* 25:559–563.

Firth, Cecil M.

1927 *The Archeological Survey of Nubia: Report for 1910–1911.* Government Press, Cairo.

Firth, Raymond W.
1973 *Symbols: Public and Private*. George Allen & Unwin, London.
Fitton, J. L. (editor)
1984 *Cycladica: Studies in Memory of N. P. Goulandris*. Proceedings of the 7th British Museum Classical Colloquium, June 1983. British Museum Publications, London.
Flannery, Kent V., and Marcus C. Winter
1976 Analyzing Household Activities. In *The Early Mesoamerican Village*, edited by K. V. Flannery, pp. 34–47. Academic Press, New York.
Fortes, M.
1938 Social and Psychological Aspects of Education in Taleland. *Africa* 11, supp. (4): 5–64.
Foster, Mary L., and Stanley H. Brandes (editors)
1980 *Symbol as Sense: New Approaches to the Analysis of Meaning*. Academic Press, New York.
Fox, A. Lane
1878 Observations on Mr. Man's Collection of Andamanese and Nicobarese Objects. *Journal of the Anthropological Institute of Great Britain and Ireland* 7:433–469.
Fraser, Douglas
1968 *Village Planning in the Primitive World.* Braziller, New York.
Frazer, J. G.
1922 *The Golden Bough.* 12 vols., 3d ed., rev. and enl. Macmillan, London.
Freeman, L. G., Jr.
1968 A Theoretical Framework for Interpreting Archeological Materials. In *Man the Hunter*, edited by R. B. Lee and I. DeVore, pp. 262–267. Aldine Publishing Co., Chicago.
Gale N. H., and Z. A. Stos-Gale
1981 Cycladic Lead and Silver Metallurgy. *Annual of the British School at Athens* 76:169–224.
Galles, Konstantinos I. (See Gallis, Kostas J.)
Gallis, Kostas J.
1982 *Kauseis Nekron apo te Neolithike Epoche ste Thessalia* (summary in English). Demosieumata tou Archaiologikou deltiou, vol. 30. Ekdose Tameiou Archaiologikon Poron kai Apollotrioseon, Athens.
1985 A Late Neolithic Foundation Offering from Thessaly. *Antiquity* 59:20–24.
1987 Die stratigraphische Einordnung der Larisa-Kultur: eine Richtigstellung. *Prähistorische Zeitschrift* 62:148–163.
Gamble, Clive
1982 Interaction and Alliance in Palaeolithic Society. *Man* 17:92–107.
Geertz, Clifford
1966 *Religion as a Cultural System.* In *Anthropological Approaches to the Study of Religion*, edited by Michael Banton, pp. 1–46. A.S.A. Monographs, vol. 3. Tavistock Publications, London .
Getz-Preziosi, Pat
1972 Traditional Canon and Individual Hand in Early Cycladic Sculpture. Ph.D. dissertation, Harvard University, Cambridge.
1977 Cycladic Sculptors and Their Methods. In *Art and Culture of the Cyclades in the Third Millennium*, edited by Jürgen Thimme, translated and edited by Pat Getz-Preziosi, pp. 71–91. University of Chicago Press, Chicago and London.
1987 *Sculptors of the Cyclades: Individual and Tradition in the Third Millennium B.C.* University of Michigan Press, Ann Arbor.

Gimbutas, Marija A.
1974a *The Gods and Goddesses of Old Europe: 7000 to 3500 BC, Myths, Legends, and Cult Images*. University of California Press, Berkeley.
1974b Achilleion: A Neolithic Mound in Thessaly; Preliminary Report on 1973 and 1974 Excavations. *Journal of Field Archaeology* 1:277–302.
1980 The Temples of Old Europe. *Archaeology* 33 (6): 41–50.
1982 *The Goddesses and Gods of Old Europe, 6500–3500 BC, Myths and Cult Images*. University of California Press, Berkeley.
1986 Mythical Imagery of Sitagroi Society. In *Excavations at Sitagroi*, vol. 1, edited by C. Renfrew, M. Gimbutas, and E. S. Elster, pp. 225–301. Monumenta Archaeologica 13. Institute of Archaeology, University of California, Los Angeles.

Gimbutas, Marija, Shan Winn, and Daniel Shimabuku
1989 *Achilleion: A Neolithic Settlement in Thessaly, Greece, 6400–5600 B.C.* Monumenta Archaeologica 14. Institute of Archaeology, University of California, Los Angeles.

Goldstein, Lynne G.
1976 *Spatial Structure and Social Organization: Regional Manifestations of Mississippian Society*. Ph.D. dissertation, Department of Anthropology, Northwestern University. University Microfilms, Ann Arbor.

Gould, Richard A.
1978 Beyond Analogy in Ethnoarchaeology. In *Explorations in Ethnoarchaeology*, edited by R. Gould, pp. 249–293. University of New Mexico Press, Albuquerque.

Gould, Richard A., and Patty J. Watson
1982 A Dialogue on the Meaning and Use of Analogy in Ethnoarchaeological Reasoning. *Journal of Anthropological Archaeology* 1:355–381.

Greub, Suzanne (editor)
1988 *Expressions of Belief: Masterpieces of African, Oceanic, and Indonesian Art from the Museum voor Volkenkunde, Rotterdam*. Rizzoli, New York.

Griaule, Marcel
1965 *Conversations with Ogotemmeli; An Introduction to Dogon Religious Ideas*. Oxford University Press, London.

Haile, Berard
1947 *Navaho Sacrificial Figurines*. University of Chicago Press, Chicago.

Halstead, Paul
1981 Counting Sheep in Neolithic and Bronze Age Greece. In *Pattern of the Past: Studies in Honour of David Clarke*, edited by I. Hodder, G. Isaac, and N. Hammond, pp. 307–339. Cambridge University Press, Cambridge.
1987a Man and Other Animals in Later Greek Prehistory. *Annual of the British School at Athens* 82:71–83.
1987b Traditional and Ancient Rural Economy in Mediterranean Europe: Plus ça Change? *Journal of Hellenic Studies* 107:77–87.

Halstead, Paul, and John O'Shea (editors)
1989 *Bad-Year Economics: Cultural Responses to Risk and Uncertainty*. Cambridge University Press, Cambridge.

Hambly, Wilfrid D.
1925 *The History of Tattooing and Its Significance*. H. F. & G. Witherby, London.

Hantman, Jeffrey L., and Stephen Plog
1982 The Relationship of Stylistic Similarity to Patterns of Material Exchange. In *Contexts*

for Prehistoric Exchange, edited by Jonathon E. Ericson and Timothy K. Earle, pp. 237–263. Academic Press, New York.

Hardin, M. A.

1977 Individual Style in San José Pottery Painting: The Role of Deliberate Choice. In *The Individual in Prehistory: Studies of Variability in Style in Prehistoric Technologies*, edited by J. N. Hill and J. Gunn, pp. 109–136. Academic Press, New York.

Harding, J. R.

1961 'Mwali' Dolls of the Wazaramo. *Man* 61:72–73.

Hauptmann, Harald

1971 Das Festland und die kleineren Inseln: Steinzeit, besonders Neolithikum *Archäologischer Anzeiger* 86:348–387.

Hawley, Florence M.

1950 Mechanics of Perpetuation of Pueblo Witchcraft. In *For the Dean; Essays in Anthropology in Honor of Byron Cummings on His Eighty-Ninth Birthday, September 20, 1950*, edited by E. K. Reed and D. S. King, pp. 143–148. Hohokam Museums Association and the Southwestern Monuments Association, Santa Fe, New Mexico: Tucson, Arizona.

Herz, Norman, and David B. Wenner

1978 Assembly of Greek Marble Inscriptions by Isotopic Methods. *Science* 199:1070–1072.

Hellstrom, Pontus

1987 *Paradeisos: A Late Neolithic Settlement in Aegean Thrace*. Medelhavsmuseet, Memoir 7, Stockholm.

Himmelheber, Hans

1960 *Negerkunst und Negerkünstler*. Bibliothek für Kunst- und Antiquitatenfreunde, vol. 40. Klinckhardt & Biermann, Braunschweig.

Hodder, Ian

1978 The Maintenance of Group Identities in the Baringo District, Western Kenya. In *Social Organisation and Settlement: Contributions from Anthropology, Archaeology, and Geography*, edited by David Green, Colin Haselgrove, and Matthew Spriggs, pp. 47–74. BAR Supplemental Series, vol. 47 (i). British Archaeological Reports, Oxford.

1979 Economic and Social Stress and Material Culture Patterning. *American Antiquity* 44:446–454.

1981 Society, Economy and Culture: An Ethnographic Case Study amongst the Lozi. In *Pattern of the Past: Studies in Honour of David Clarke*, edited by I. Hodder, G. Isaac, and N. Hammond, pp. 67–95. Cambridge University Press, Cambridge.

1982 *Symbols in Action: Ethnoarchaeological Studies of Material Culture*. Cambridge University Press, Cambridge.

1988 Response to N. David, J. Sterner, and K. Gavua: Why Pots are Decorated. *Current Anthropology* 29:382–383.

Holmberg, Erik J.

1944 *The Swedish Excavations at Asea in Arcadia*. Schrifter utgivna av svenska institutet i Rom.; regni sueciae XI. C. W. K. Gleerup, Lund.

Hourmouziadis, G. Ch.

1973 *I Anthropomorphi Idoloplastiki tis Neolithikis Thessalias*. Volos.

Immerwahr, Sara A.

1971 *The Athenian Agora XIII: The Neolithic and Bronze Ages*. The American School of Classical Studies in Athens, Princeton.

Jacobsen, Thomas W.

1969 Excavations at Porto Cheli and Vicinity, Preliminary Report II: The Franchthi Cave, 1967–1968. *Hesperia* 38:343–381.

1973a Excavations in the Franchthi Cave, 1969–1971, Part I. *Hesperia* 42:45–88.

1973b Excavations in the Franchthi Cave, 1969–1971, Part II. *Hesperia* 42:253–283.

1976 17,000 Years of Greek Prehistory. *Scientific American* 234:76–87.

1979 Excavations at Franchthi Cave, 1973–1974. *Archaiologikon Deltion* 29B (1973–1974) (Chronika): 268–282.

1981 Franchthi Cave and the Beginning of Settled Village Life in Greece. *Hesperia* 50:303–319.

1984a Investigations at Franchthi Cave. *Archaiologikon Deltion* 31 (1976) (Chronika): 75–78.

1984b Seasonal Pastoralism in Southern Greece: A Consideration of the Ecology of Neolithic Urfirnis Pottery. Chapter 3 in *Pots and Potters: Current Approaches in Ceramic Archaeology*, edited by P. M. Rice, pp. 27–43. Institute of Archaeology Monograph 24. University of California, Los Angeles.

1985 Another Modest Proposal: Ethnoarchaeology in Greece. In *Contributions to Aegean Archaeology: Studies in Honor of William A. McDonald*, edited by N. C. Wilkie and W. D. E. Coulson, pp. 91–107. Publications in Ancient Studies No. 1. Center for Ancient Studies, University of Minnesota, Minneapolis.

Jacobsen, Thomas W., and Tracey Cullen

1981 A Consideration of Mortuary Practices in Neolithic Greece: Burials from Franchthi Cave. In *Mortality and Immortality: The Anthropology and Archaeology of Death*, edited by S. C. Humphreys and H. King, pp. 79–101. Academic Press, London.

Jacobsen, Thomas W., and William R. Farrand

1987 *Franchthi Cave and Paralia: Maps, Plans, and Sections*. Excavations at Franchthi Cave, Greece, fasc. 1. Indiana University Press, Bloomington and Indianapolis.

James, E. O.

1957 *Prehistoric Religion: A Study in Prehistoric Archaeology*. Praeger, New York.

1959 *The Cult of the Mother Goddess: An Archaeological and Documentary Study*. Praeger, New York.

1960 *The Ancient Gods: The History and Diffusion of Religion in the Ancient Near East and the Eastern Mediterranean*. Weidenfeld and Nicolson, London.

Joyce, Rosemary A.

1988 Response to N. David, J. Sterner, and K. Gavua: Why Pots are Decorated. *Current Anthropology* 29:383–384.

Kano, Tadao, and Kokichi Segawa

1956 *An Illustrated Ethnography of Formosan Aborigines*. Vol. 1, *The Yami*. rev. ed. Maruzen Co., Tokyo.

Kelly, Roger E., Richard W. Lang, and Harry Walters

1972 *Navaho Figurines Called Dolls*. Museum of Navaho Ceremonial Art, Santa Fe, New Mexico.

Kjersmeier, Carl

1934 Habbe-Kunst. *Ymer* 54:59–68.

Kluckhohn, Clyde

1944 *Navaho Witchcraft*. Papers of the Peabody Museum of Archaeology and Ethnology, vol. 22, no. 2. The Museum, Cambridge, Mass.

Kosmopoulos, Leslie W.

1948 *The Prehistoric Inhabitation of Corinth*. Münchner-Verlag, Munich.

Lambert, Nicole
1974 Grotte de Kitsos (Lavrion). *Bulletin de correspondance hellénique* 98:723–758.
LeBar, Frank M.
1963 *The Material Culture of Truk*. Human Relations Area Files, New Haven.
Lee, R. B., and I. Devore (editors)
1968 *Man the Hunter*. Aldine Press, Chicago.
Leonard, Robert D, and George T. Jones (editors)
1988 *Quantifying Diversity in Archaeology*. Cambridge University Press, Cambridge.
Lem, F. H.
1948 *Sculptures Sudanaises*. Arts et Métiers Graphiques, Paris.
Loeb, Edwin M.
1926 *Pomo Folkways*. University of California Publications in American Archaeology and Ethnology, vol. 19, no. 2. University of California Press, Berkeley.
1935 *Sumatra; Its History and People*. Institut für Völkerkunde der Universität Wien, Vienna.
McDougall, Lorna
1977 Symbols and Somatic Structures. In *The Anthropology of the Body*, edited by John Blacking, pp. 391–406. Academic Press, New York.
McGhee, R.
1977 Ivory for the Sea Woman: The Symbolic Attributes of a Prehistoric Technology. *Canadian Journal of Archaeology* 1:141–149.
Macintosh, N. W. G.
1977 Beswick Creek Cave Two Decades Later: A Reappraisal. In *Form in Indigenous Art: Schematisation in the Art of Aboriginal Australia and Prehistoric Europe*, edited by P. J. Ucko, pp. 191–197. Gerald Duckworth, London.
Makkay, J.
1983 Foundation Sacrifices in Neolithic Houses of the Carpathian Basin. In *Prehistoric Art and Religion, Valcamonica Symposium '79*, edited by E. Anati et al., pp.157–167. International Symposium on the Intellectual Expressions of Prehistoric Man, Art, and Religion. Edizioni del Centro, Capo di Ponte. Editoriale Jaca, Milan.
Massé, Henri
1954 *Persian Beliefs and Customs*. Translated by C. A. Messner. Human Relations Area Files, New Haven. Originally published as *Croyances et coutumes persanes: suivies de contes et chansons populaires* (Maisonneuve, Paris, 1938).
Maurer, Evan M., and Allen F. Roberts
1985 *Tabwa: The Rising of a New Moon, a Century of Tabwa Art*. University of Michigan Museum of Art, Ann Arbor.
Mauss, Marcel
1973 Techniques of the Body. *Economy and Society* 2:70–88.
Meighan, Clement W.
1953 Ancient Pottery Figurines and Their Significance in the Study of Prehistory. Ph.D. dissertation, Department of Anthropology, University of California, Berkeley.
Meillassoux, Claude
1973 On the Mode of Production of the Hunting Band. In *French Perspectives in African Studies*, edited by Pierre Alexandre, pp. 187–203. Oxford University Press, London.
Mellaart, James
1970 *Excavations at Hacilar*. 2 vols. The British School of Archaeology at Ankara Occasional Publication No. 9. Edinburgh University Press, Edinburgh.

Morales, Vivian Broman
1990 *Figurines and Other Clay Objects from Sarab and Çayönü.* Oriental Institute Communications No. 25. The Oriental Institute of the University of Chicago, Chicago.
Morss, Noel
1954 *Clay Figurines of the American Southwest.* Papers of the Peabody Museum of American Archaeology and Ethnology, vol. 49, no. 1. The Museum, Cambridge.
Morton-Williams, Peter
1960 Yoruba Responses to the Fear of Death. *Africa* 30:34–40.
Muhly, J. D.
1985 Beyond Typology: Aegean Metallurgy in Its Historical Context. In *Contributions to Aegean Archaeology: Studies in Honor of William A. McDonald,* edited by N. C. Wilkie and W. D. E. Coulson, pp. 109–141. Publications in Ancient Studies No. 1. Center for Ancient Studies, University of Minnesota, Minneapolis.
Müller, Kurt F.
1938 *Die Urfirniskeramik.* Vol. 4 of *Tiryns: Die Ergebnisse der Ausgrabungen des Instituts.* Reprint. Deutsches Archaeologisches Institut in Athen. F. Bruckmann, München. Reprint, P. von Zabern, Mainz/Rhein, 1976.
Mylonas, George E.
1929 *Excavations at Olynthus.* Part I, *The Neolithic Settlement.* Edited by D. M. Robinson. Johns Hopkins University Studies in Archaeology No. 6. Johns Hopkins Press, Baltimore.
1932 *Proistorike Eleusis.* Demosieumata Archaiologikou Tmematos Hypergeiou Paideias, Athens.
Nandris, John
1970 The Development and Relationships of the Earlier Greek Neolithic. *Man,* n.s. 5:192–213.
Needham, Rodney
1973 *Right and Left: Essays on Dual Symbolic Classification.* University of Chicago Press, Chicago.
Oates, Joan
1966 The Baked Clay Figurines from Tell Es-Sawwan. *Iraq* 28:146–153.
Oosterom, M. G.
1968 Mineralogical Investigation of Archaeological Specimens from Saliagos. Appendix II in *Excavations at Saliagos near Antiparos,* edited by J. D. Evans and C. Renfrew, pp. 99–100. British School of Archaeology at Athens, Supplementary Volume 5. Thames & Hudson, London.
Oustinoff, Elizabeth
1984 The Manufacture of Cycladic Figurines: A Practical Approach. In *Cycladica: Studies in Memory of N. P. Goulandris,* edited by J. L. Fitton, pp. 38–47. Proceedings of the Seventh British Museum Classical Colloquium, June 1983. British Museum Publications, London.
Papathanasopoulos, G. A.
1971 Spilaia Dirou: Ai Anaskaphai tou 1970–1971. (French summary) *Archaiologika Analekta ex Athenon* 4:12–26.
Parrinder, Edward Geoffrey
1967 *African Mythology.* Paul Hamlyn, London.
Parsons, Elsie Clews
1919 Increase by Magic: A Zuñi Pattern. *American Anthropologist* 21:279–286.

Parsons, Mary H.

1972 Aztec Figurines from the Teotihuacan Valley, Mexico. In *Miscellaneous Studies in Mexican Prehistory*, by M. Spence, J. R. Parsons, and M. H. Parsons. Anthropological Papers 45, Museum of Anthropology. University of Michigan, Ann Arbor.

Payne, Sebastian

1975 Faunal Change at Franchthi Cave from 20,000 B.C. to 3,000 B.C. In *Archaeozoological Studies*, edited by A. T. Clason, pp. 120–131. Elsevier, Amsterdam.

1982 Faunal Evidence for Environmental/Climatic Change at Franchthi Cave (Southern Argolid, Greece), 25000 B.P. to 5000 B.P.—Preliminary Results. In *Palaeoclimates, Palaeoenvironments and Human Communities in the Eastern Mediterranean Region in Later Prehistory,* edited by J. L. Bintliff and W. van Zeist, pp. 133–136. BAR International Series, vol. 133. British Archaeological Reports, Oxford.

Peltenburg, E. J.

1988 Prähistorische Religion in Zypern: Die rituelle Hortfund von Kissonerga. *Antike Kunst* 3:2–15.

Peltenburg, Edgar, and Elizabeth Coring

1991 Terracotta Figurines and Ritual at Kissonerga-Mosphilia. In *Cypriote Terracottas.* Proceedings of the First International Conference of Cypriote Studies, Brussels–Liège–Amsterdam, 29 May–1 June, 1989. Edited by F. Vandenabeele and R. Laffineur. A. G. Leventis Foundation, Vrije Universiteit Brussels–Université de Liège, Brussels–Liège.

Perey, Arnold

1975 Body and World in Oksapmin Kin Terms. *Oceania* 45:235–236.

Perlès, Catherine

1989 *From Stone Procurement to Neolithic Society in Greece.* The David Skomp Distinguished Lectures in Anthropology, February 1989. Indiana University, Bloomington.

Phelps, William W.

1975 The Neolithic Pottery Sequence in Southern Greece. Ph.D. dissertation, Institute of Archaeology, University of London.

1987 Prehistoric Figurines from Corinth. *Hesperia* 56:233–253.

Plass, Margaret W.

1956 *African Tribal Sculpture.* The University Museum, University of Pennsylvania, Philadelphia.

Plog, Stephen

1980 *Stylistic Variation in Prehistoric Ceramics: Design Analysis in the American Southwest.* Cambridge University Press, Cambridge.

Ploss, Hermann H., Maximilian C. Bartels, and Paul R. A. Bartels

1927 *Das Weib in der Natur- und Völkerkunde,* vol 1. Neufeld und Henius, Berlin.

Posner, Michael I.

1973 *Cognition: An Introduction.* Scott, Foresman, Glenview, Illinois.

Preziosi, Donald

1979 *Architecture, Language and Meaning.* Approaches to Semiotics, vol. 49. Mouton, The Hague.

Reese, David

1982 The Use of Cone Shells in Neolithic and Bronze Age Greece. *Archaiologika Analekta ex Athenon* 15:125–129.

Reichel-Dolmatoff, Gerardo

1961 Anthropomorphic Figurines from Columbia, Their Magic and Art. In *Essays in Pre-*

Columbian Art and Archaeology, by Samuel K. Lothrop et al., pp. 229–241. Harvard University Press, Cambridge.

Renfrew, Colin

1973 Trade and Craft Specialisation. In *Neolithic Greece*, by D. Theocharis, edited by S. Papadopoulos, pp. 179–200. The National Bank of Greece, Athens.

1985 *The Archaeology of Cult: The Sanctuary at Phylakopi*. The British School of Archaeology at Athens, London.

1986 A Neolithic Head from the Cyclades. *Antiquity* 60:134–135.

Renfrew, Colin, and John F. Cherry (editors)

1986 *Peer Polity Interaction and Socio-political Change*. Cambridge University Press, Cambridge.

Richards, Audrey I.

1956 *Chisungu: A Girls' Initiation Ceremony Among the Bemba of Northern Rhodesia*. Faber and Faber, London.

Richards, Audrey I., and J. F. Schofield

1945 Pottery Images or *Mbusa* Used at a Chisungu Ceremony of the Bemba People of North-Eastern Rhodesia. *South African Journal of Science* 41:444–458.

Ricoeur, Paul

1972 The Symbol Gives Rise to Thought. In *Ways of Understanding Religion,* by Walter H. Capps, pp. 309–317. Macmillan, New York.

Ridley, Cressida, and K. Rhomiopoulou

1972 Prehistoric Settlement of Servia (W. Macedonia). Excavations 1971. *Archaiologika Analekta ex Athenon* 5:27–34.

Ridley, Cressida, and K. A. Wardle

1979 Rescue Excavations at Servia 1971–1973: A Preliminary Report. *Annual of the British School at Athens* 74:185–230.

Robb, John

1991 Gender Ideology and the Evolution of Inequality in Prehistoric Italy. Unpublished manuscript, Anthropology Department, University of Michigan.

Rodden, Robert J.

1962 Excavations at the Early Neolithic Site of Nea Nikomedeia, Greek Macedonia (1961 Season). *Proceedings of the Prehistoric Society* 28:267–288.

1965 An Early Neolithic Village in Greece. *Scientific American* 212 (4): 82–92.

Rodden, Robert J., and J. M. Rodden

1964 A European Link with Chatal Huyuk: the 7th Millennium Settlement of Nea Nikomedeia in Macedonia. Part II—Burials and the Shrine. *The Illustrated London News*, April 18, Archaeology Section 2180, 604–606.

Runnels, Curtis N.

1981 *A Diachronic Study and Economic Analysis of Millstones from the Argolid, Greece*. Ph.D. dissertation, Program in Classical Archaeology, Indiana University, Bloomington. University Microfilms, Ann Arbor.

1983 Trade and Communication in Prehistoric Greece. *Ekistics: The Problems and Science of Human Settlements* 50:417–420.

1985 Trade and the Demand for Millstones in Southern Greece in the Neolithic and Bronze Age. In *Prehistoric Production and Exchange: The Aegean and Eastern Mediterranean*, edited by A. B. Knapp and T. Stech, pp. 30–43. Institute of Archaeology Monograph 25. University of California, Los Angeles.

Runnels, Curtis N., and Tj. H. van Andel
1987 The Evolution of Settlement in the Southern Argolid, Greece: An Economic Explanation. *Hesperia* 56:303–334.
Saraswati, Baidyanath, and Nab K. Behura
1966 *Pottery Techniques in Peasant India.* Memoir No. 13. The Anthropological Survey of India, Calcutta.
Saxe, Arthur
1970 *Social Dimensions of Mortuary Practices.* Ph.D. dissertation, Department of Anthropology, University of Michigan, Ann Arbor. University Microfilms, Ann Arbor.
Schaeffer, Marguerite C.
1977 An Attribute Analysis and Formal Typology of the Ornaments from Franchthi Cave, Greece. Master's thesis, Program in Classical Archaeology, Indiana University, Bloomington.
Schiffer, Michael B.
1976 *Behavioral Archeology.* Academic Press, New York.
Schortman, Edward M.
1989 Interregional Interaction in Prehistory: The Need for a New Perspective. *American Antiquity* 54:52–65.
Segy, Ladislas
1958 *African Sculpture.* Dover Publications, New York.
Shackleton, Judith C.
1988 *Marine Molluscan Remains from Franchthi Cave.* Excavations at Franchthi Cave, Greece, fasc. 4. Indiana University Press, Bloomington and Indianapolis.
Shanks, Michael, and Tilley, Christopher
1987 *Re-constructing Archaeology: Theory and Practice.* Cambridge University Press, Cambridge.
Shaw, E. M.
1948 Fertility Dolls in Southern Africa. *NADA: Native Affairs Department Annual* 25:62–68.
Shaw, W. H., and L. R. Ashley
1983 Analogy and Inference. *Dialogue* 22:415–432.
Shepard, Anna O.
1956 *Ceramics for the Archaeologist.* Publication 609. Carnegie Institution of Washington, Washington, D.C.
Sieber, Roy
1972 *African Textiles and Decorative Arts.* Museum of Modern Art, New York.
Simon, Arleyn W., and William A. Coghlan
1989 The Use of Indentation Testing to Obtain Precise Hardness Measurements from Prehistoric Pottery. *American Antiquity* 54:107–122.
Stanislawski, Michael B.
1974 The Relationships of Ethnoarchaeology, Traditional and Systems Archaeology. In *Ethnoarchaeology*, edited by C. B. Donnan and C. W. Clewlow, Jr., pp. 15–26. Archaeological Survey, Monograph 4. Institute of Archaeology, University of California, Los Angeles.
Stannus, Hugh S.
1922 *The Wayao of Nyasaland.* Peabody Museum of Harvard University, Cambridge. Reprinted from *Harvard African Studies* 3:229–372.
Sutherland, Anne
1977 The Body as a Social Symbol Among the Rom. In *The Anthropology of the Body*, edited by John Blacking, pp. 375–390. Academic Press, New York.

Talalay, Lauren E.

1982 A Neolithic Mystery: The Halving of Anthropomorphic Figurines. Paper delivered at the 84th General Meeting of the Archaeological Institute of America, Philadelphia. Abstract: *American Journal of Archaeology* 87 (1983): 264.

1983a Neolithic Figurines of Southern Greece: Their Form and Function. Ph.D. dissertation, Program in Classical Archaeology, Indiana University, Bloomington.

1983b Implications of an Early Sculptural Canon in the Greek Neolithic. Paper delivered at the 48th Annual Meeting of the Society for American Archaeology, Pittsburgh.

1983c Neolithic Initiation Rites: A New Interpretation of Anatolian Figurines. Paper delivered at the 85th General Meeting of the Archaeological Institute of America, Cincinnati. Abstract: *American Journal of Archaeology* 88 (1984): 262.

1984a Beyond Artifacts: Interpreting Human Images in the Prehistoric Aegean. Paper delivered at the 86th General Meeting of the Archaeological Institute of America, Toronto. Abstract: *American Journal of Archaeology* 89 (1985): 353.

1984b The Case of the Silent Figurines: Interpreting Human Images in Prehistory. Paper delivered at the Sixth Annual Eastern European Archaeology Meeting, Los Angeles.

1986 Life After Death: New Light on the Cemetery at Kephala, Greece. Paper delivered at the 88th General Meeting of the Archaeological Institute of America, San Antonio. Abstract: *American Journal of Archaeology* 91 (1987): 294.

1987 Rethinking the Function of Clay Figurine Legs from Neolithic Greece: An Argument by Analogy. *American Journal of Archaeology* 91:161–169.

1989 Herding and Magic: Neolithic Economy and Zoomorphic Images in Southern Greece. Paper delivered at the First Joint Archaeological Congress, Baltimore. Abstract: *American Journal of Archaeology* 93 (1989): 271.

1991 Body Imagery of the Ancient Aegean. *Archaeology* 44 (4): 46–49.

Talalay, Lauren E., and R. Handler

1985 The Present in the Past: Archaeological Objectivity and the Interpretation of Stone Age Figurines. Paper delivered at the 87th General Meeting of the Archaeological Institute of America,Washington D.C. Abstract: *American Journal of Archaeology* 90 (1986): 185.

Teit, James A.

1930 *Tattooing and Face and Body Painting of the Thompson Indians, British Columbia.* Edited by Franz Boas. Bureau of American Ethnology Annual Report, vol. 45. Smithsonian Institution. USGPO, Washington, D.C.

Tessmann, Gunter

1913 *Die Pangwe.* 2 vols. E. Wasmuth, Berlin.

Theocharis, Dimitrios R.

1954 Anaskaphe Neolithikou Synoikismou en Nea Makri, Attikis. *Praktika tes en Athenais Archaiologikes Hetairias* —:114–122.

1956 Nea Makri: Eine grosse neolithische Siedlung in der Nähe von Marathon. *Athenische Mitteilungen* 71:1–29.

1973 *Neolithic Greece.* Edited by S. Papadopoulos. The National Bank of Greece, Athens.

Thimme, Jürgen (editor)

1977 *Art and Culture of the Cyclades in the Third Millennium B.C.* Translated and edited by Pat Getz-Preziosi. University of Chicago Press, Chicago and London.

Thomas, Northcote W.

1913 *Anthropological Report on the Ibo-Speaking Peoples of Nigeria.* Part 4, *Law and Custom of the Ibo of the Asaba District, S. Nigeria.* Harrison and Sons, London.

Torrence, Robin
1986 *Production and Exchange of Stone Tools: Prehistoric Obsidian in the Aegean.* Cambridge University Press, Cambridge.
Tringham, Ruth
1971 *Hunters, Fishers and Farmers of Eastern Europe, 6000–3000 B.C.* Hutchinson and Co., Ltd., London.
Tsountas, Ch.
1908 *Hai Proistorikai Akropoleis Diminiou kai Sesklou.* Bibliotheke tes en Athenais Archaiologikes Hetaireias, vol. 43. Sakellarios, Athens.
Turner, Victor W.
1967 *The Forest of Symbols; Aspects of Ndembu Ritual.* Cornell University Press, Ithaca, N.Y.
1969 *The Ritual Process: Structure and Anti-Structure.* The Lewis Henry Morgan Lectures. Aldine Publishing Co., Chicago.
1974 *Drama, Fields, and Metaphors; Symbolic Action in Human Society.* Cornell University Press, Ithaca, N.Y.
1975 Symbolic Studies. In *Annual Review of Anthropology* 4:145–161.
Turner, Victor W. (editor)
1982 *Celebration, Studies in Festivity and Ritual.* Smithsonian Institution Press, Washington, D.C.
Turner, W. Y.
1878 On the Ethnology of the Motu. *Journal of the Anthropological Institute of Great Britain and Ireland* 7:470–497.
Ucko, Peter J.
1962 Prehistoric Anthropological Figurines of the Ancient Near East and the Aegean. Ph.D. dissertation, University of London.
1968 *Anthropomorphic Figurines.* Royal Anthropological Institute. Occasional Papers, no. 24. A. Szmidla, London.
1969 Ethnography and Archaeological Interpretation of Funerary Remains. *World Archaeology* 1:262–280.
Vaillant, George C.
1930 *Excavations at Zacatenco.* Anthropological Papers of the American Museum of Natural History, vol. 32, pt. 1. The Trustees, New York.
Valente, Waldemar
1955 *Sincretismo Religioso Afro-Brasileiro.* Biblioteca Pedagógica brasileira. Sér. 5: Brasiliana, vol. 280. Companhia Editora Nacional, São Paulo.
Valmin, Mattias Natan
1938 *The Swedish Messenia Expedition.* Acta Reg. Societatis Humaniorum Litterarum Lundensis 26. C. W. K. Gleerup, Lund.
van Andel, Tj. H., and C. N. Runnels
1987 *Beyond the Acropolis: A Rural Greek Past.* Stanford University Press, Stanford.
1988 An Essay on the "Emergence of Civilization" in the Aegean World. *Antiquity* 62:234–247.
van Andel, Tj. H., and C. J. Vitaliano
1987 Water and Other Resources. In *Landscape and People of the Franchthi Region*, by Tj. H. van Andel and S. B. Sutton, pp. 17–20. Excavations at Franchthi Cave, Greece, fasc. 2. Indiana University Press, Bloomington and Indianapolis.

Verger, Pierre

1954 *Dieux d'Afrique*. Hartmann, Paris.

Vitelli, K. D.

1974 *The Greek Neolithic Patterned Urfirnis Ware from the Franchthi Cave and Lerna*. Ph.D. dissertation, Department of Classical Archaeology, University of Pennsylvania, Philadelphia. Xerox University Microfilms, Ann Arbor.

1984a Social Implications of the EN Pottery Assemblage at Franchthi. Paper delivered at the Sixth Annual Eastern European Archaeology Meeting, Los Angeles.

1984b Greek Neolithic Pottery by Experiment. Chapter 9 in *Pots and Potters: Current Approaches in Ceramic Archaeology,* edited by P. M. Rice, pp. 113–131. Institute of Archaeology Monograph 24. University of California, Los Angeles.

1991 (Not About) Possible Uses of Plant Extracts by Prehistoric Potters. Paper delivered at the 56th Annual Meeting of the Society for American Archaeology, New Orleans.

Forthcoming *Franchthi Neolithic Pottery*. Vol. 1, *Classification and Ceramic Phases 1 and 2*. Excavations at Franchthi Cave, Greece, fasc. 8. Indiana University Press, Bloomington and Indianapolis.

Wace, A. J. B., and M. S. Thompson

1912 *Prehistoric Thessaly*. University Press, Cambridge.

Weinberg, Saul S.

1947 Aegean Chronology: Neolithic Period and Early Bronze Age. *American Journal of Archaeology* 51:165–182.

1951 Neolithic Figurines and Aegean Interrelations. *American Journal of Archaeology* 55:121–133.

1970 The Stone Age in the Aegean. Chapter 10 of *The Cambridge Ancient History.* 3d ed. Vol. 1, pt. 1, *Prolegomena and Prehistory,* edited by I. E. Edwards, C. J. Gadd, and N. L. Hammond, pp. 517–618, 664–672. Cambridge University Press, Cambridge.

1977 Anthropomorphic Stone Figurines from Neolithic Greece. In *Art and Culture of the Cyclades in the Third Millennium B.C.,* edited by Jürgen Thimme, translated and edited by Pat Getz-Preziosi, pp. 52–58. University of Chicago Press, Chicago and London.

Welbourn, A.

1984 Endo Ceramics and Power Strategies. In *Ideology, Power and Prehistory*, edited by D. Miller and C. Tilley, pp. 17–24. Cambridge University Press, Cambridge.

Welter, Gabriel

1938 *Aigina*. Gebr. Mann, Berlin.

1954 Aeginetica XXV–XXXVI. *Archäologischer Anzeiger* 69:28–48.

Whalen, Michael E.

1981 *Excavations at Santo Domingo Tomaltepec: Evolution of a Formative Community in the Valley of Oaxaca, Mexico*. Memoirs of the Museum of Anthropology No. 12. University of Michigan, Ann Arbor.

Whittle, Alasdair W. R.

1985 *Neolithic Europe: A Survey*. Cambridge University Press, Cambridge.

Wickens, Jere M.

1986 *The Archaeology and History of Cave Use in Attica, Greece from Prehistoric Through Late Roman Times*. 2 vols. Ph.D. dissertation, Program in Classical Archaeology, Indiana University, Bloomington. University Microfilms, Ann Arbor.

Wijnen, Marie-Hélène J. M. N.

1982 *The Early Neolithic I Settlement at Sesklo: An Early Farming Community in Thessaly, Greece*. Analekta Praehistorica Leidensia, vol. 14. Universitaire Pers Leiden, Leiden.

Wolters, Paul
1891 Marmorkopf auf Amorgos. *Athenische Mitteilungen* 16:46–58.
Wylie, Alison M.
1982 An Analogy by Any Other Name is Just as Analogical: A Commentary on the Gould–Watson Dialogue. *Journal of Anthropological Archaeology* 1:382–401.
1985 The Reaction Against Analogy. In *Advances in Archaeological Method and Theory*, vol. 8, edited by M. B. Schiffer, pp. 63–111. Academic Press, New York.
Young, David E., and Robson Bonnichsen
1983 *Understanding Stone Tools: A Cognitive Approach.* Peopling of the Americas, Process series, vol. 1. Center for the Study of Early Man, University of Maine, Orono.

Plates

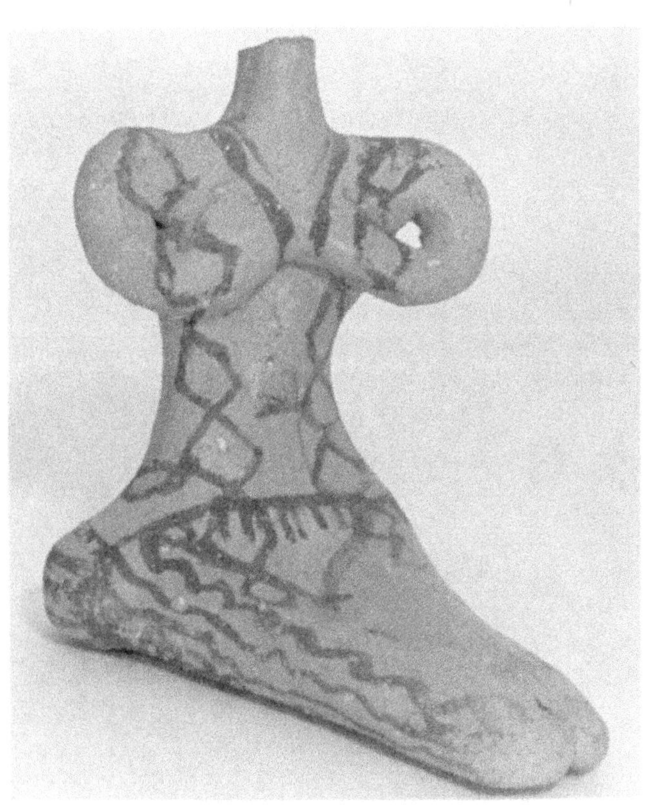

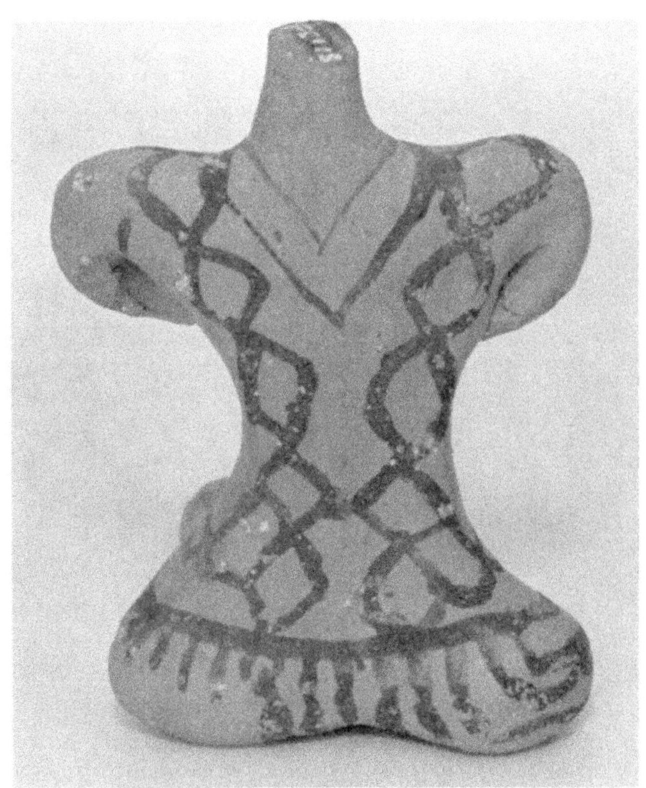

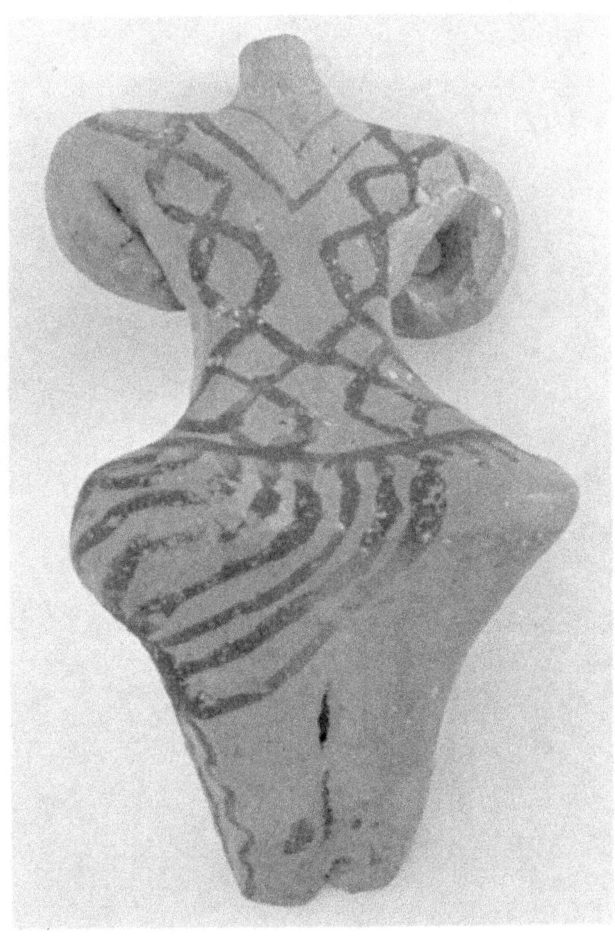

Plate 1. FC 118. Scale 1:1.

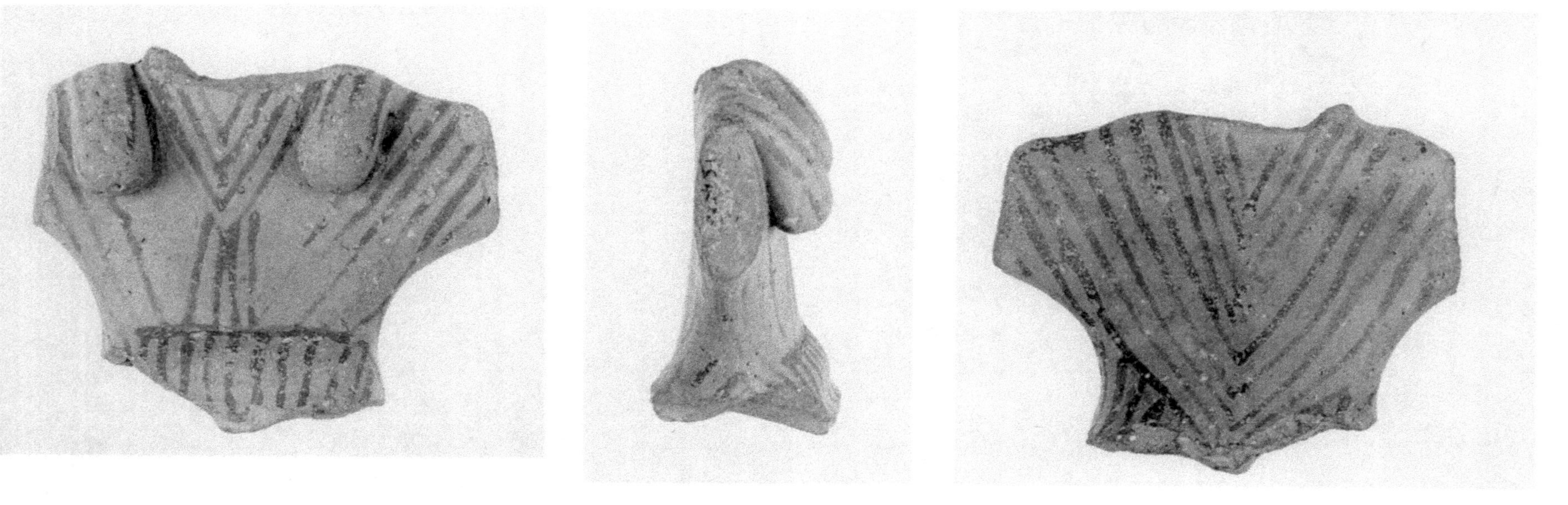

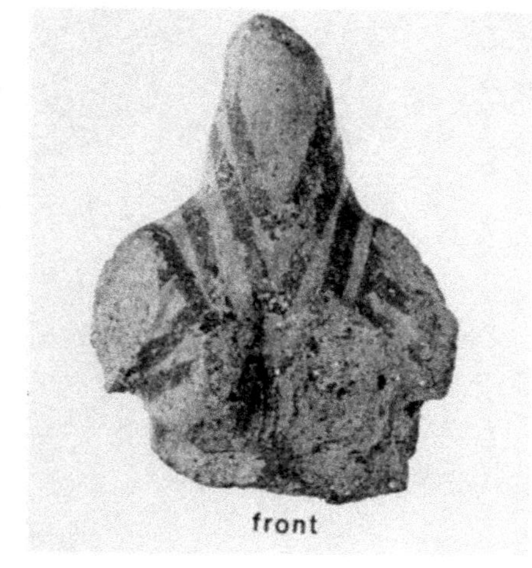

Plate 2. (a) FC 42: front, side, back; (b) FC 167. Scale 1:1.

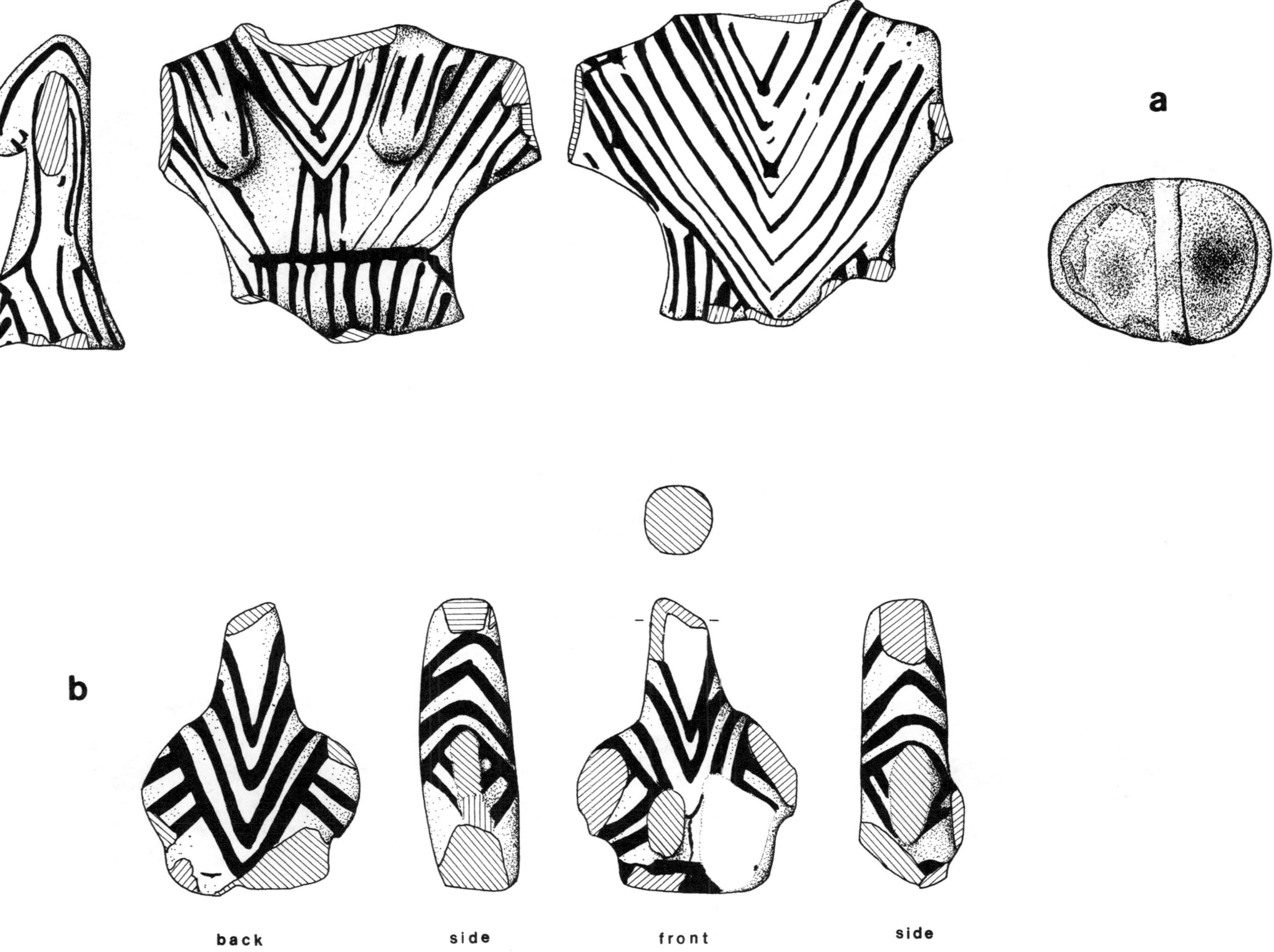

Plate 3. Drawings of (a) FC 42: side, front, back, underside; (b) FC 167. Scale 1:1.

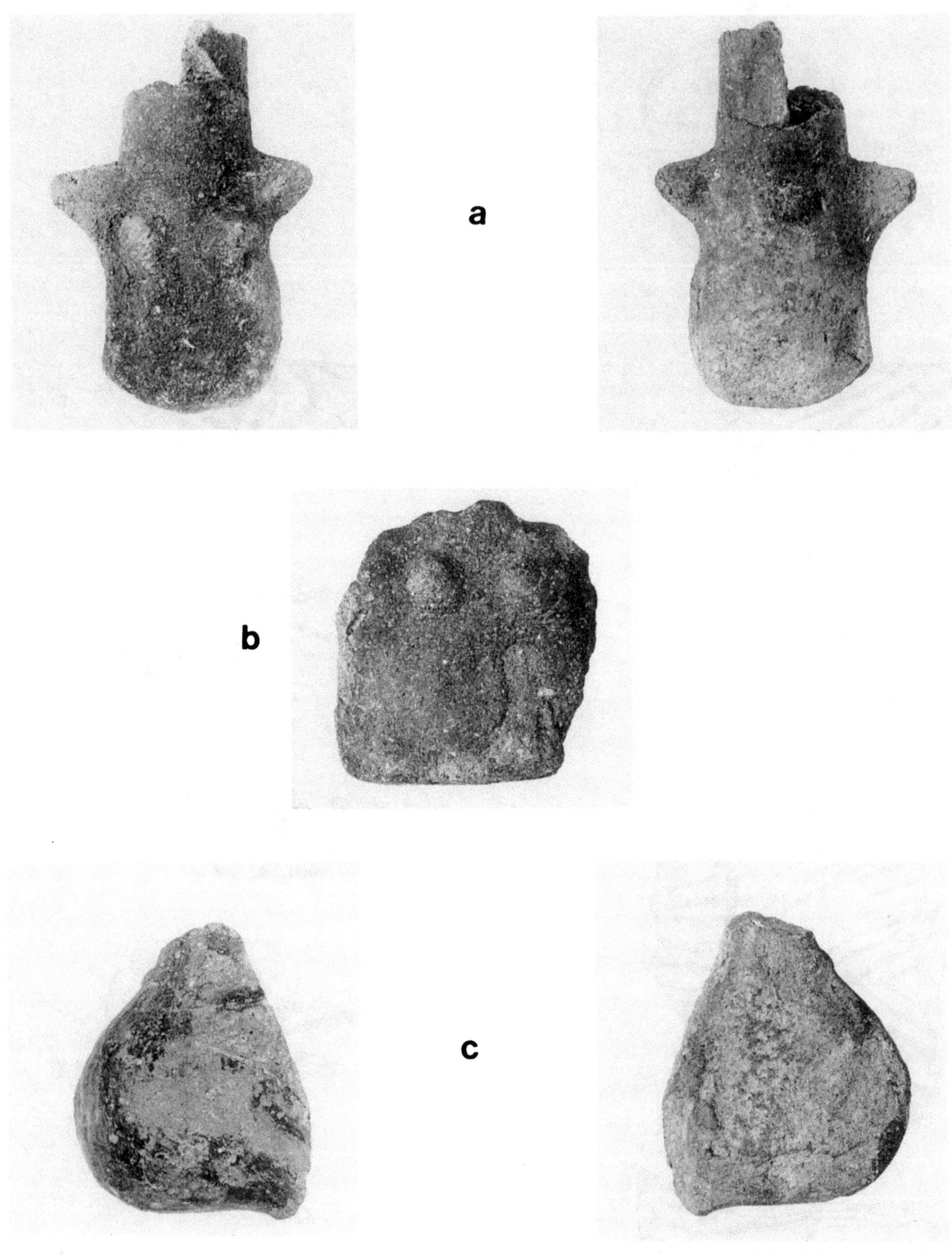

Plate 4. (a) FC 112: front, back; (b) FC 4: front; (c) FC 12: side, medial side. Scale 1:1.

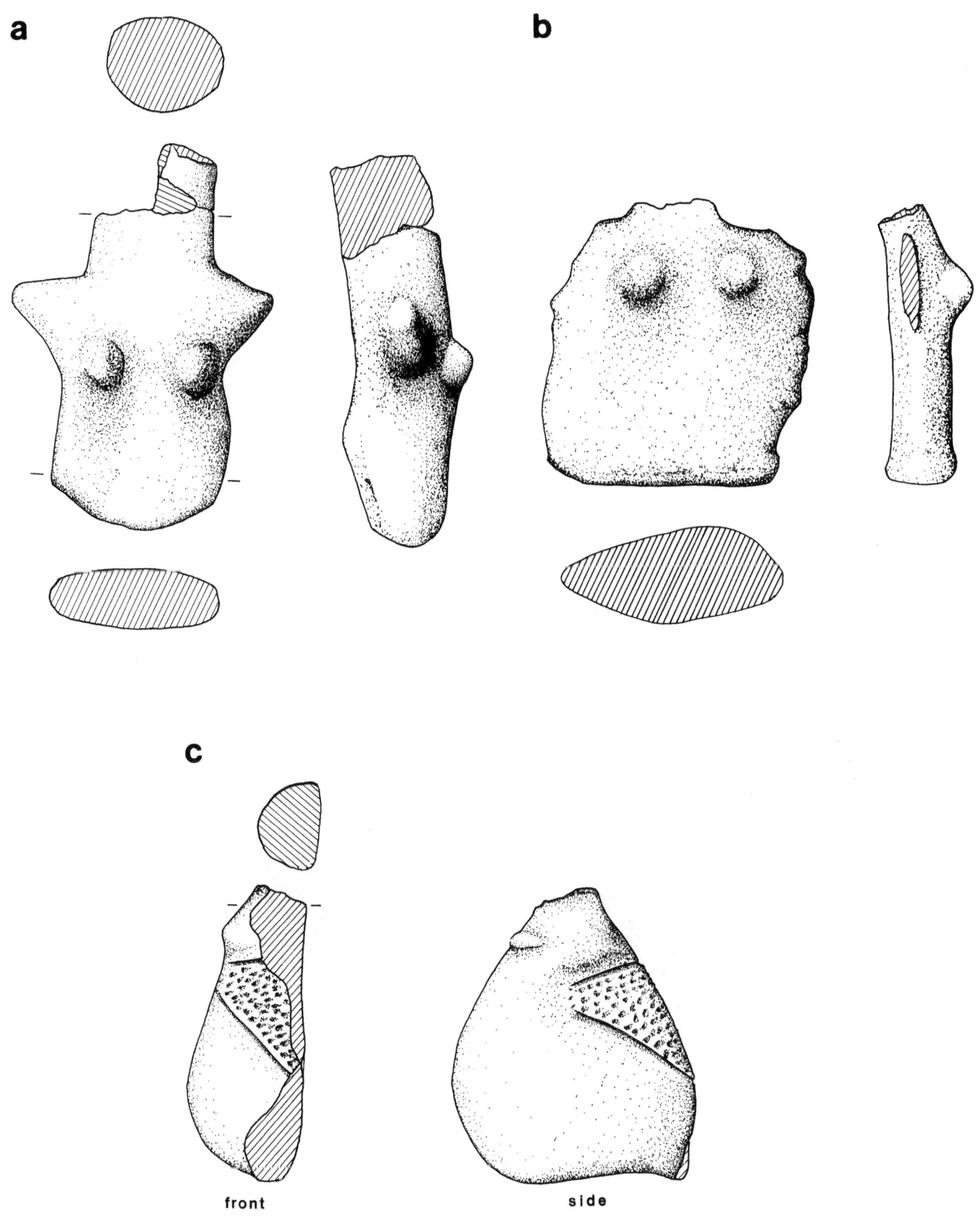

Plate 5. Drawings of (a) FC 112: front, side; (b) FC 4: front, side; (c) FC 12. Scale 1:1.

a

b

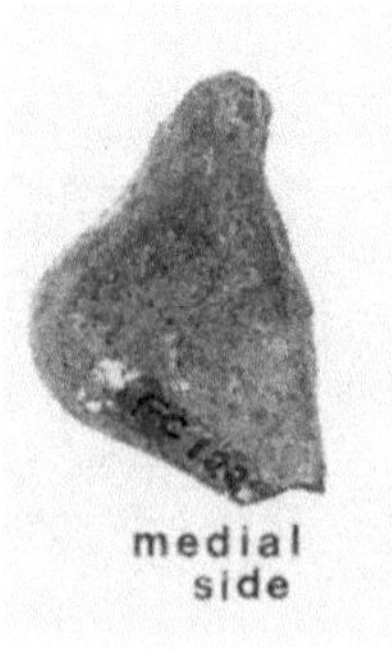

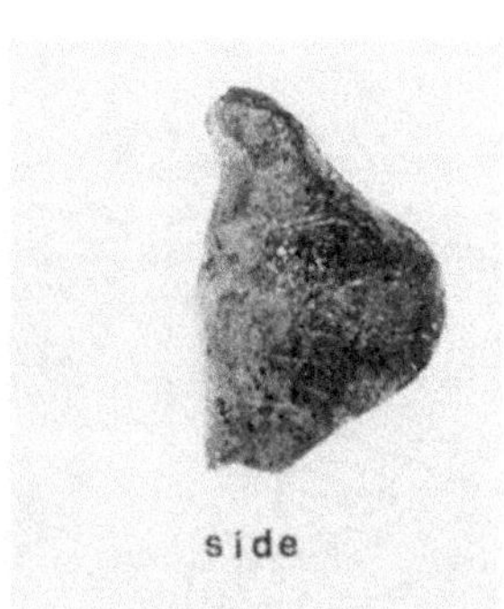

c

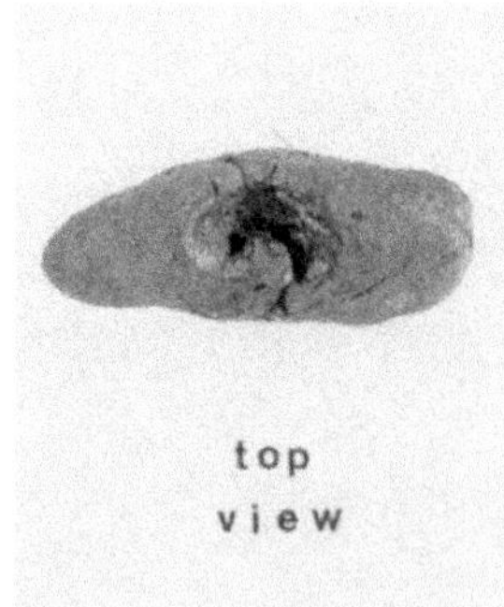

Plate 6. (a) FC 28: front, back; (b) FC 122; (c) FC 190. Scale 1:1.

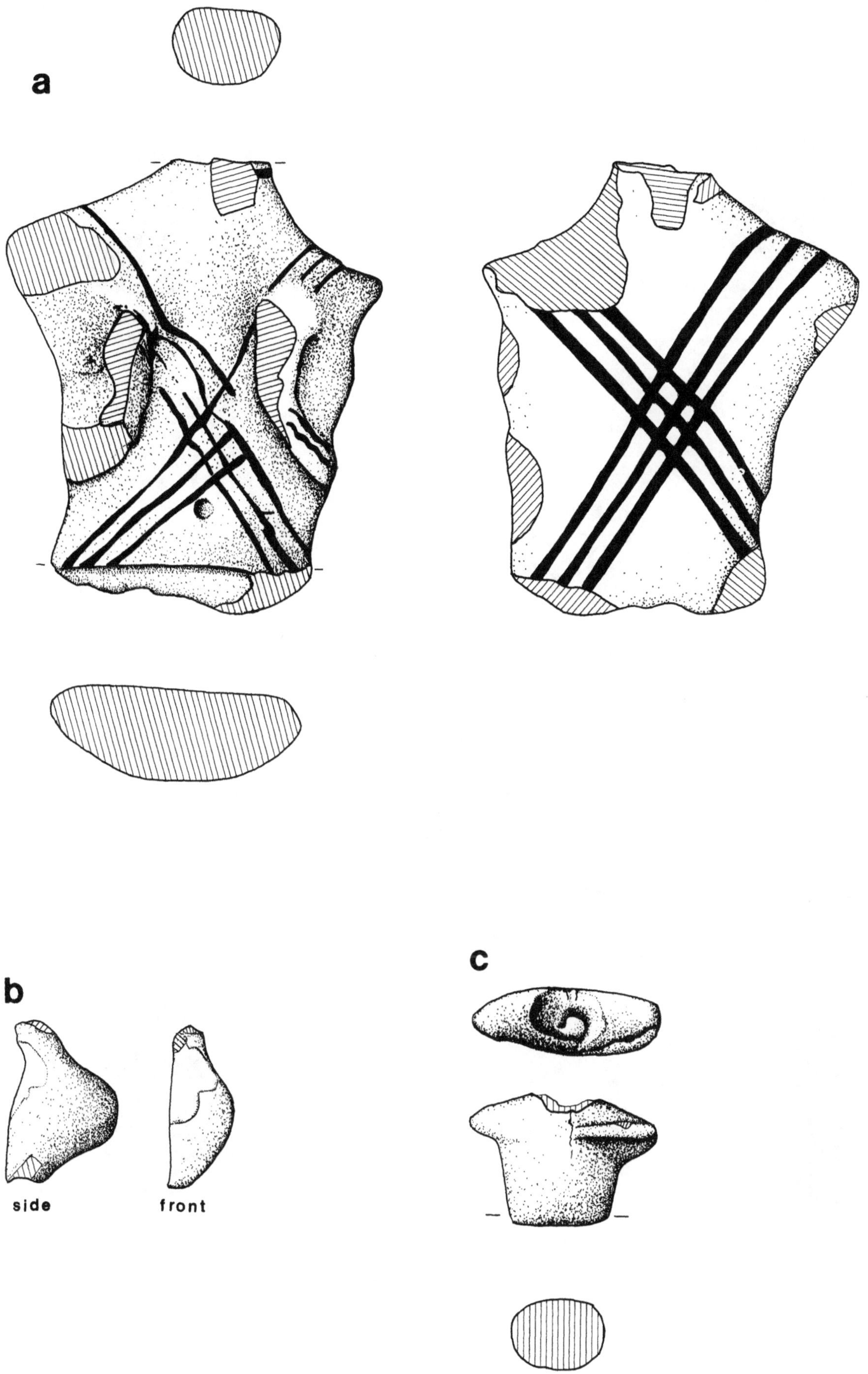

Plate 7. Drawings of (a) FC 28: front, back; (b) FC 122; (c) FC 190: top, front. Scale 1:1.

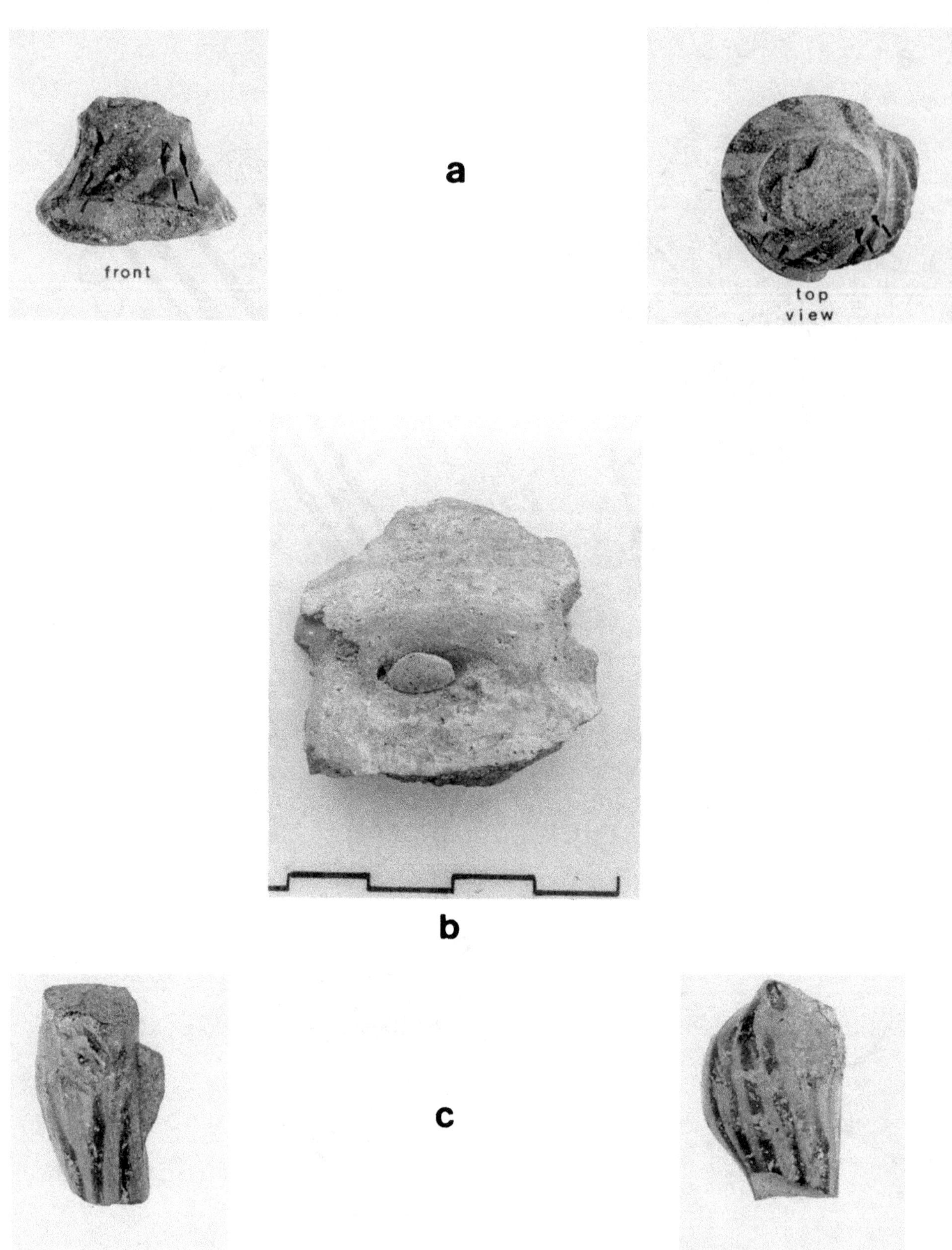

Plate 8. (a) FC 208, scale 1:1; (b) FP 173: front, scale in cm; (c) FC 124: front, side, scale 1:1.

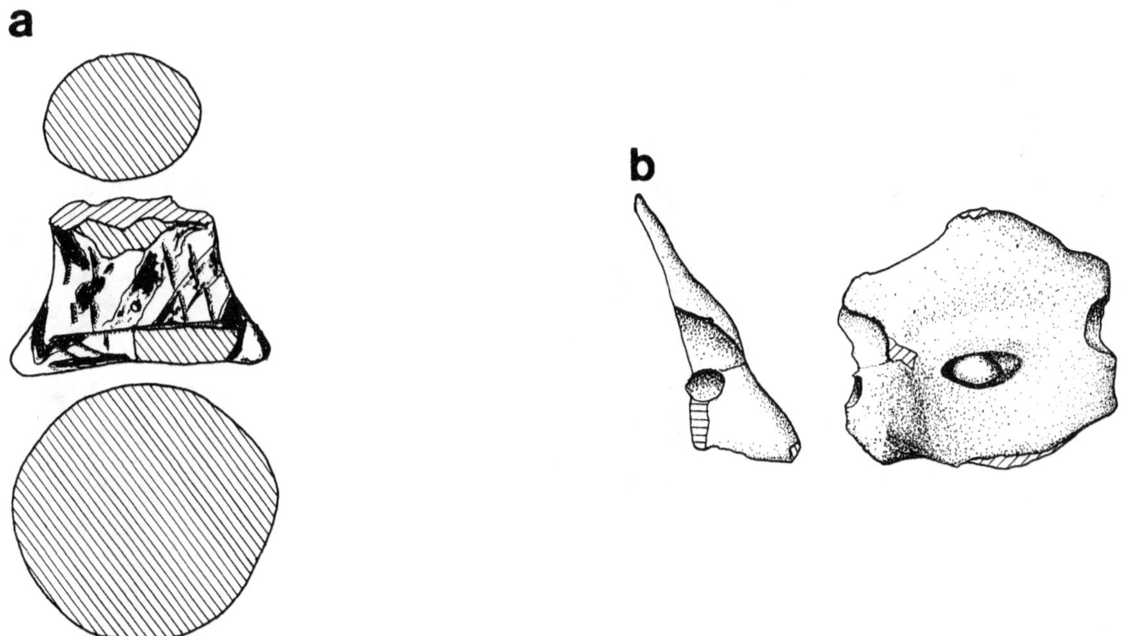

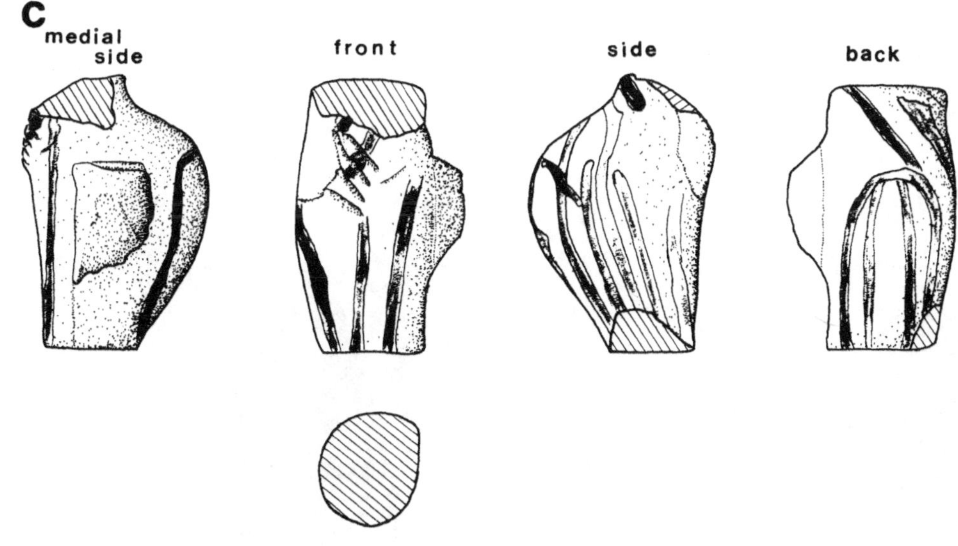

Plate 9. Drawings of (a) FC 208: front; (b) FP 173: side, front; (c) FC 124. Scale 1:1.

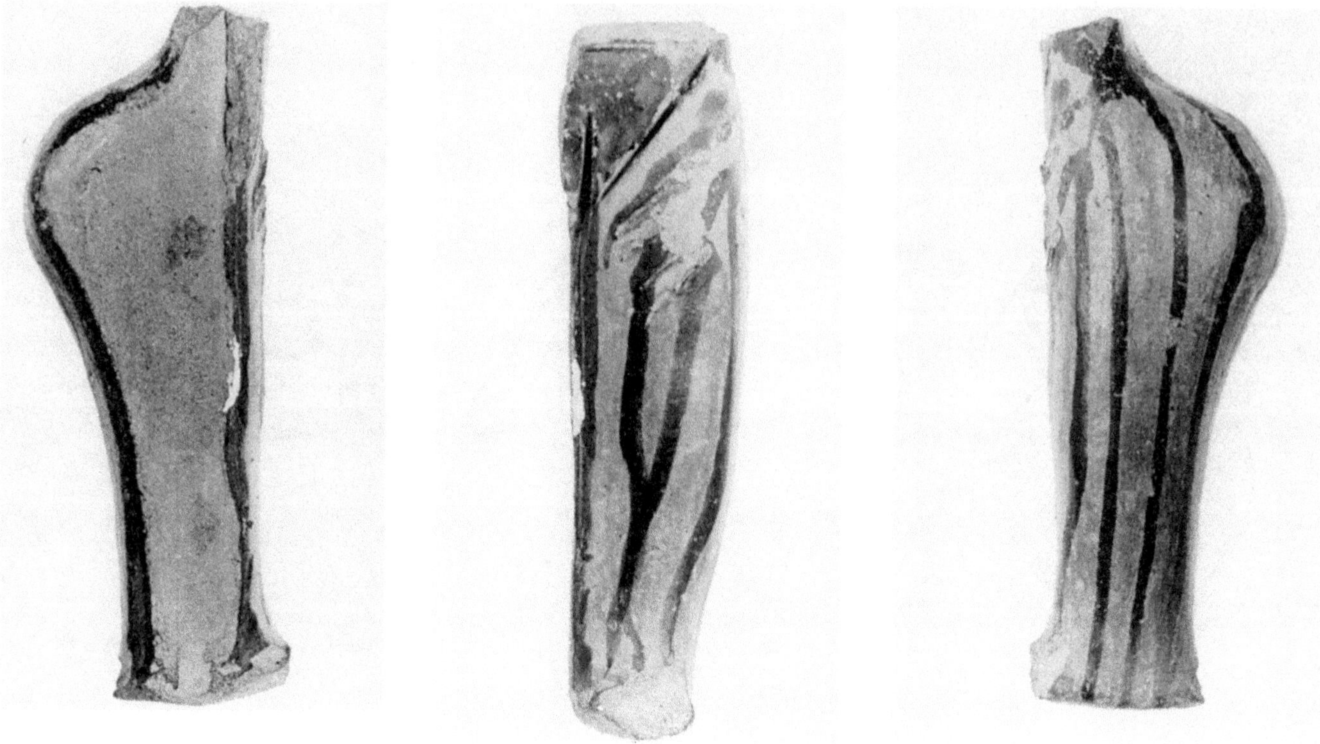

a

Plate 10. (a) FC 68: medial side, front, side; (b) FC 57: side, front. Scale 1:1.

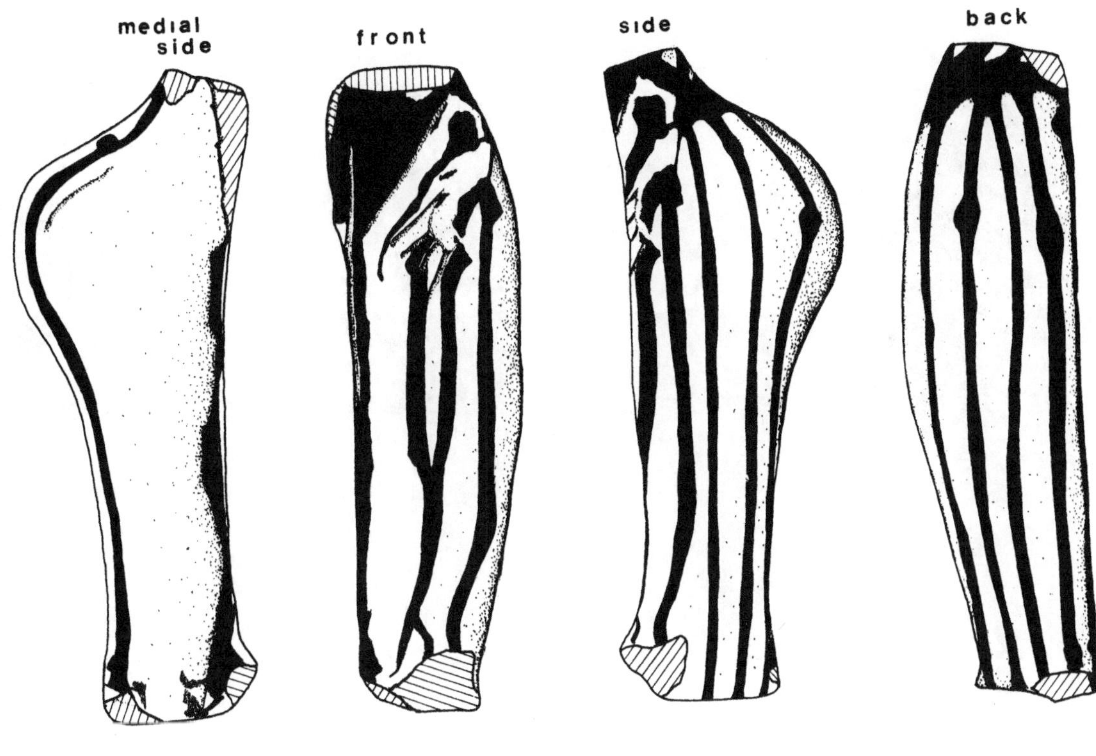

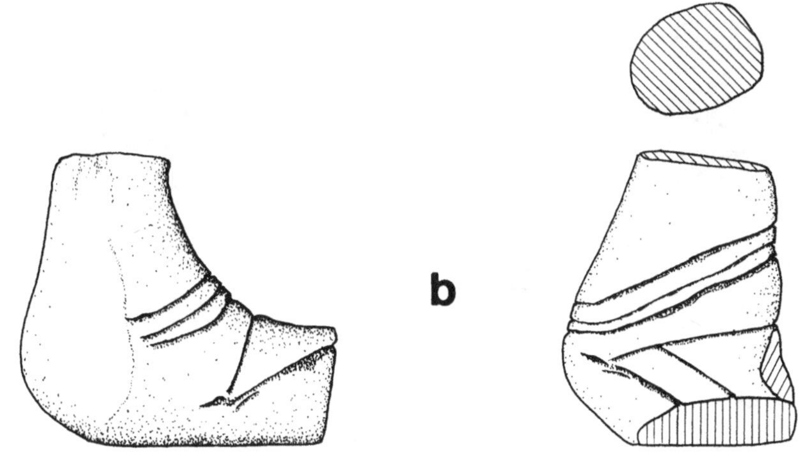

Plate 11. Drawings of (a) FC 68; (b) FC 57: side, front. Scale 1:1.

a

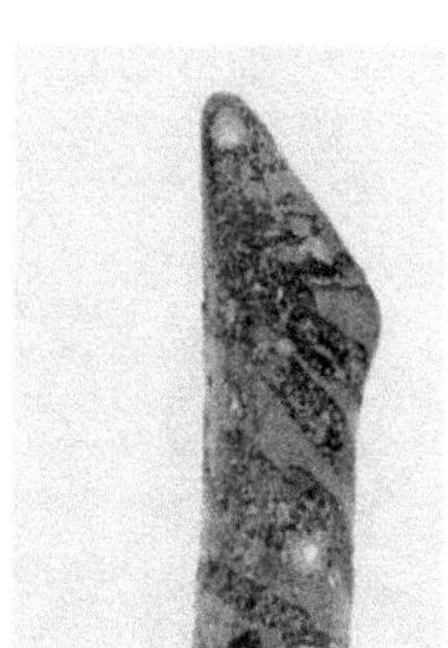
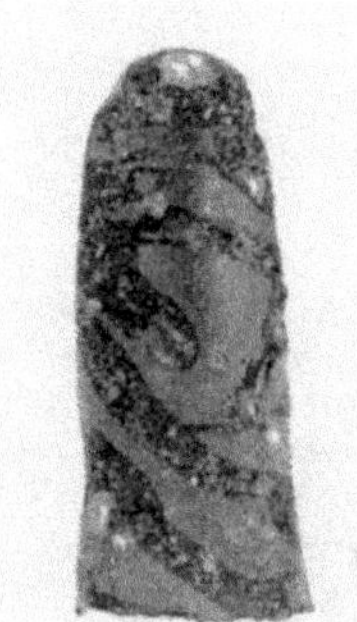

b

Plate 12. (a) FC 117: front, side, back; (b) FC 101: side, front. Scale 1:1.

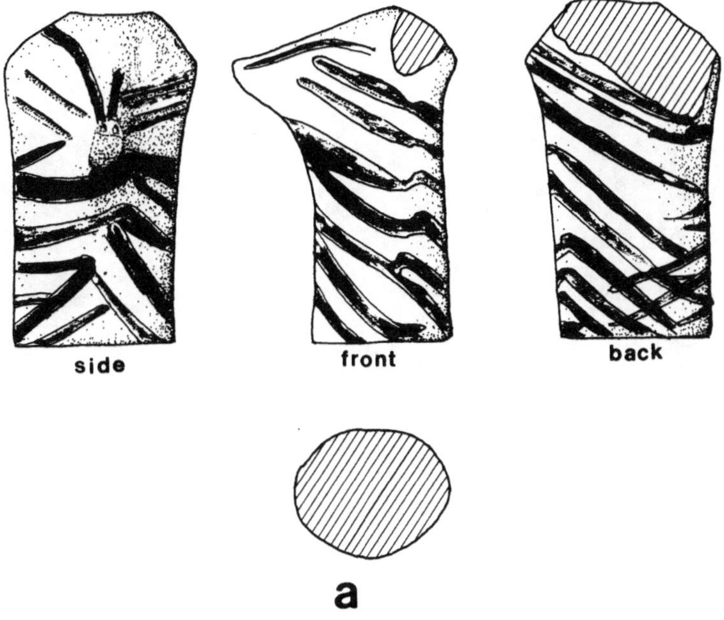

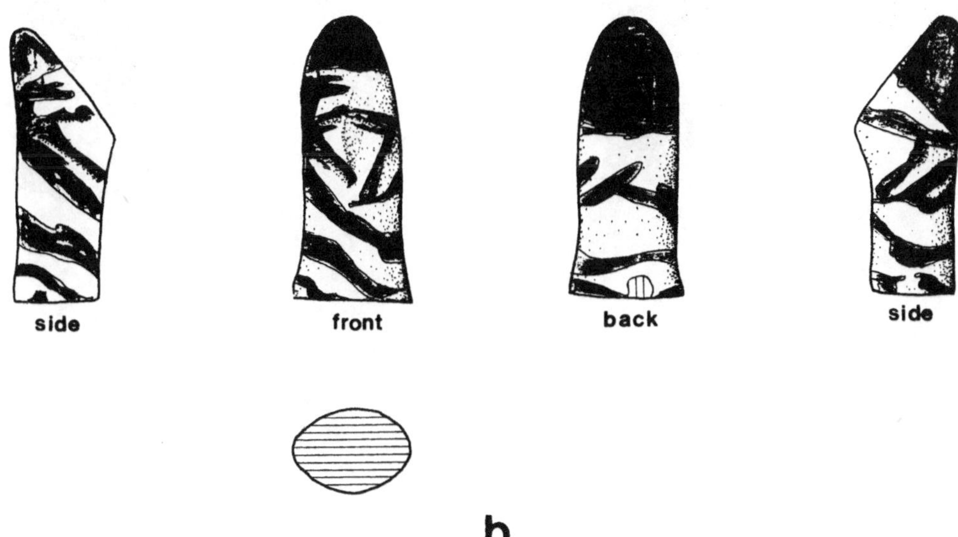

Plate 13. Drawings of (a) FC 117; (b) FC 101. Scale 1:1.

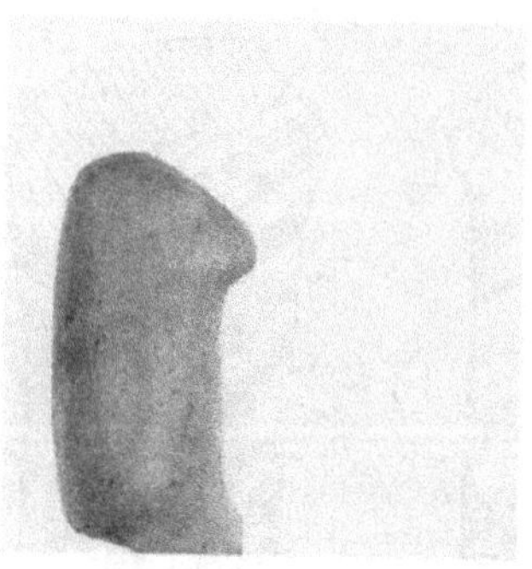

a

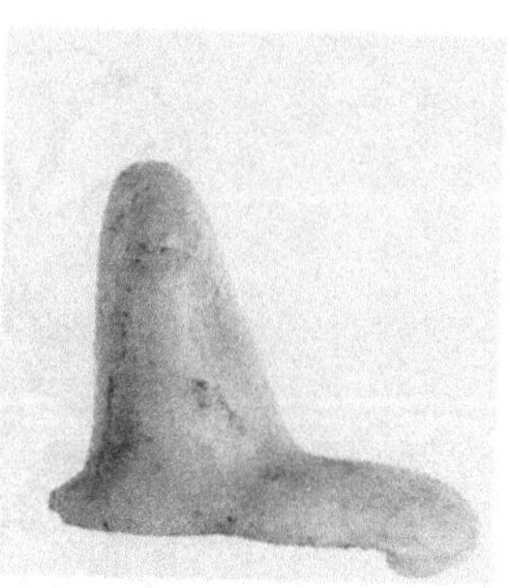

b

Plate 14. (a) FS 101: side, front; (b) FC 60: front, side. Scale 1:1.

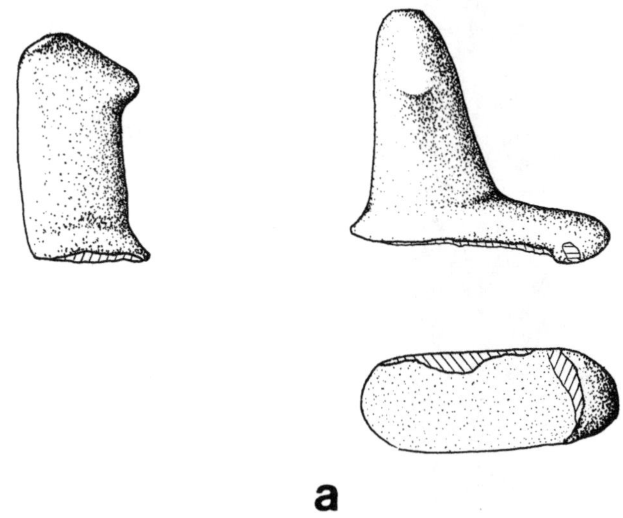

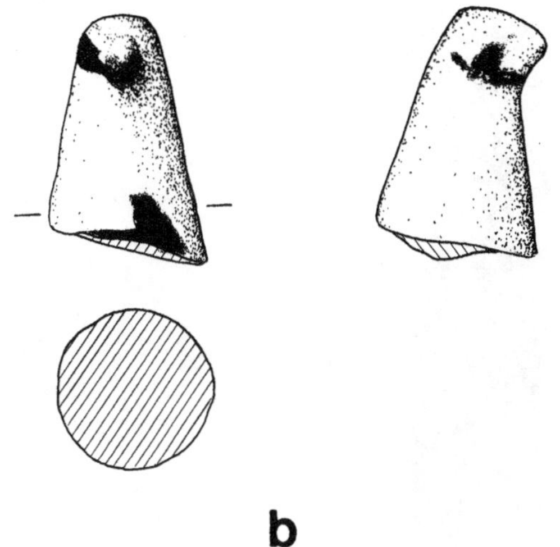

Plate 15. Drawings of (a) FS 101: side, front; (b) FC 60: front, side. Scale 1:1.

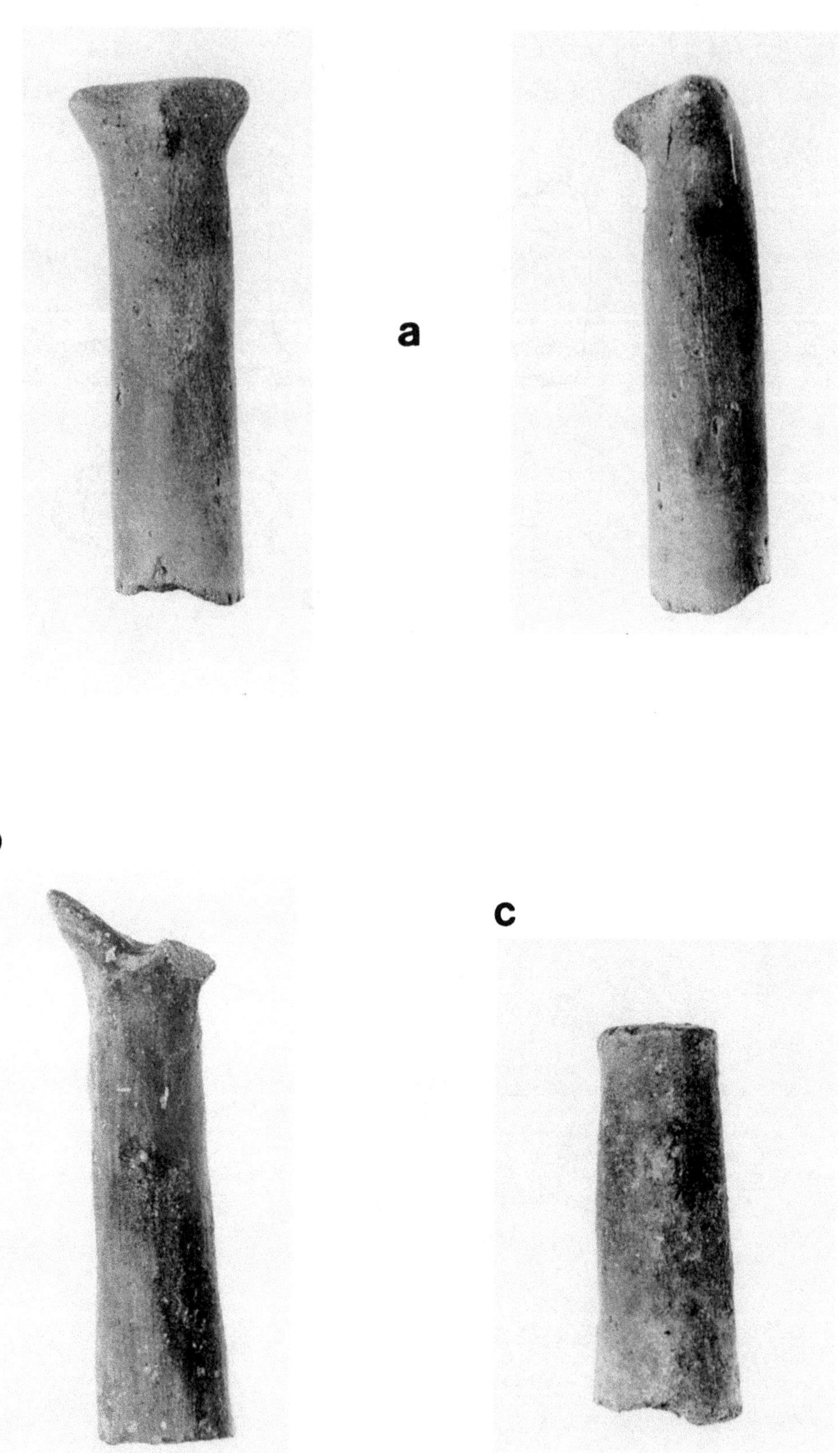

Plate 16. (a) FC 31: front, side; (b) FC 30: front; (c) FC 11: front. Scale 1:1.

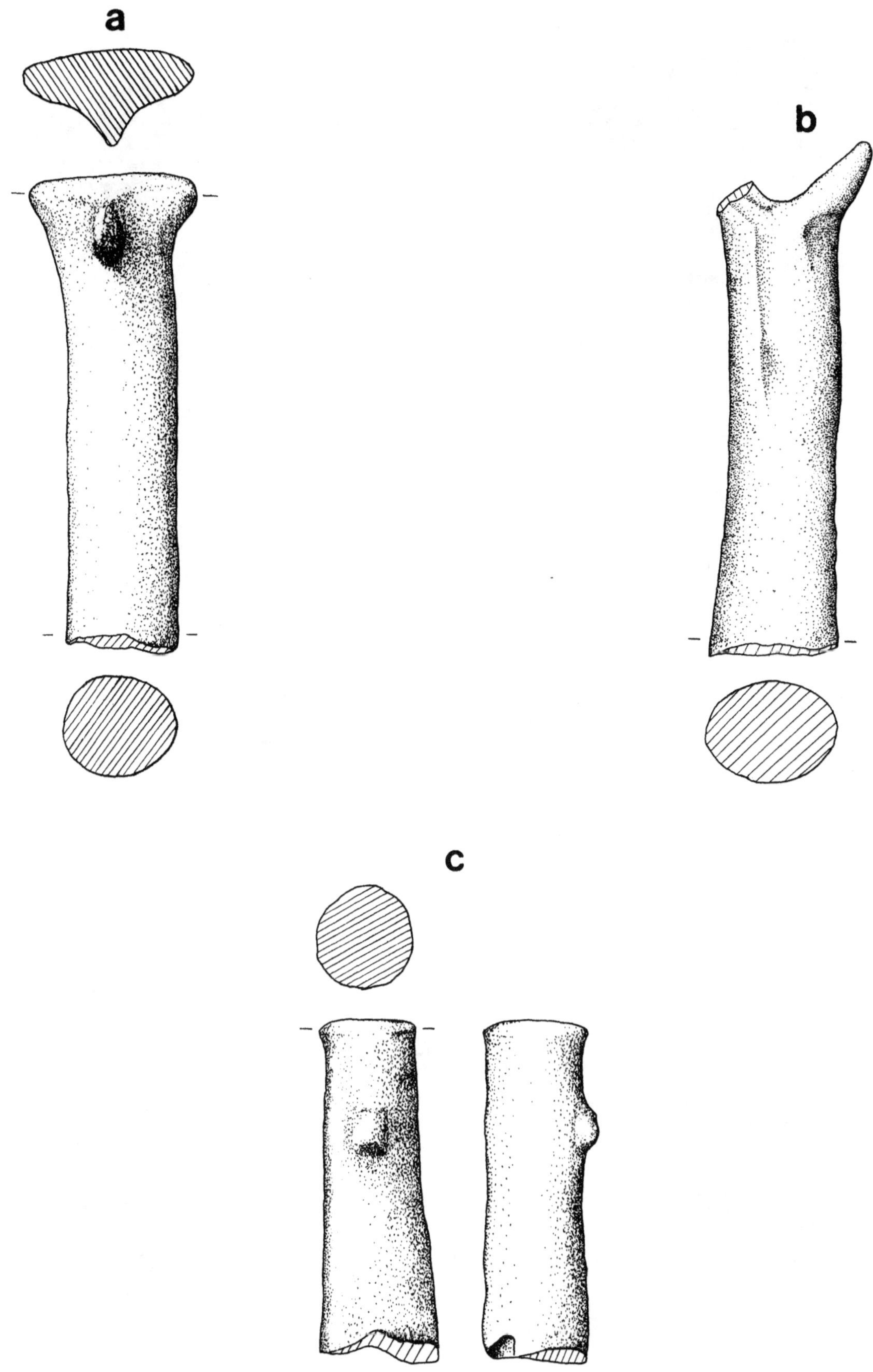

Plate 17. Drawings of (a) FC 31: front; (b) FC 30: front; (c) FC 11: front, side. Scale 1:1.

a

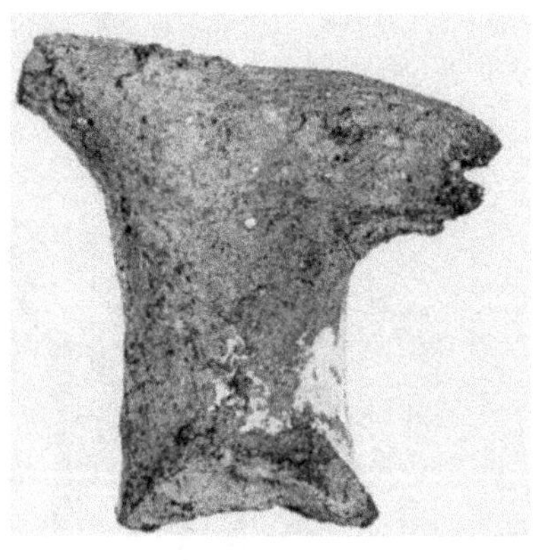

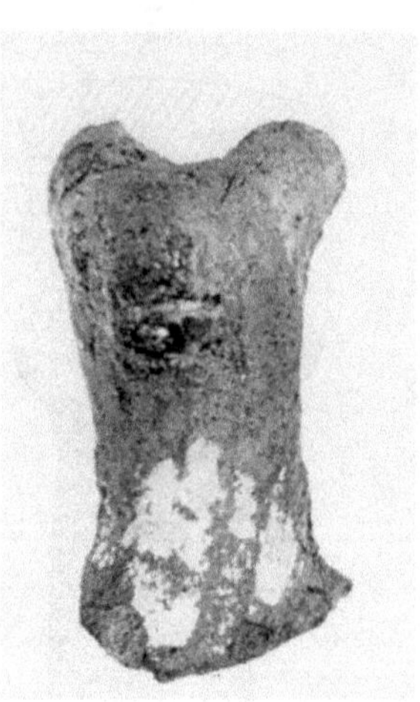

b

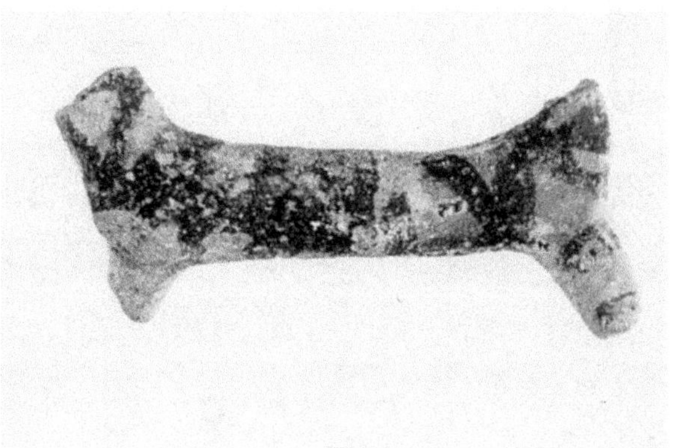

c

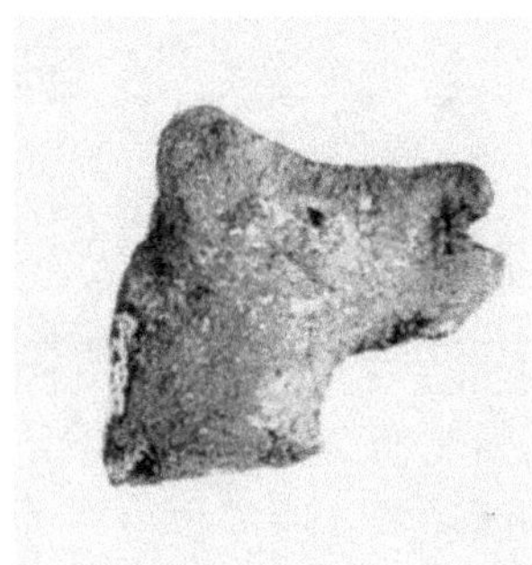

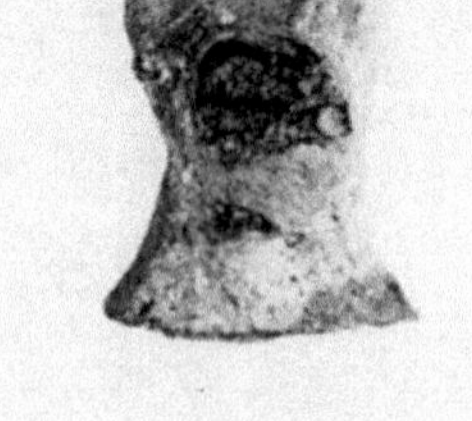

Plate 18. (a) FC 41: side, front; (b) FC 177, side; (c) FC 88: side, front. Scale 1:1.

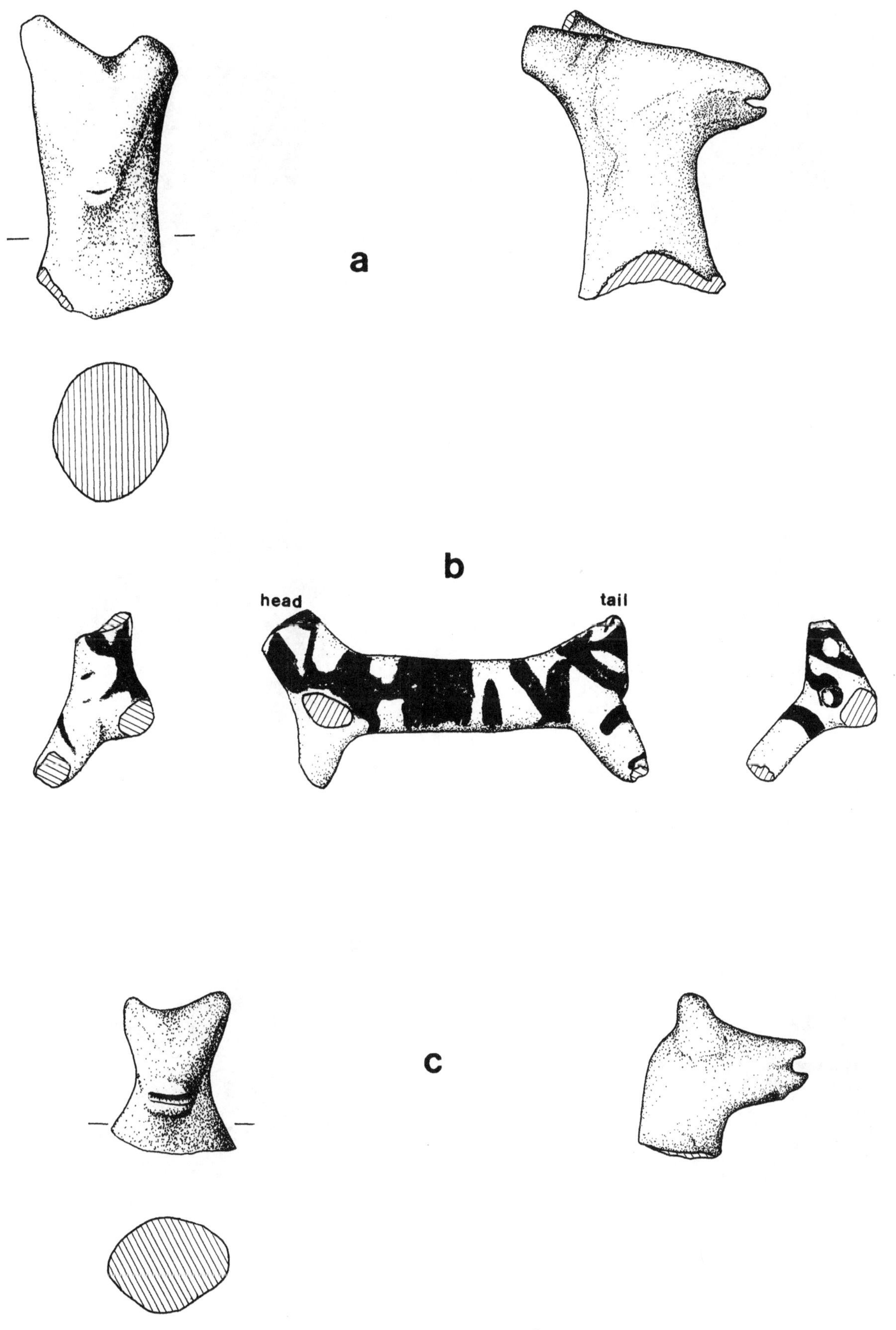

Plate 19. Drawings of (a) FC 41: front, side; (b) FC 177: front, side, back; (c) FC 88: front, side. Scale 1:1.

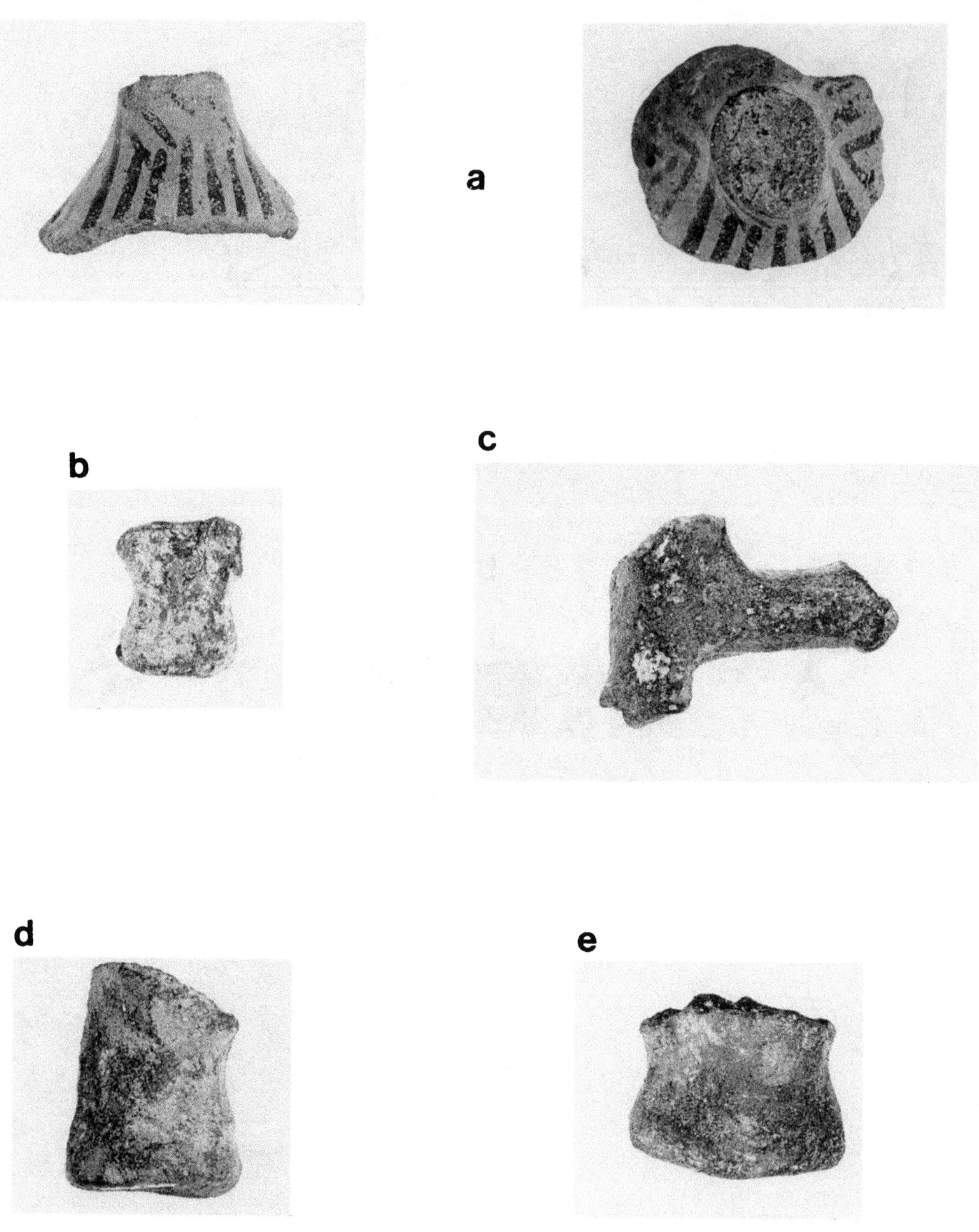

Plate 20. (a) FC 178; (b) FC 176; (c) FC 204; (d) FC 45; (e) FC 114. Scale 1:1.

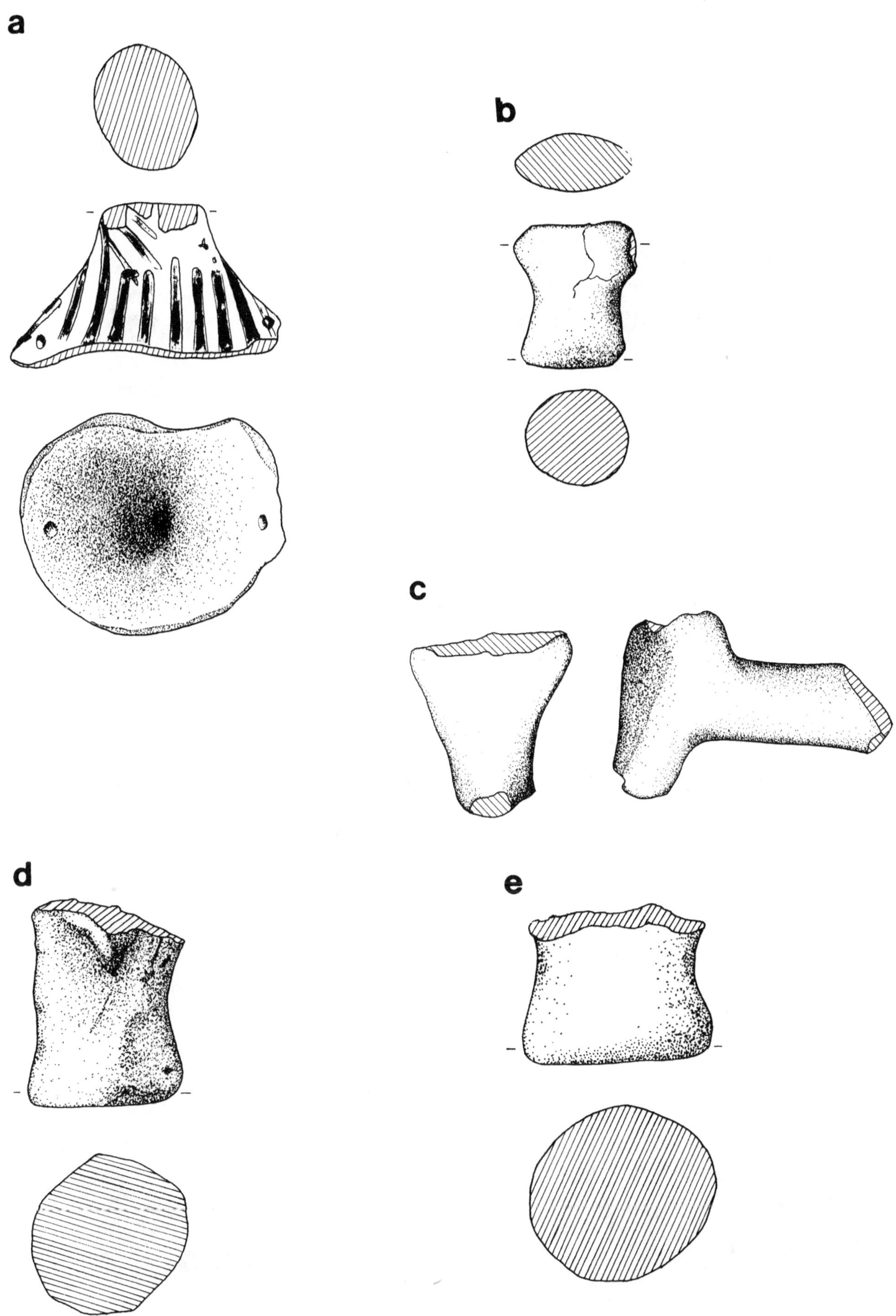

Plate 21. Drawings of (a) FC 178; (b) FC 176; (c) FC 204; (d) FC 45; (e) FC 114. Scale 1:1.

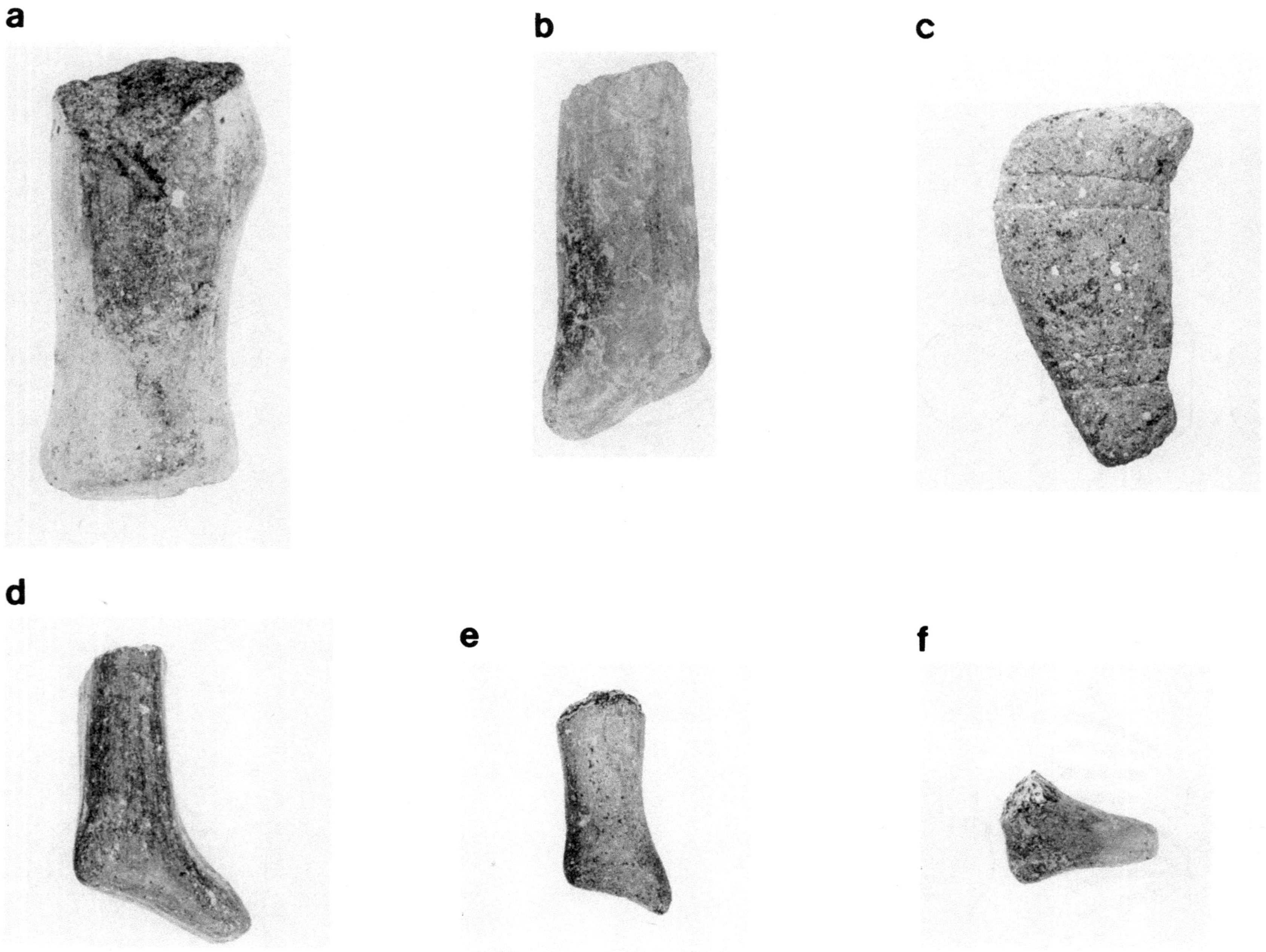

a

b

c

d

e

f

Plate 22. (a) FC 27; (b) FC 195; (c) FC 29; (d) FC 130; (e) FC 181; (f) FC 180. Scale 1:1.

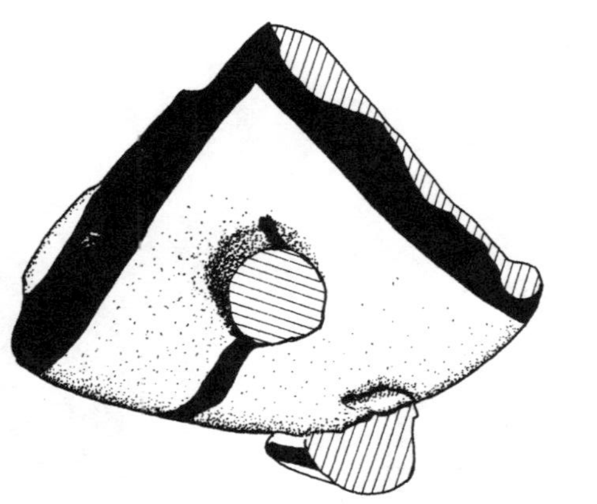
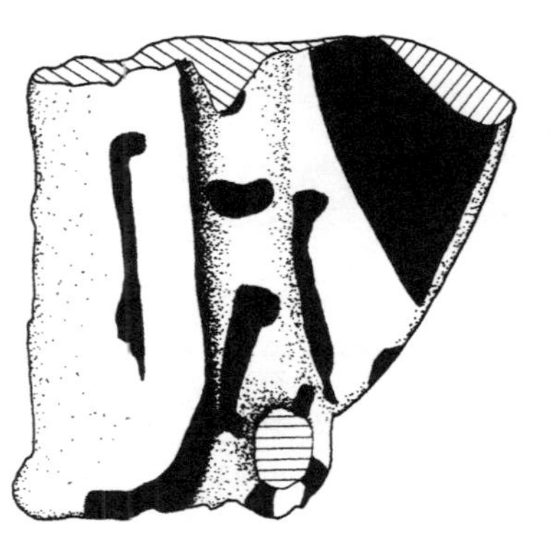

Plate 23. Photographs and drawings of FP 80. Scale 1:1.

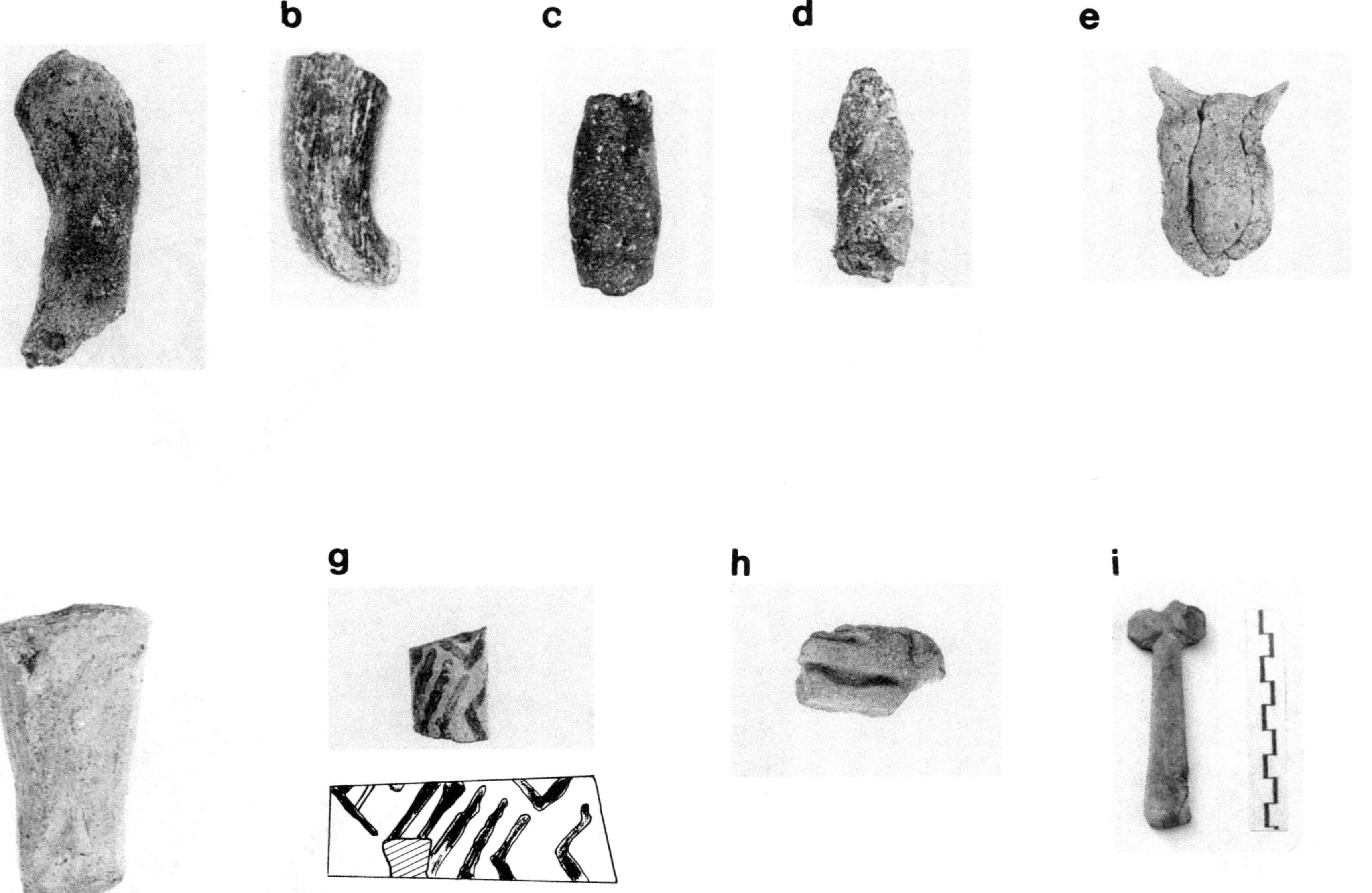

Plate 24. (a) FC 97; (b) FC 191; (c) FC 98; (d) FC 202; (e) FC 194; (f) FC 175; (g) FC 170; (h) FC 131; (i) FB 82. All scales 1:1, except FB 82; scale in cm

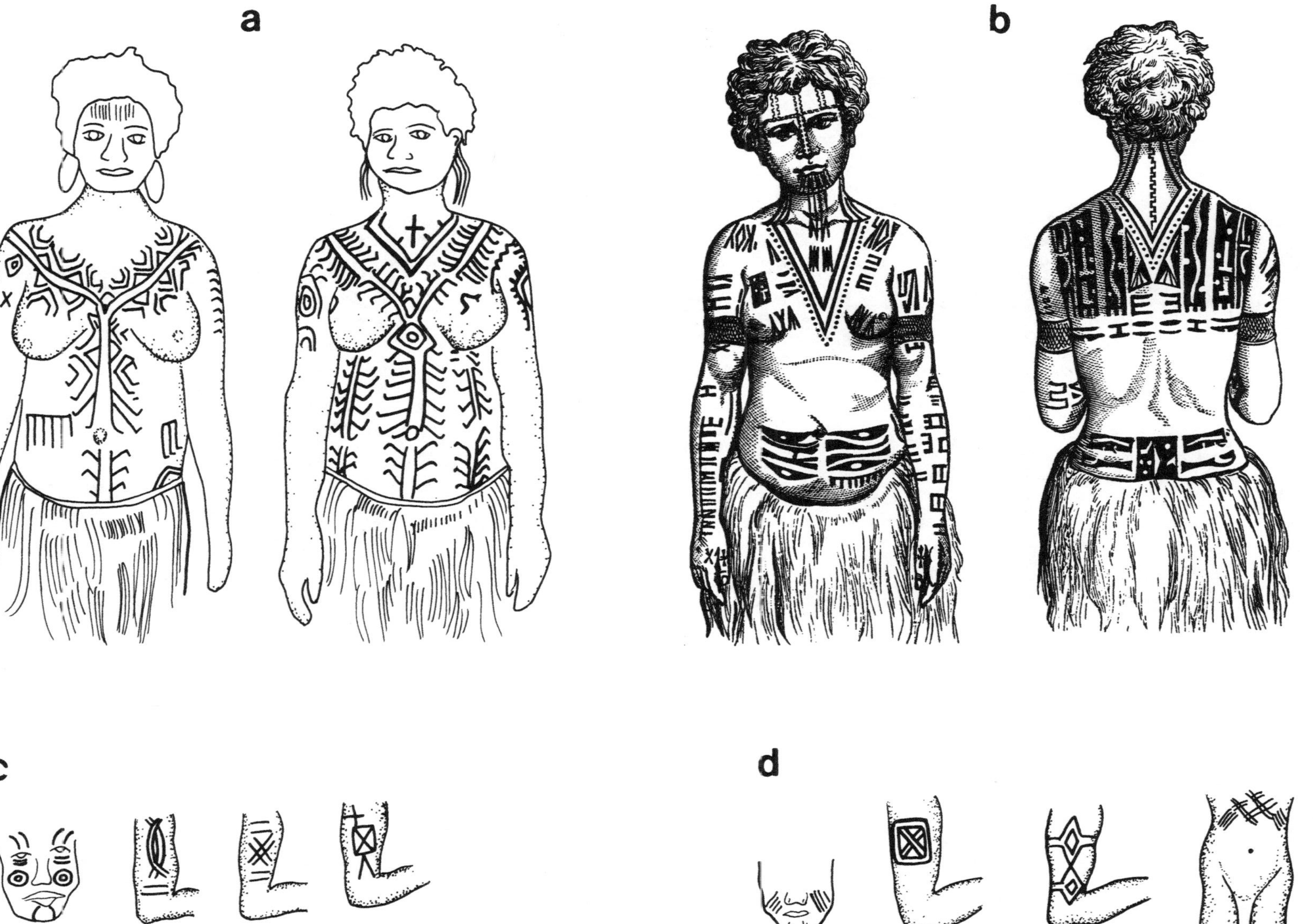

Plate 25. (a) Pre- and post-betrothal markings, Makeo district, New Guinea (after Hambly 1925:30); (b) pre- and post-menses markings, Motu (after Turner 1878:480); (c) body designs, Somali (after Hambly 1925:184); (d) body designs, Galla (after Hambly 1925:184).

www.ingramcontent.com/pod-product-compliance
Lightning Source LLC
LaVergne TN
LVHW082004060826
844660LV00031B/1276
9780253319814